DAVID BUSCH'S CANON® POWERSHOT® G1 X

GUIDE TO DIGITAL PHOTOGRAPHY

David D. Busch

Course Technology PTR

A part of Cengage Learning

COURSE TECHNOLOGY
CENGAGE Learning·

Australia, Brazil, Japan, Korea, Mexico, Singapore, Spain, United Kingdom, United States

**David Busch's Canon® PowerShot® G1 X
Guide to Digital Photography
David D. Busch**

**Publisher and General Manager,
Course Technology PTR:**
Stacy L. Hiquet

Associate Director of Marketing:
Sarah Panella

Manager of Editorial Services:
Heather Talbot

Senior Marketing Manager:
Mark Hughes

Executive Editor:
Kevin Harreld

Project Editor:
Jenny Davidson

Series Technical Editor:
Michael D. Sullivan

Interior Layout Tech:
Bill Hartman

Cover Designer:
Mike Tanamachi

Indexer:
Katherine Stimson

Proofreader:
Mike Beady

For product information and technology assistance, contact us at **Cengage Learning Customer & Sales Support, 1-800-354-9706.**

For permission to use material from this text or product, submit all requests online at **cengage.com/permissions**. Further permissions questions can be emailed to **permissionrequest@cengage.com**.

Canon and PowerShot are registered trademarks of Canon, Inc. All other trademarks are the property of their respective owners.

All images © David D. Busch unless otherwise noted.

Library of Congress Control Number: 2012936602

ISBN-13: 978-1-285-08456-5

ISBN-10: 1-285-08456-X

Course Technology, a part of Cengage Learning
20 Channel Center Street
Boston, MA 02210
USA

Cengage Learning is a leading provider of customized learning solutions with office locations around the globe, including Singapore, the United Kingdom, Australia, Mexico, Brazil, and Japan. Locate your local office at: **international.cengage.com/region**.

Cengage Learning products are represented in Canada by Nelson Education, Ltd.

For your lifelong learning solutions, visit **courseptr.com**.

Visit our corporate website at **cengage.com**.

Printed in the United States of America
1 2 3 4 5 6 7 12 13 14

For Cathy

Acknowledgments

Once again thanks to the folks at Course Technology PTR, who have pioneered publishing digital imaging books in full color at a price anyone can afford. Special thanks to executive editor Kevin Harreld, who always gives me the freedom to let my imagination run free with a topic, as well as my veteran production team, including project editor, Jenny Davidson and technical editor, Mike Sullivan. Also thanks to Bill Hartman, layout; Katherine Stimson, indexing; Mike Beady, proofreading; Mike Tanamachi, cover design; and my agent, Carole Jelen, who has the amazing ability to keep both publishers and authors happy. I'm also grateful for the chance to have worked with Alexander S. White, my co-author on my earlier PowerShot books. His research and suggestions formed the foundation for some of the descriptions in this new volume.

Also, big thanks to the folks at Campus Camera (www.campuscamera.net), who obtained one of the first Canon PowerShot G1 X cameras available for me when even Canon had none to provide. Their help made it possible for me to be using this great camera and putting together this book while many eager potential owners were still waiting for delivery.

Thanks again to master photographer Nancy Balluck (www.nancyballuckphotography.com) for the back cover photo of yours truly.

About the Author

With more than a million books in print, **David D. Busch** is the #1 best-selling camera guide author, and the originator of popular series like *David Busch's Pro Secrets, David Busch's Compact Field Guides,* and *David Busch's Quick Snap Guides.* He has written more than 50 hugely successful guidebooks for Canon and other digital camera models, including the all-time #1 best-sellers for several different cameras, additional user guides for other camera models, as well as many popular books devoted to digital photography, including *Mastering Digital SLR Photography, Third Edition* and *Digital SLR Pro Secrets.* As a roving photojournalist for more than 20 years, he illustrated his books, magazine articles, and newspaper reports with award-winning images. He's operated his own commercial studio, suffocated in formal dress while shooting weddings-for-hire, and shot sports for a daily newspaper and upstate New York college. His photos have been published in magazines as diverse as *Scientific American* and *Petersen's PhotoGraphic,* and his articles have appeared in *Popular Photography & Imaging, Rangefinder, The Professional Photographer,* and hundreds of other publications. He's also reviewed dozens of digital cameras for CNet and *Computer Shopper.*

When About.com named its top five books on Beginning Digital Photography, debuting at the #1 and #2 slots were Busch's *Digital Photography All-In-One Desk Reference for Dummies* and *Mastering Digital Photography.* In the last week of 2011, he had a total of 18 books listed in the Top 100 of Amazon.com's Digital Photography Best-seller list—simultaneously! Busch's 150-plus other books published since 1983 include best-sellers like *David Busch's Quick Snap Guide to Using Digital SLR Lenses.*

Busch is a member of the Cleveland Photographic Society (www.clevelandphoto.org), which has operated continuously since 1887.

Visit his website at http://www.dslrguides.com/blog.

Contents

PART I: GETTING STARTED WITH YOUR CANON POWERSHOT G1 X

Chapter 3
Canon PowerShot G1 X Roadmap   43

Chapter 4
Setting Up Your Canon PowerShot G1 X   67

PART II: GETTING THE MOST FROM YOUR CANON POWERSHOT G1 X

Chapter 5
Fine-Tuning Exposure   131

Chapter 6
Mastering the Mysteries of Autofocus   171

Chapter 7
Movie Making with Your Canon
PowerShot G1 X   193

PART III: ADVANCED TOOLS

Chapter 8
Advanced Shooting with Your Canon
PowerShot G1 X   213

Chapter 9
Getting the Most from Your Zoom   233

Chapter 10
Making Light Work for You   251

Chapter 11
Downloading and Editing Your Images　　　281

Preface

You don't want good pictures from your new Canon PowerShot G1 X—you demand *outstanding photos*. After all, the PowerShot G1 X is the most advanced compact digital camera that Canon has ever introduced. It boasts 14.3 megapixels of resolution, blazing-fast automatic focus, and a collection of special Scene modes that make it easy to take pictures under any type of conditions. But your gateway to pixel proficiency is dragged down by the slim little book included on the CD in the box. You know everything you need to know is in there, somewhere, but you don't know where to start. In addition, the camera manual doesn't offer much information on photography or digital photography. Nor are you interested in spending hours or days studying a comprehensive book on digital camera photography that doesn't necessarily apply directly to your G1 X.

What you need is a guide that explains the purpose and function of the G1 X's basic controls, how you should use them, and *why*. Ideally, there should be information about file formats, resolution, exposure, and special autofocus modes, but you'd prefer to read about those topics only after you've had the chance to go out and take a few hundred great pictures with your new camera. Why isn't there a book that summarizes the most important information in its first two or three chapters, with lots of illustrations showing what your results will look like when you use this setting or that?

Now there is such a book. If you want a quick introduction to the G1 X's focus controls, flash, how to use the focal lengths available with the 4X optical zoom lens, or which exposure modes are best, this book is for you. If you can't decide on what basic settings to use with your camera because you can't figure out how changing ISO or white balance or focus defaults will affect your pictures, you need this guide.

Introduction

Canon has done it again! It's packaged up many of the most alluring features of its advanced digital SLR cameras and stuffed them into the compact confines of the Canon PowerShot G1 X camera. It has a layout similar to earlier models in the PowerShot G series (including the latest PowerShot G12). Your new camera is loaded with capabilities that few would have expected to find in a "point-and-shoot" digital camera. The G1 X gets the most image quality out of its 14.3-megapixel sensor with astounding high-sensitivity performance that tops out at ISO 12800!

Yet, the G1 X retains the ease of use that smoothes the transition for those new to digital photography. For those just dipping their toes into the digital pond, the experience is warm and inviting. The PowerShot G1 X isn't a snapshot camera—it's a point-and-shoot (if you want to use it in that mode) for the thinking, creative photographer.

But once you've confirmed that you made a wise purchase decision, the question comes up, *how do I use this thing?* All those cool features can be mind numbing to learn, if all you have as a guide is the manual furnished with the camera. Help is on the way. I sincerely believe that this book is your best bet for learning how to use your new camera, and for learning how to use it well.

If you're a Canon PowerShot G1 X owner who's looking to learn more about how to use this great camera, you've probably already explored your options. There are DVDs and online tutorials—but who can learn how to use a camera by sitting in front of a television or computer screen? Do you want to watch a movie or click on HTML links, or do you want to go out and take photos with your camera? Videos are fun, but not the best answer.

There's always the manuals furnished with the G1 X. The main manual, unfortunately, is furnished on CD only, which means you can consult it only when seated at your computer, or when reading the PDF on your laptop, tablet, or smart phone. This book is available in e-book form, too, including a Kindle edition you can share between all your compatible devices, but I think most G1 X users will want a hard copy to page through and annotate.

Of course the "official" G1 X manual is filled with information, but there's really very little about *why* you should use particular settings or features, and its organization may make it difficult to find what you need. Multiple cross-references may send you flipping back and forth between two or three sections of the book to find what you want to know. The basic manual is also hobbled by black-and-white line drawings and tiny monochrome pictures that aren't very good examples of what you can do.

Also available are third-party guides to the G1 X, like this one. I haven't been happy with some of these guidebooks, which is why I wrote this one. The existing books range from skimpy and illustrated by black-and-white photos to lushly illustrated in full color but too generic to do much good. Photography instruction is useful, but it needs to be related directly to the Canon PowerShot G1 X as much as possible.

I've tried to make *David Busch's Canon PowerShot G1 X Guide to Digital Photography* different from your other G1 X learn-up options. The roadmap sections use larger, color pictures to show you where all the buttons and dials are, and the explanations of what they do are longer and more comprehensive. I've tried to avoid overly general advice, including the two-page checklists on how to take a "sports picture" or a "portrait picture" or a "travel picture." Instead, you'll find tips and techniques for using all the features of your Canon PowerShot G1 X to take *any kind of picture* you want. If you want to know where you should stand to take a picture of a quarterback dropping back to unleash a pass, there are plenty of books that will tell you that. This one concentrates on teaching you how to select the best autofocus mode, shutter speed, f/stop, or flash capability to take, say, a great sports picture under any conditions.

This book is not a lame rewriting of the manual that came with the camera. Some folks spend five minutes with a book like this one, spot some information that also appears in the original manual, and decide "Rehash!" without really understanding the differences. Yes, you'll find information here that is also in the owner's manual, such as the parameters you can enter when changing your G1 X's operation in the various menus. Basic descriptions—before I dig in and start providing in-depth tips and information—may also be vaguely similar. There are only so many ways you can say, for example, "Hold the shutter release down halfway to lock in exposure."

David Busch's Canon PowerShot G1 X Guide to Digital Photography is aimed at both Canon and digital camera veterans as well as newcomers to digital photography and digital cameras. Both groups can be overwhelmed by the options the G1 X offers, while underwhelmed by the explanations they receive in their user's manual. The manuals are great if you already know what you don't know, and you can find an answer somewhere in a booklet arranged by menu listings and written by a camera vendor employee who last threw together instructions on how to operate a camcorder.

Why the Canon PowerShot G1 X Needs Special Coverage

The Canon PowerShot G1 X is deceptively similar to earlier models in the PowerShot G lineup, but it has some special capabilities tucked into its slightly larger form factor. The most important change is the larger sensor, which by itself nearly justifies the several hundred dollar premium Canon has placed on this upscale G-series camera's price tag.

As you can see below, the G1 X's sensor is *much* larger than the one found in cameras like the earlier G12. Indeed, it's more than *six times* the size of the G12's sensor, and almost *80 percent* the size of sensors found on digital SLR models like the Canon EOS 7D. In fact, if you cropped the 7D's 18MP sensor to the size of the sensor found in the G1 X, you'd end up with the same 14.3MP resolution found in the PowerShot.

What does this mean to you, the PowerShot G1 X owner? The (relatively) huge sensor in your camera delivers a double benefit. It has more useful resolution (14.3MP vs. 10MP) than most earlier G-series PowerShots. (The exception was the ill-fated G10, which offered 14.7 megapixels, but was crippled at higher ISO settings due to an intolerable amount of noise.) You'll find that the modest bump in resolution is accompanied by improved image quality.

The large sensor found in the Canon EOS 7D (upper left), cropped to the same dimensions found in the PowerShot G1 X's image-grabber, would have the same resolution. Both are many times larger than the tiny sensor found in the earlier PowerShot G12.

Canon EOS dSLR
22.3 x 14.9mm

PowerShot G1 X
18.7 x 14mm

PowerShot G12
7.44 x 5.58mm

Part of that enhanced image quality comes from the reduction in visual noise that the larger sensor offers, with its larger light-gathering pixels. While the PowerShot G12 offered ISO setting only up to ISO 3200, the multi-colored specks we call noise became intrusive at any setting of ISO 1250 or higher. You should be able to use your G1 X at ISO 3200 routinely, and, in a pinch, it includes settings all the way up to ISO 12800!

The larger sensor is only one of the strengths that make the PowerShot G1 X an upper-tier G-series camera worthy of its own book. It boasts a faster 4.5 frames-per-second continuous shooting rate, making the G1 X a better choice for sports photography, as well as fast-moving subjects like children. It offers extensive manual controls and 14-bit RAW format shooting (I'll explain them all later in this book) that cater to the creative photographer in you. And, unlike many of the point-and-shoot cameras on the market today, it has an optical viewfinder, so you can compose your shot with the camera held up to your eye, if you like, rather than held at arm's length. For those moving up from a snapshot camera who don't need an interchangeable lens "mirrorless" model, and dSLR owners looking for a compact camera for walk around and back-up use, the Canon PowerShot G1 X is a serious contender.

Who This Book Is For

There are many general digital photography books on the market that will teach you basic techniques and concepts. Why do I concentrate on books about specific digital cameras like the PowerShot G1 X? One reason is that I feel digital photographers who are learning to use their cameras deserve books tailored to their equipment.

When I started writing digital photography books in 1995, digital cameras cost as much as $30,000 and few people other than certain professionals could justify them. Most of my readers more than 15 years ago were stuck using the point-and-shoot low-resolution digital cameras of the time—even if they were advanced photographers. I took tons of digital pictures with an Epson digital camera with 1024 × 768 (less than 1 megapixel!) resolution, and which cost $500. It was the best way to acquire digital images that could be manipulated in a computer without shooting film and then scanning negatives, slides, or prints.

Today, roughly the same amount of money (adjusted for inflation) buys you a sophisticated model like the Canon PowerShot G1 X. The digital camera is no longer the exclusive bailiwick of the professional, the wealthy, or the serious photography addict willing to scrimp and save to acquire a dream camera. Advanced digital cameras have become the favored tool for anyone who wants to go beyond point-and-shoot capabilities. And Canon cameras have enjoyed a dominating position among digital cameras because of Canon's innovation in introducing affordable cameras with interesting features and outstanding performance (particularly in the area of high ISO image quality).

You've selected your camera of choice, and you belong in the Canon camp if you fall into one of the following categories:

- Individuals who want to get better pictures, or perhaps transform their growing interest in photography into a full-fledged hobby or artistic outlet with a PowerShot G1 X and advanced techniques.

- Those who want to produce more professional-looking images for their personal or business website, and feel that the PowerShot G1 X will give them more control and capabilities than the typical fully automatic point-and-shoot camera.

- Small business owners with more advanced graphics capabilities who want to use the PowerShot G1 X to document or promote their business.

- Corporate workers who may or may not have photographic skills in their job descriptions, but who work regularly with graphics and need to learn how to use digital images taken with a Canon PowerShot G1 X for reports, presentations, or other applications.

- Professional webmasters with strong skills in programming (including Java, JavaScript, HTML, Perl, etc.) but little background in photography, but who realize that the G1 X can be used for sophisticated photography.

- Graphic artists and others who already may be adept in image editing with Photoshop or another program, and who may already be using a less sophisticated camera (Canon or otherwise), but who need to learn more about digital photography and the special capabilities of the G1 X digital camera.

Who Am I?

After spending years as the world's most successful unknown author, I've become slightly less obscure in the past few years, thanks to a horde of camera guidebooks and other photographically oriented tomes. You may have seen my photography articles in *Popular Photography & Imaging* magazine. I've also written about 2,000 articles for magazines like *Petersen's PhotoGraphic* (which is now defunct through no fault of my own), plus *Rangefinder, Professional Photographer,* and dozens of other photographic publications. You might have caught my advice on National Public Radio's *All Tech Considered.* But, first, and foremost, I'm a photojournalist and made my living in the field until I began devoting most of my time to writing books.

Although I love writing, I'm happiest when I'm out taking pictures, which is why I invariably spend several days each week photographing landscapes, people, close-up subjects, and other things. I spend a month or two each year traveling to events, such as Native American "powwows," Civil War re-enactments, county fairs, ballets, and sports (baseball, basketball, football, and soccer are favorites). Recently, I took 14 days for a solo visit to Europe, strictly to shoot photographs of the people, landscapes, and monuments that I've grown to love. And in the months prior to starting on this book, I spent time in Arizona, catching up on baseball Spring Training and natural wonders like the Sedona Red Rocks and the Grand Canyon. I can offer you my personal advice on how to take photos under a variety of conditions because I've had to meet those challenges myself on an ongoing basis.

Like all my digital photography books, this one was written by someone with an incurable photography bug. My first Canon camera was a Pellix back in the 1960s, and I've used a variety of newer models since then. I've worked as a sports photographer for an Ohio newspaper and for an upstate New York college. I've operated my own commercial studio and photo lab, cranking out product shots on demand and then printing a few hundred glossy 8 × 10s on a tight deadline for a press kit. I've served as a photo-posing instructor for a modeling agency. People have actually paid me to shoot their weddings and immortalize them with portraits. I even prepared press kits and articles on photography as a PR consultant for a large Rochester, N.Y., company, which gave me a first-hand look at the development of digital photography, even if that company failed to cash in fully on the evolution away from film. My trials and travails with imaging and computer technology have made their way into print in book form an alarming number of times, including a few dozen on scanners and photography.

Like you, I love photography for its own merits, and I view technology as just another tool to help me get the images I see in my mind's eye. But, also like you, I had to master this technology before I could apply it to my work. This book is the result of what I've learned, and I hope it will help you master your PowerShot G1 X digital camera, too.

In closing, I'd like to ask a special favor: let me know what you think of this book. If you have any recommendations about how I can make it better, visit my website at www.dslrguides.com/blog, click on the E-Mail Me tab, and send your comments, suggestions on topics that should be explained in more detail, or, especially, any typos. (The latter will be compiled on the Errata page you'll also find on my website.) I really value your ideas, and appreciate it when you take the time to tell me what you think! Some of the content of the book you hold in your hands came from suggestions I received from readers like yourself. If you found this book especially useful, tell others about it. Visit http://www.amazon.com/dp/128508456X and leave a positive review. Your feedback is what spurs me to make each one of these books better than the last. Thanks!

Part I

Getting Started with Your Canon PowerShot G1 X

This part consists of four chapters designed to help you get up and running with the Canon PowerShot G1 X. Of course, there's a distinct possibility that you've already *done* that prior to opening this book for the first time. You may have taken a few hundred or a few thousand photos with your PowerShot already. Indeed, this camera appeals directly to the sort of avid photographer who is likely to have jumped in and conducted some warmly rewarding experiments with the camera before deciding to buckle down with this book and learn all its features.

Why not? The PowerShot is incredibly easy to use. The initial steps, including charging the battery and inserting a Secure Digital memory card aren't exactly rocket science. Every control you need to begin snapping pictures is nestled on the top surface. There's a power button (cleverly labeled ON/OFF); the shutter release button; a large mode dial that includes an Auto position labeled with green text (plus other settings including one that looks suspiciously like an old-time movie camera); and a zoom lever, located concentrically with the shutter release. The rawest neophyte can turn on the camera, spin the dial to one of those settings, and begin shooting. If you are an old hand with some experience with digital cameras, getting started with the G1 X is even more of a no-brainer.

But, even if you didn't march out of a camera store with a G1 X box under one arm, and my book in hand, you're probably ready to learn more. It's not a bad idea, once you've taken a few (hundred) orientation pictures with your camera, to go back and review the basic operations of the camera from the beginning, if only to see if you've missed something. This part is my opportunity to review the setup procedures for the camera for those among you who are already veteran users, and to help ease the more timid (and those who have never worked with a digital camera before). For the uninitiated, as easy as it is to use initially, the PowerShot *does* have lots of dials and buttons and settings that might not make sense at first, but will surely become second nature after you've had a chance to review the instructions in this chapter and the next one.

Other camera guides I've seen throw you off the dock into deep water and expect you to learn how to swim before you go under for the third time. I've found that a more gentle approach works better. Depending on your experience level, you can either skim through the four chapters in this part quickly or pore over them attentively, soaking up the information you need to hit the ground running. (Don't worry: the PowerShot includes a feature called *image stabilization* that will help you avoid blurry images if you try to shoot while hitting the ground and/or running. Your Canon is more than a match for any metaphor!)

Start with any of these four chapters:

- **If you need help in setting up your camera, read:** *Chapter 1: Your New Canon PowerShot G1 X.* This chapter introduces you to the Canon PowerShot, and will help sort out the array of things found in the compact box your camera came in as you prep the camera for your first shots. I'll explain what each and every item is, how'll you'll be using it, and provide a list of must-have items you'll want to check out as soon as possible. You'll find a summary of a few nice-to-have accessories to consider, too. By the time you finish this brief chapter, you'll have your camera's battery charged and inserted, your digital "film" ready to capture photos, and a basic understanding of the camera and its key accessories.

- **If you want a quick start to snapping great shots right away, begin with:** *Chapter 2: Taking Your First Canon PowerShot G1 X Photos.* Here, I'll guide you through a pre-flight checklist of actually taking your first pictures. Rather than bog you down with excessive detail, I'll leave discussions of the more advanced features for the other parts of the book. Indeed, I'm going to tell you just what you absolutely *must* understand, accompanied by some interesting tidbits that will help you become acclimated. I'll go into more depth and even repeat some of what I explain here in later chapters, so you don't have to memorize everything you see. Just relax, follow a few easy steps, and then go out and begin taking your best shots—ever.

- **If you know the basics and want a quick introduction to the controls, go to:** *Chapter 3: Canon PowerShot G1 X Roadmap.* There are lots of buttons and dials on your PowerShot camera. That may be intimidating but, actually, this is a *good* thing, because your G1 X provides direct control over many functions, such as shooting mode, sensor sensitivity, and exposure adjustments. Many lesser cameras (including most point-and-shoot models) send you off to a command buried in a menu each time you want to change some of these functions. This chapter provides a street-level roadmap of all those controls.

- **If you want to jump ahead and begin customizing the camera's settings, start with:** *Chapter 4: Setting Up Your Canon PowerShot G1 X.* The PowerShot G1 X has so many cool features that you will need to access its well-designed menu system to use some of them. This chapter explains all the Shooting menu settings (which you'll adjust from time to time as you take pictures), the Setup menu settings (which you can often set and forget, until you need to change how your camera behaves), and even ways to design your own Custom menu with the commands that you use most often.

1

Your New Canon PowerShot G1 X

Your PowerShot G1 X represents the latest technology in the Canon PowerShot G series, and judging by the reception afforded by serious photographers, the G1 X and its predecessors in this series (most recently, the G12) are easily the most popular cameras in the PowerShot line yet. That's because they combine the small size, portability, and ease of use of point-and-shoot digital cameras with the high image quality and control that avid photographers—both professional and amateur—demand. Indeed, the G1 X and its recent precursors are among the first cameras in a long time that are serious contenders as a "second" or "walk-around" camera for those who use a more advanced digital SLR, too.

That's why I purchased my G1 X. I wanted a smaller camera to carry around all the time, but I wasn't willing to give up image quality or creative control. Many other happy PowerShot G-series owners are photographers who are stepping up from a less-capable point-and-shoot-type camera, because they need the options and extra capabilities, including the 14.2 megapixel (MP) resolution, low-light performance, and HD video capability, among other features, that this camera offers. No other cameras I've seen have been as popular among serious shooters of all types as the PowerShot G-series. In fact, I decided to write my first G-series book (for the G10) after overhearing a "pro" photographer at a camera club explaining why he loved the PowerShot cameras to several dedicated amateur photographers—who also had selected similar Canon models as their no-compromise "pocket" camera.

TECHIE ALERT

I'll explain about megapixels, LCD displays, telephoto/wide-angle zoom ranges, and movie-making as we continue with this book. I included technical gobbledygook in this introduction as a summary for the photo-techie types the PowerShot G1 X seems to attract. If you're not of that ilk, you can learn these terms later, as you don't need to understand them to continue with this chapter.

Of course, the Canon PowerShot G1 X does not really fit in a pocket, unless you're sporting a photo vest or are of the marsupial persuasion. This camera, to a certain extent, follows in the tradition of the 35mm *rangefinder* film camera, including the pioneering Leica models, which were solid, well-made compact cameras prized for their image quality, quiet operation, precision construction, and versatility. The G1 X departs from that model substantially. For example, it comes equipped with a 28–112mm (full frame equivalent) non-interchangeable automatic-focus zoom lens instead of a complement of Leica-style fixed focal length manual-focus non-zoom lenses. Nor is there a rangefinder focus viewfinder, although the G1 X does retain a vestigial optical window for framing pictures. Instead, most viewing of images prior to exposure is done using a swiveling 3-inch LCD, which does triple duty as the display for pictures *after* they've been taken (something not possible with a film camera at all) and for showing menus used to select camera features.

Contents of the Table

You probably spread out on a table or desk the contents of the handsome box that transported the Canon PowerShot from its birthplace in Japan. The box is filled with stuff, including connecting cords, booklets, a CD, and lots of paperwork. The first thing you should do (or the *next* thing you should do, if you've already been taking pictures with your camera), is to double-check the contents of the box to make sure nothing was left out, or accidentally removed by the retailer. Someone might have checked out the camera for you as a quality assurance method, or a curious store employee might have rooted through the box to see what this cool new camera actually looks like. In either case, it's entirely possible that something went astray, and it's good to know that *now*, when you can easily bring any missing pieces to the attention of the store that sold you the camera. Otherwise, a month down the road, you're going to decide to see what the output of your PowerShot looks like on your TV screen, and discover that the video cable you *thought* you had has gone AWOL at some unknown time.

So, check the box at your earliest convenience, and make sure you have (at least) the following:

- **Canon PowerShot G1 X camera.** This is hard to miss. The camera is the main reason you laid out the big bucks, and it is tucked away inside a soft envelope you should save for protection in case the G1 X ever needs to be sent in for repair.

- **Battery pack NB-10L (with terminal cover).** The power source for your PowerShot G1 X is packaged separately. You'll need to charge this 7.4V, 920mAh (milliampere hour) battery before using it. It should be charged as soon as possible (as described next) and inserted in the camera. Save the protective cover. If you transport a battery outside the camera, it's a good idea to re-attach the cover to prevent the electrical contacts from shorting out.

- **Battery charger CB-2LC or CB-2LCE.** One of these two battery chargers will be included. They are similar, except that the CB-2LZ plugs directly into the wall, while the CB-2LZE uses a cord.

- **Neck strap NS-DC9.** Canon provides you with a suitable neck strap, emblazoned with discreet Canon advertising proclaiming the brand name. Unlike the straps provided with some other cameras, the Canon strap is low-key enough that it doesn't attract unwanted attention from potential thieves. It's entirely acceptable as a "starter" strap. However, if you want a strap that won't easily slip off your shoulder, I recommend the UPstrap RF/DC, which is made especially for smaller cameras like the Leica M series and Canon PowerShot G-series. It has a patented non-slip pad and 3/8-inch webbed strap, and can be found at www.upstrap.com. Figure 1.1 shows the slightly beefier SG strap with the Vectran quick-release ends

Figure 1.1
You'll probably like a non-slip premium strap like the UPstrap better than the one Canon furnishes with the G1 X.

that I use. Either strap offers reassuring traction and eliminates the contortions we sometimes go through to keep the camera from slipping off. I know several photographers who refuse to use anything else. If you do purchase an UPstrap, be sure you mention to photographer-inventor Al Stegmeyer that I sent you hence. You won't get a discount, but Al will get yet another confirmation of how much I like his marvelous neck straps.

- **Interface cable IFC-400PCU.** You can use this USB cable to transfer photos from the camera to your computer, although I don't recommend using that mode extensively, because direct transfer uses a lot of battery power. It is a standard cable, so you may be able to use it with other cameras you own, or keep it as a spare.

- **Lens cap (with cord).** Unlike previous PowerShot models, the lens of the G1 X does not retract into the body when the camera is powered down. You'll need to cover the lens with this cap to protect it. You won't want to lose the lens cap, so Canon provides you with a (not-so) handy cord to tether the cap to the G1 X's neck strap. As soon as I can obtain a couple inexpensive replacements for this cap, I'm going to cut the cord, because I prefer to tuck a lens cap in my pocket rather than walk around with something dangling from my camera. Unfortunately, the G1 X does not accept a standard lens cap or filters (you need to purchase the FA-58C adapter, a tube-like device with a 58mm filter thread on its front for that). The "threads" on the stock G1 X are smaller than standard 46mm lens caps, and larger than standard 43mm accessories. It's likely that any accessories smaller than 58mm in diameter that would fit the lens would cause vignetting (darkening) in the corners, anyway.

- **Canon Digital Camera Solution CD.** The disc contains useful software that will be discussed in more detail in Chapter 11.

- **Instruction manuals.** These include the printed Canon PowerShot G1 X Getting Started pamphlet, and, on the CD, the Camera User Guide, the Software Guide, and the Personal Printing Guide, in PDF format. Even if you have this book, you'll probably want to check the user's guides that Canon provides, if only to check the actual nomenclature for some obscure accessory, or to double-check an error code. The CD-based user's guide at pages 226–233 contains a mind-numbing eight-page matrix that shows each of the functions available/not available in all of the G1 X's Shooting/Scene/Movie modes. If you have an old SD card that's too small to be usable on a modern camera (I still have some 128MB and 256MB cards), you can copy the PDF of the user's guide to that. But an even better choice is to put the manual on a low-capacity USB "thumb" drive, which you can buy for less than $10. You'll then be able to access the reference anywhere you are, because you can always find someone with a computer that has a USB port and Adobe Acrobat Reader available. You might not be lucky enough to locate a computer with an SD card reader.

■ **Warranty and Canon Customer Support leaflet.** Don't lose these! You can register your Canon PowerShot G1 X by mail or online. You don't really need to register the camera in order to keep your warranty in force, but you may need the information in this paperwork (plus the purchase receipt/invoice from your retailer) should you require Canon service support.

Don't bother rooting around in the box for anything beyond what I've listed previously. There are a few things that are not included with your camera that Canon classifies as optional accessories, even though you (and I) might consider some of them essential. Here's a list of what you *don't* get in the box, but might want to think about as an impending purchase. I'll list them roughly in the order of importance:

■ **Secure Digital (SD) card.** First-time digital camera buyers are sometimes shocked that their new tool doesn't come with a memory card. Why should it? The manufacturer doesn't have the slightest idea of how much storage you require, or whether you want a slow/inexpensive card or one that's faster/more expensive, so why should they pack one in the box and charge you for it? Plan on buying one right away if you don't already own one. For a camera like the PowerShot G1 X, with a generous-sized 14.3 MP of resolution and the ability to record RAW files and HD video, both of which eat up storage space voraciously, you shouldn't consider any card smaller than 4GB. This means you need an SDHC or SDXC card (HC is for high capacity; XC is for Extended Capacity), not an ancient SD card, which come in sizes only up to 2GB. A larger 8GB to 32GB card is an even better idea, especially if you travel on vacation or business and won't be able to transfer your photos from the camera to a computer on a daily basis. You can read about some of the latest memory card options in the section that follows this one.

■ **Extra battery pack NB-10L.** Even though you might get 250–700 or more shots from a single battery, you very well may need to take more images than that on a single charge, especially given burst shooting, and not to mention recording video scenes, all of which can drain a battery before you know it. Batteries can unexpectedly fail, too, or simply lose their charge from sitting around unused for a week or two. Buy an extra, keep it charged, and free your mind from worry.

■ **AV cable AVC-DC400ST.** Although with previous models Canon formerly included a cable for linking your camera to a television, the divergence of TV types means that most people will need either this cable (for a standard TV) or one for an HDTV (described next). Rather than provide both cables or risk including the wrong cable, Canon elected to save some money and include neither with your G1 X. This one allows you to view your camera's LCD output on a larger television screen, monitor, or other device with a yellow RCA composite video input jack. Note that this cable has two audio connectors—red and white—because the G1 X has been enhanced with stereo sound for its movies.

- **HDMI cable HTC-100.** This is the one you need to output to a high-definition television.

- **Add-on Speedlite.** Your Canon PowerShot's built-in electronic flash is fine for snapshots or as fill for inky shadows when shooting in daylight. But it can produce the dreaded "red-eye" effect (or yellow/green eyes in some animals) when people are looking directly at the camera lens, especially in a darkened environment. And, the built-in flash only illuminates a scene out to about 23 feet (at best). You may want an add-on electronic flash, such as the small Canon Speedlite 270EX, which I'll describe in Chapter 10.

- **AC adapter kit ACK-DC80.** This item can power the G1 X independently of the battery. There are several typical situations where this capability can come in handy: when indoors shooting tabletop photos, portraits, class pictures, and so forth for hours on end; when using your G1 X for remote shooting as well as time-lapse photography (using external timer/remotes that are readily available from third parties); for extensive review of images on your television; or for file transfer to your computer. These activities all use prodigious amounts of power, which can be provided by this AC adapter.

- **Remote switch RS60-E3.** This "cable release"-style control (for you old-timers) electronically triggers the camera's shutter when its button is pressed, allowing you to take an exposure without actually touching the camera and thereby creating blur-causing vibrations.

- **Filter adapter FA-DC58C.** This adapter allows you to mount 58mm filters in front of the lens of the G1 X, or the LH-DC70 lens hood (to prevent extraneous light from causing flaring in your image). But not at the same time, unfortunately.

- **Other stuff.** There are other accessories you might find useful, including brackets, off-camera shoe cords for flash units, printers, and waterproof cases for underwater shooting, but I'll describe these as appropriate in other chapters as we go along.

Memory Card Variations

Nowadays, all new computers should be compatible with SDHC cards, which come in sizes from 4GB to 32GB. You might need to get a new card reader if you are using a reader more than a year or two old, because the older SD card readers cannot read SDHC cards. If you really want to flex your storage muscles, you can spring for one of the newest types of SD card, called the SDXC, for extended capacity. One of the enhanced capabilities of the PowerShot G1 X is its ability to use these new super-storage cards. SDXC cards are currently available in capacities of 64GB or 128GB, which is more than enough for any application, except maybe doing photo IDs for the entire population of a small city. Theoretically, these cards can be made in capacities up to 2TB (terabytes), the equivalent of about 2,000GB. If you feel like splurging (which you'll have to do at current prices of up to $200) for an SDXC card, you need to be careful about compatibility, not just with the card reader (you'll likely need a new one), but with your computer.

As of this writing, SDXC cards can be read by most computers using Windows 7, but many Macintosh computers cannot read these cards without a software patch. (Mac OS X Lion and Mountain Lion should fix this for those who upgrade.) My MacBook Pro was unable to read an SDXC card at all (even through a USB connection to the camera) until I purchased a 21-in-1 Multimedia Memory Card Reader & Writer for ExpressCard/34 by a company called Sonnet (www.sonnettech.com). Luckily, my computer has an ExpressCard/34 slot to accommodate the reader; many computers don't have that type of slot. Also, I had to download a special driver from Sonnet's website to enable the computer to read the SDXC card, even with that new reader. Once I downloaded the driver, though, the MacBook Pro could read the card even when the images were transferred to the computer through a USB connection to the camera. The message here is to be very careful about computer compatibility before investing in an SDXC card.

Finally, there's one other option you may want to consider for your storage card. The PowerShot G1 X provides compatibility with the Eye-Fi card, a special type of SDHC card that includes a tiny transmitter for transferring images directly to your computer over a wireless (Wi-Fi) network. The card works just like any other SDHC card, but, once the camera records an image (or video), the card immediately connects to your network and starts sending the image to your computer; you will see a little window open up on your computer's screen, and the file will be available for editing or viewing within a number of seconds or minutes, depending on its size. This is a terrific technology that can provide a real boost to your productivity if you shoot a lot of images, such as in a studio or laboratory environment.

Initial Setup

The initial setup of your Canon PowerShot G1 X is fast and easy. Basically, you just need to charge the battery, attach the strap, and insert a memory card. I'll address each of these steps separately, but if you already feel you can manage these setup tasks without further instructions, feel free to skip this section entirely. You should at least skim its contents, however, because I'm going to list a few options that you might not be aware of.

Battery Included

Your Canon PowerShot is a sophisticated hunk of machinery and electronics, but it needs a charged battery to function, so rejuvenating the NB-10L lithium-ion battery pack furnished with the camera should be your first step. A fully charged power source should be good for approximately 250 or more shots under normal temperature conditions, or up to 700 shots if the LCD is switched off. (In that case, you'd be using the optical viewfinder to frame your images, and not reviewing them after they are taken.) If you use the built-in flash, expect to achieve fewer shots per battery charge. Remember that things like picture review, playing with menus, and using the image stabilization features of your camera can use up more power than you might expect. If your pictures are important to you, always take along one spare, fully charged battery.

And remember that all rechargeable batteries undergo some degree of self-discharge just sitting idle in the camera or in the original packaging. Lithium-ion power packs of this type typically lose a few percent of their charge every few days, even when the camera isn't turned on. So, it's very likely that the battery purchased with your camera, even if charged at the factory, has begun to poop out after the long sea voyage on a banana boat (or, more likely, a trip by jet plane followed by a sojourn in a warehouse), so you'll want to revive it before going out for some serious shooting.

There are many situations in which you'll be glad you have that spare battery:

- **Remote locales.** If you like to backpack and will often be far from a source of electricity, rechargeable cells won't be convenient. They tend to lose some charge over time, even if not used, and will quickly become depleted as you use them. You'll have no way to recharge the cells, lacking a solar-powered charger that might not be a top priority for your backpacking kit.

- **Unexpected needs.** Perhaps you planned to shoot landscapes one weekend, and then are given free front-row tickets to a Major League Soccer game. Instead of a few dozen pictures of trees and lakes, you find yourself shooting hundreds of images of David Beckham and company, which may be beyond the capacity of the single battery you own. If you have a spare battery, you're in good shape.

- **Unexpected failures.** I've charged up batteries and then discovered that they didn't work when called upon, usually because the rechargeable cells had gone past their useful life, the charger didn't work, or because of human error. (I *thought* I'd charged them!) That's one reason why I always carry two (or three) times as many batteries as I think I will need.

- **Long shooting session.** Perhaps your niece is getting married, and you want to photograph the ceremony, receiving line, and reception. Several extra batteries will see you through the longest shooting session.

Power Options

Multiple battery chargers and power sources are available for the Canon PowerShot G1 X. The compact CB-2LC, shown in Figure 1.2, plugs directly into a wall socket and is commonly furnished with the camera. Canon also provides the CB-2LCE, which is similar, but has a cord. Purchasing one of the optional charging devices offers more than some additional features: You gain a spare that can keep your camera running until you can replace your primary power rejuvenator. Here's a list of your power options:

- **CB-2LC.** The standard charger for the G1 X, this one is the most convenient, because of its compact size and because, with its built-in wall plug prongs that connect directly into your power strip or wall socket, it requires no cord. This charger, as well as the CB-2LCE, has a switching power module that is fully compatible with 100V to 240V 50/60 Hz AC power, so you can use it outside the U.S. with no problems. When I travel to Europe, for example, I take my charger and an adapter to convert the plug shape for the European sockets. No voltage converter is needed. (Actually, I take a very small power strip with four outlets, so a single plug adapter allows me to connect multiple chargers and accessories.)

- **CB-2LCE.** This unit is similar to the CB-2LC, and also charges a single battery, but requires a cord. That can be advantageous in certain situations. For example, if your power outlet is behind a desk or in some other semi-inaccessible location, the cord can be plugged in and routed so the charger itself sits on your desk or another more convenient spot. The cord itself is a standard one that works with many different chargers and devices (including the power supply for my laptop), so I purchased several of them and leave them plugged into the wall in various locations. I can connect my charger, my laptop computer's charger, or any one of several other electronic components to one of these cords without needing to crawl around behind the furniture. The cord itself draws no power when it's not plugged into a charger.

- **AC adapter kit ACK-DC80.** This kit allows you to operate your PowerShot directly from AC power, with no battery required. Studio photographers need this capability because they often snap off hundreds of pictures for hours on end and want constant, reliable power. The camera is probably plugged into a flash sync cord (or radio device), and the studio flash units are plugged into power packs or AC power, so the extra tether to this adapter is no big deal in that environment. You also might want to use the AC adapter when viewing images or videos on a TV connected to your camera, or when shooting remote or time-lapse photos.

Charging the Battery

To charge your battery, just follow these steps:

1. **Remove battery.** If the battery is already in the camera, remove it by sliding open the battery cover door (move it toward the nearest outer edge of the camera) and pressing the red/brown lever inside toward that same edge of the camera. The battery will pop out. (See Figure 1.3.)

2. **Insert in charger.** Tilt the battery downward so that the gray triangle on the battery is aligned with the matching white triangle on the socket in the battery charger. (You can't insert the battery if you try to stuff the aft end in first.) The battery will click when in place.

3. **Connect to power.** Flip out the plug on the back of the CB-2LC charger or, if you're using the CB-2LCE, attach the supplied cord. Plug the charger into a power outlet.

4. **Charge battery.** The upper LED, labeled CHARGE, will begin to glow red/orange, and will continue to illuminate while the charging process continues. When charging is complete, the CHARGE LED will turn off, and the lower, FULL LED will glow green. The process will take about 2 hours and 20 minutes.

Figure 1.3 Press the red-brown lever toward the outside edge of the camera to remove the battery.

Figure 1.4 Insert the battery into the camera with the Canon logo facing the back.

5. **Remove battery.** Extract the battery from the charger by lifting up on the back end, using the semi-circle cutout area for access.

6. **Insert in camera.** Unfortunately, Canon neglected to "key" the NB-10L battery, so there are four different ways you can insert it into the bottom of the PowerShot. Three of them are wrong, and won't let you seat the battery fully. The end with the gold contacts goes into the battery cavity first, and the side with the large Canon logo faces the back of the camera; the "fine print" information faces the front. (See Figure 1.4.)

7. **Close door.** When the battery is seated fully, flip the door shut, and slide it toward the center of the camera to lock it.

Final Steps

Your Canon PowerShot G1 X is almost ready to fire up and shoot. You'll need to adjust the viewfinder for your vision, and insert a memory card. Each of these steps is easy, and if you've used any Canon camera (or most other brands) in the past, you already know exactly what to do. I'm going to provide a little extra detail for those of you who are new to the Canon or digital camera worlds.

Adjusting Diopter Correction

Those of us with less than perfect eyesight can often benefit from a little correction in the optical viewfinder (which is rather tiny and difficult to view through in any case). Your contact lenses or glasses may provide all the correction you need, but if you are a glasses wearer and want to use the optical viewfinder of the PowerShot without your glasses, or use your glasses with your camera's optical window and can benefit from some additional correction, you can take advantage of the camera's built-in diopter adjustment. It can be varied from −3 to +1 correction. Look through the viewfinder and aim at something that lets you focus sharply and definitely, such as text on a computer screen or in a book, then rotate the adjacent diopter adjustment wheel (see Figure 1.5) while looking through the window until the image appears sharp and is comfortable to view without squinting. If more than one person uses your camera, and each requires a different diopter setting, you can save a little time by noting the number of clicks and direction (clockwise to increase the diopter power; counterclockwise to decrease the diopter value) required to change from one user to the other. There are 10 detents in all.

Figure 1.5
Viewfinder diopter correction from −3 to +1 can be specified with this dial.

Inserting a Memory Card

You can't take photos without a memory card inserted in your PowerShot. The LCD will scold you with a No Memory Card warning at its upper edge if you try. So, your final step will be to insert a memory card, which fits in the same compartment as the battery. Slide the door on the underside of the body toward the near outer edge of the camera to release the cover, and then open it. You should only remove the memory card when the camera is switched off. If you open the compartment door when not actively shooting, the camera switches off automatically; if you try that while actually taking pictures, the G1 X will beep a warning before turning off. (The beep is your cue to expect that you might have just lost the most recent shot you took.) In practice, we rarely try to replace a battery or memory card while in the midst of shooting, so in most cases your images will be safe.

To remove a memory card that's already in the camera, press down on the edge of the card. It will pop right out. Insert a memory card with the label facing the front of the camera (toward the battery), as shown in Figure 1.6, oriented so the edge with the gold contacts goes into the slot first.

Figure 1.6
The memory
card is inserted
with the label
facing the front
of the camera.

WRITE PROTECT?

Some (but by no means all) SD, SDHC, and SDXC cards have a notch on the long side opposite the one with the diagonal cutout. If the notch is exposed (that is, the write-protect slide is in the lower position, or not present), the card cannot be used by the camera to store photographs. A Memory Card Locked message appears on the upper edge of the LCD screen. Not all devices recognize the write-protect notch (which is an optional feature for SD/SDHC/SDXC cards), but the PowerShot G1 X does.

Formatting a Memory Card

There are four ways to create a blank SD card for your G1 X, and three of them are at least partially wrong. Here are your options, both correct and incorrect:

- **Erase images in the camera.** The Playback menu (discussed in Chapter 4 of this book) allows you to select individual images to delete, or to choose them by range, date, or folder. You can create a blank memory card by selecting All Images for deletion using this menu option. This method won't give you a truly blank card, however, as it doesn't affect files you've labeled as Protected (using the Protect Images function in the Playback menu). Nor does it identify and lock out parts of your memory card that have become corrupted or unusable since the last time you formatted the card.

- **Transfer (move) files to your computer.** When you transfer (rather than copy) all the image files to your computer from the SD card (either using a direct cable transfer or with a card reader, as described later in this chapter), the old image files are erased from the card, leaving the card blank. Theoretically. As with the Erase Images function, this method does *not* remove files that you've labeled as Protected, nor does it "freshen" your card as the Format command (found in the Setup menu) does. The main reason for erasing or transferring images is when you *want* to leave the protected/unerased images on the card for awhile longer, say, to share with friends, family, and colleagues.

- **(Don't) Format in your computer.** With the SD card inserted in a card reader or card slot in your computer, you can use Windows or Mac OS to reformat the memory card. Don't! The operating system won't necessarily arrange the structure of the card the way the camera likes to see it (in computer terms, an incorrect *file system* may be installed). The only way to ensure that the card has been properly formatted for your camera is to perform the format in the camera itself. The only exception to this rule is when you have a seriously corrupted memory card that your camera refuses to format. Sometimes it is possible to revive such a corrupted card by allowing the computer's operating system to reformat it first, then trying again in the camera.

- **Setup menu format.** The best way to create a blank card is to use the recommended method to format a memory card, using the Setup menu.

To format a memory card, just follow these steps:

1. **Turn on the camera.** Since you won't necessarily be taking a photo at the moment, the fastest way to switch the camera on is to press the Playback button on the back of the camera (with the blue right-pointing triangle), next to the optical viewfinder. You can also turn on the camera by pressing the ON/OFF button, because the Setup menu you'll be using is available in either playback or shooting mode.

MODES FOR MENUS

When you turn the camera on using the Playback button, the lens remains retracted, and the Playback, Print, and Setup menus become available when you press the MENU button. If you turn on the camera using the ON/OFF button on the top panel, the lens pops out so you can take a picture, and the available menus that pop up when you press the MENU button are the Shooting, Setup, and My Menu options. In that mode, you can also press the Playback button followed by the MENU button to switch to the second complement of menus. Just remember that to access the Shooting and My Menu options, the camera must be in *shooting* mode; to access the Playback and Print menus, the camera must be in *playback* mode. The Setup menu is always available in either mode.

2. **Press the MENU button.** The button is located in the lower-right corner of the back of the camera. The main menu appears. Locate the right cursor button (which has a lightning bolt on it, because it is also used for other things, including Flash functions). Press this cursor button once or twice until the Setup menu (with wrench and mallet icons) is highlighted. Figure 1.7 shows the Setup menu as it appears when accessed from playback mode; the menu is located one tab to the left when you access it from shooting mode.

3. **Rotate the control dial.** It's the ridged wheel located concentric with the cursor pad on the back of the camera. This dial has several uses; one of them is to scroll up and down through the menu screens. Continue scrolling down with the control dial until the Format command is highlighted. (If you prefer, you can press the down cursor button to scroll down.) Then press the FUNC./SET button, in the center of the cursor pad. You'll see a screen like the one in Figure 1.8.

4. **Choose OK.** Cancel will be highlighted, so you'll need to press the right cursor button to highlight OK. Then press the FUNC./SET button one more time. You will now see a final confirmation screen warning you that all data on the card will be erased. Use the up cursor button or the control dial to highlight OK, and press FUNC./SET to start the formatting process.

Figure 1.7
Navigate to the Format command in the Setup menu.

Figure 1.8
Choose your
Format options
and press the
FUNC./SET
button to begin.

LOW-LEVEL FORMAT

When the Format screen appears, you can also use the up or down cursor button (or the
control dial) to navigate to the Low Level Format box. Press the left or right cursor button to mark or unmark this box. Activating this option tells the G1 X to perform an
additional, more thorough, formatting of the card after the initial format is finished.
The low-level format serves to remove data from all writable portions of your memory
card while locking out "bad" sectors, and can be used to restore a memory card that is
slowing down as it "trips" over those bad sectors. This extra step takes a bit longer than a
standard reformat, and need not be used every time you format your card. I recommend
doing it after every 10 or so uses of the memory card.

Powering Up/Setting Date and Time

Tap the On/Off switch on top of the camera to switch the camera on, if you intend to
take a picture. Or, if you just want to review shots already on your memory card, or
need to access a menu, press the blue right-pointing triangle that marks the Playback
button on the back of the camera to the right of the optical viewfinder. As I mentioned,
this action powers up the camera, but doesn't cause the lens to pop out.

The first time you use the PowerShot, it may ask you to enter the time and date. (If it doesn't, this information may have been set by someone checking out the camera on your behalf prior to sale.) Just follow these steps:

1. **Press the MENU button.** The button is located in the lower-right corner of the back of the camera. The main menu appears. Press the right cursor button until the yellow Setup menu icon (with the wrench and mallet) is highlighted.

2. **Rotate the control dial.** Scroll down through the Setup menu screens with the control dial (or with the down cursor button) until the Date/Time command is highlighted. Then press the FUNC./SET button. The screen shown in Figure 1.9 appears. The time zone you've currently selected will be indicated by an icon next to the Set Date/Time entry. Either the House icon (Home) or Airplane icon (World Time) will appear. The sidebar that follows explains a little more about this option.

3. **Select the values for your currently selected time zone.** There are seven values you can change: Month, Day, Year, Hour, Minutes, Date Format, and Daylight Savings Time (On or Off). Use the left/right cursor buttons to move the gold selection box until it highlights the value you want to change. A pair of up/down pointing triangles appears above and below the value. A 24-hour clock is used when making settings, to help distinguish A.M. from P.M. hours.

Figure 1.9
Choose the Date/Time options from the Setup menu.

4. **Modify the values.** Press the up/down keys (or turn the control dial) to adjust the value up or down.

5. **Change other values.** Repeat steps 3 and 4 for each of the other values you want to change. The date format can be switched from the default mm/dd/yy to yy/mm/dd or dd/mm/yy.

6. **Confirm your settings.** When finished, press the FUNC./SET button to confirm, or the MENU button to cancel your changes and return to the Setup menu.

HOME AND WORLD TIME ZONES

You can set the correct Time Zone for your Canon PowerShot G1 X using the Time Zone entry in the Setup menu. Two settings appear: Home and World zones. Use the cursor buttons or the control dial to choose either the Home (House icon) or World (Airplane icon) option, and select the city from a scrolling map. Then, you can switch back and forth between them at any time. Perhaps you spend most of your time on the East Coast of the United States, but frequently visit an exotic location, like Cairo or Los Angeles, on business. Specify one location for your Home zone, and the second for your World (travel) zone, and switch between them easily. If you hop around a lot, you can change your World setting as many times as you want. I'll have some more to say about this useful adjustment in Chapter 4.

Taking Your First Canon PowerShot G1 X Photos

If you've read Chapter 1, or have decided to begin with this chapter because your camera is all set up and ready to go, you'll find all the basic information you need to take your first photos with your PowerShot G1 X. In the first part of this chapter, I'm going to give you the 52-Second No-Option Quick Tour that will have you taking great pictures in less than a minute. Then, in the second part of this chapter, you'll find the 10-Minute Introduction, which allows you to make a few choices that will have you taking even better photos with only a few minutes prep.

This chapter is strictly an introduction to some basic features. You'll learn how to make simple settings, and, later in the chapter, select the easiest exposure, metering, and autofocus modes. After you've finished either of this chapter's crash courses and taken a few pictures, you can return to this book with Chapters 3 and 4 to learn more about how your Canon PowerShot G1 X operates, as you work your way toward Part II, which *really* looks at the camera's great features in depth.

But first, let's get snapping.

52-Second No-Option Quick Tour for Still Photos

To begin taking still photos immediately (once you have charged the battery and inserted a formatted memory card), just follow these easy steps:

1. **Remove the lens cap and press the ON/OFF switch on top of the camera.** The lens extends from the camera body, a green LED illuminates in the center of the power button, the start-up sound plays through the speaker on the left side of the

camera body, and the start-up image displays briefly on the LCD monitor on the back of the camera before the scene in front of the camera shows up on the screen. I'll show you how to change the start-up sound and image (or to disable them) in Chapter 4.

2. **Set the fully automatic shooting mode.** Rotate the mode dial (the tallest dial on the right top of the camera) to the green Smart Auto setting. (See Figure 2.1.) The PowerShot makes all the exposure settings for you at this setting, choosing a Scene mode and displaying an icon that indicates which mode has been selected. But, as you'll learn later, you can make some changes.

3. **Frame your image.** First, make sure you've rotated the LCD on its hinges into viewing position. Once you have the viewing surface facing out from the camera's back, view the image on the LCD. It will look something like Figure 2.2. Some of the information overlaid on the image may differ, depending on the modes the camera chooses. Reframe, as desired, by rotating the zoom lever located concentric with the shutter release button: a clockwise push zooms in; counterclockwise zooms out.

Figure 2.1
These are the shooting controls located on the top of the camera that you'll use to take your first pictures and movies.

Microphone   Exposure   Mode   Power   Shutter   Movie   Zoom
             compensation dial   switch   release   button   lever
                 dial

Figure 2.2
Frame your still photo using the color LCD.

4. **Focus.** When the image is composed the way you want, press the shutter release button halfway to set the focus. Frames will appear on the LCD showing the subject(s) the camera has detected. The upper LED to the immediate right of the optical viewfinder window will flash green, and you'll hear a beep (unless the camera has been set to Mute) when focus is achieved. If the lighting is so dim that the Raise the Flash message appears on the screen, press the flash switch on the upper-left edge of the camera to pop up the camera's built-in electronic flash.

5. **Take your best shot.** Press the shutter release down the rest of the way to take the picture. The same green LED that indicated focus will flash as the picture is being stored on your memory card. The admonition "Busy" may appear on the bottom edge of the LCD at the same time.

6. **Review your result.** Continue to hold down the shutter release button after you've taken a picture and your shot will display on the LCD until you release the button. If you release the button immediately, the picture will be displayed for review for about two seconds. (I'll show you how to increase this display time in Chapter 4.)

52-Second No-Option Quick Tour for Movies

To begin taking movies immediately, just follow these easy steps:

1. **Remove the lens cap and press the ON/OFF switch on top of the camera.** The lens pops out of the camera body, a green LED illuminates in the center of the power button, the start-up sound plays through the speaker on the left side of the camera body, and the start-up image displays briefly on the LCD monitor on the back of the camera before the scene in front of the camera shows up on the screen. I'll show you how to change the start-up sound and image (or to disable them) in Chapter 4.

2. **Press and release the red Movie shooting button.** It's located at the upper-right edge of the back of the camera. *You do not need to rotate the mode dial to the movie position.* The G1 X will shoot movies when the camera is set for *any* mode. Just press the button to begin capturing video. The camera should beep once as movie shooting begins and a red ● Rec indicator will appear on the LCD along with the elapsing time (see Figure 2.3). Other icons may appear depending on the mode dial position. For example, if the camera is set to the green Smart Auto icon, you may see focus mode and anti-shake icons in the upper-right corner. Black bars at the top and bottom of the frame show you the image area being captured.

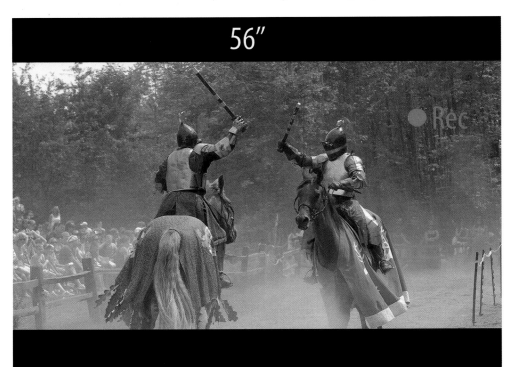

Figure 2.3
Indicators on the LCD show that you're shooting a video clip, and display the elapsed time.

3. **Press the red Movie shooting button again to stop.** Use the zoom lever to zoom in and out, if you like. When finished capturing a clip, press the red Movie button again. The camera beeps twice and the indicators in the screen vanish.

4. **View the clip you just shot.** Press the Playback button, and then the FUNC./SET button to reveal a series of VCR-type controls. Press the green arrow for playback, and playback or tap the shutter release to cancel.

Your 10-Minute Introduction

If you have more than 52 seconds to spare, read or skim through this section to begin shooting, and apply a few options that will make your images even better. You'll learn how to choose a shooting mode, metering mode, focusing mode, and make other simple settings.

That's a lot of modes! Here's what each of the main types of settings does for you:

- **Shooting modes.** These are set using the large raised dial on the top-right side of the G1 X. They include the semi-automatic Av (Aperture priority/value), Tv (Time/ Shutter priority), P (Program auto exposure/AE), and M (Manual) modes. Also on this dial are automatic exposure modes like the special Smart Auto, Scene (SCN), Creative Filters, and the Movie setting. The G1 X also has two custom setting modes that store and retrieve your own personalized shooting options in slot positions labeled C1 and C2 on the mode dial.

- **Metering modes.** Three metering modes are available that allow you to choose what areas of the image the PowerShot G1 X uses to calculate correct exposure. They include Evaluative (which combines information from several different zones within the image); Center weighted averaging (which meters the entire image but places the emphasis on the subject matter in the center); and Spot AE (which calculates exposure based on a small area, either the center of the frame or the current point being used to calculate autofocus). You make this selection by pressing the metering mode button, located to the lower left of the control dial on the back of the camera.

- **Focusing modes.** The PowerShot G1 X has two different types of AF (autofocus) options. The first option, AF mode, determines *when* the camera locks in focus. You can choose Continuous AF, which adjusts focus for whatever subject is in the frame at all times, or Servo AF, which focuses only when the shutter release is pressed (which saves battery power). The second option, AF Frame mode, determines *where* in the scene the camera focuses—that is, what areas of the image are used to calculate focus. You make your selections of AF mode and AF Frame mode using the Shooting menu, as described in Chapter 4.

Selecting a Shooting Mode

You choose your shooting method from the mode dial located on the top right of the Canon PowerShot G1 X. (See Figure 2.4.) This dial has 10 different settings, which let you select the various shooting modes. These modes have various levels of automation and a variety of features. The P, Tv, Av, and M settings—for Program (P), Time/Shutter speed value (Tv), Aperture value (Av), and Manual (M)—are your key creative tools, with the maximum amount of flexibility and adjustments. I'll be discussing those shooting modes and the settings to make when using them in considerable detail in later chapters.

The G1 X also offers a collection of other shooting modes including the Smart Auto and SCN (for Scene) modes. Finally, there are more specialized modes that are designed for particular purposes, including Creative Filter, and Movie mode. I'll explain each of these modes also, though I'll be concentrating most heavily on the P, Tv, Av, and M settings, because it's with those settings that you'll have the opportunity to use your knowledge of photographic principles to the greatest extent.

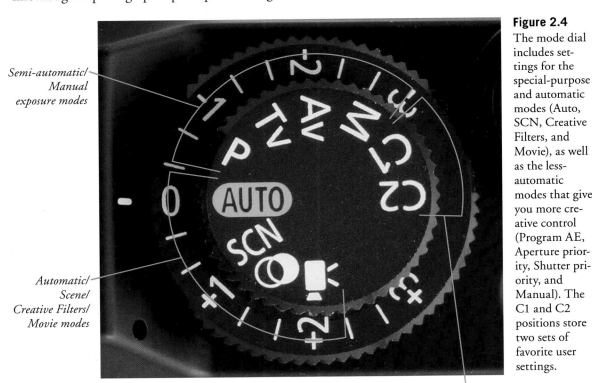

Semi-automatic/
Manual
exposure modes

Automatic/
Scene/
Creative Filters/
Movie modes

User settings

Figure 2.4
The mode dial includes settings for the special-purpose and automatic modes (Auto, SCN, Creative Filters, and Movie), as well as the less-automatic modes that give you more creative control (Program AE, Aperture priority, Shutter priority, and Manual). The C1 and C2 positions store two sets of favorite user settings.

If you're very new to digital photography, you might want to set the camera to Smart Auto (highlighted in green on the mode dial) or P (Program AE mode) and start snapping away. Either mode will make all the appropriate settings for you for many shooting situations. If you have a specific type of picture you want to shoot, you can try out one of the Scene types by turning the mode dial to the SCN setting, then pressing the FUNC./SET button and choosing from the menu that appears at the bottom of the screen. (See Figure 2.5.) In this chapter, I'll provide a quick introduction to each shooting mode. I'll follow up with more details in later chapters.

Figure 2.5
The icons for the Scene modes indicate what type of picture each is suited for.

Tip

If you want a more complete discussion of the various shooting modes, and the differences between them, jump to Chapter 5.

First, the special-purpose and automatic modes. Select the Auto, SCN, Creative Filter, and Movie modes by turning the mode dial to their respective icons. For the Scene modes, there's one further step. Once the mode dial is set to the SCN position, press the FUNC./SET button, then, with the most-recently selected Scene mode at the top of the menu on the left of the LCD, use the right cursor button or rotate the rear control dial (the knurled ring to the right of the LCD, shown at right in Figure 2.6) to navigate through the menu of Scene types on the bottom of the screen until the one you want is highlighted. Once it is, press FUNC./SET, and the icon for that Scene type will be shown in the upper-right corner of the LCD when you return to shooting mode. The special-purpose and automatic modes follow. First, Scene modes:

- **Smart Auto.** With the mode dial set to this position, the G1 X makes all the exposure decisions for you, and will ask you to pop up the flash if necessary under low light conditions.

- **Movie Digest.** When this Scene mode is active, the G1 X will record a 2–4 second movie clip to accompany each still photograph you take. While the still pictures will be stored as separate files on your memory card, each of the movie clips captured *during a particular day* will be appended to the end of a single movie file. At the end of the day, you'll end up with a series of still pictures and a movie file with matching video snapshots.

- **Portrait.** Use the Portrait option when you're taking a picture of a subject standing relatively close to the camera and want to de-emphasize the background, maximize sharpness, and produce flattering skin tones.

- **Landscape.** Select this mode when you want extra sharpness and rich colors of scenes.

- **Kids & Pets.** An "action" scene mode for capturing fast-moving pets and children without subject blur. The camera may boost the ISO to a higher level than normal to allow a fast shutter speed.

Front control dial

Rear control dial

Figure 2.6
The G1 X has two control dials, a front control dial on the hand grip (left) and rear control dial (right) located on the back panel.

- **Sports.** Use this mode to freeze fast-moving subjects. Again, a high ISO setting may be used.

- **Smart Shutter.** This setting is not so much of a Scene type as a way to set the camera's automatic face detection features. I'll provide details about its operation in Chapter 5.

- **High Speed Burst HQ.** This Scene mode switches the camera to continuous shooting at up to 4.5 frames per second, for up to 6 total shots.

- **Handheld Night Scene.** Helps you produce great night images without a tripod by taking several consecutive shots and combining them to reduce image shake not countered by the G1 X's image stabilization, and compensate for visual image noise.

- **Beach.** This setting provides properly exposed human subjects against a bright background of water, sand, and reflected sunlight.

- **Underwater.** This setting is intended specifically for use under the surface with the optional Canon Waterproof Case WP-DC34. It removes bluish color casts and reduces the intensity of the flash. The camera may use a high ISO setting to compensate for the reduced amount of light underwater.

- **Foliage.** Another saturation-rich setting for shooting trees and leaves, with emphasis on bright and vivid greens.

- **Snow.** Like Beach, this setting properly exposes people and other subjects, despite glaring ice and snow, while removing the blue tinge often caused by snow backgrounds.

- **Fireworks.** Offers vivid photos of fireworks with a longer exposure to capture an entire burst.

- **Stitch Assist 1 and 2.** These last two settings in SCN mode (one for left-to-right shots and the other for right-to-left) help you expose two or more overlapping images (up to 26 in total) that are merged to create a panorama on your computer with the supplied PhotoStitch program.

You can also select Creative Filter modes from the Function menu in a similar way, by pressing the FUNC./SET button and scrolling among the following options arrayed at the bottom of the screen. I'll show you how to use each of these in Chapter 5.

- **HDR.** This is Canon's setting for producing in-camera processing of a High Dynamic Range image, by taking three pictures in one sequence at different exposures, and then combining them into a final product that uses the most clearly exposed portions of the different shots. I'll discuss this mode, and provide further information about HDR in general, in Chapter 5.

- **Nostalgic.** This setting lets you ramp down the saturation of the colors in your images, giving the appearance of a faded, antique photograph.

- **Fish-eye Effect.** This setting simulates the bulging, distorted view produced by an extreme wide-angle "fish-eye" lens.

- **Miniature Effect.** This setting lets you select a portion of the image to be shown clearly, while blurring the top and bottom, resulting in an effect like viewing a miniaturized model.

- **Toy Camera Effect.** Vignetted, darkened, and blurred corners and garish colors similar to the results you get with a cheap toy camera are produced by this setting.

- **Monochrome.** Creates black-and-white, sepia, or blue-and-white images.

- **Super Vivid.** This setting increases the saturation of the colors in a scene, making them appear much richer and more intense than normal. Use it for dramatic effect, but you'll probably want to use this one sparingly, because it could wear out its welcome rapidly.

- **Poster Effect.** This setting, like the previous one, is not intended for a specific type of scene; rather, it imposes a particular type of processing on the image. In this case, it provides a degree of "posterization," increasing contrast with bright color effects.

- **Color Accent.** Creates a special effect: Choose one color on the LCD, and all the other colors in an image are converted to black-and-white. I'll explain how it works in Chapter 5.

- **Color Swap.** Changes one color to another. If you want to see Kentucky bluegrass that's *really* blue, this is the mode for you.

If you have more photographic experience, you might want to opt for one of the less specialized, less automatic settings. These, too, are described in more detail in Chapter 5. These modes, which let you apply a little more creativity to your camera's settings, are indicated on the mode dial by letters M, Av, Tv, and P. There are also two custom setting positions on the mode dial, labeled C1 and C2, which can be used to store a group of settings, including any of the less automatic modes along with current menu settings, plus additional parameters, like the zoom and manual focus settings at the time you load the settings into C1 or C2, and your customized My Menu settings. I'll explain how to use the C1 and C2 modes in Chapter 4. Here is a brief introduction to the "creative" shooting modes:

- **M (Manual).** Select when you want full control over the shutter speed and lens opening, either for creative effects or because you are using a studio flash or other flash unit not compatible with the PowerShot's automatic flash metering.

- **Av (Aperture priority).** Choose when you want to use a particular lens opening, especially to control sharpness or how much of your image is in focus. The G1 X will select the appropriate shutter speed for you. Av stands for *aperture value.*

- **Tv (Shutter priority).** This mode (Tv stands for *time value*) is useful when you want to use a particular shutter speed to stop action or produce creative blur effects. The camera will select the appropriate f/stop for you.

- **P (Program).** This mode allows the G1 X to select the basic exposure settings, but you can still override the camera's choices to fine-tune your image.

Choosing a Metering Mode

Metering mode determines what areas of the frame are used when calculating exposure. You might want to select a particular metering mode for your first shots, although the default Evaluative metering (which is set automatically when you choose one of the more automatic shooting modes, such as Smart Auto or SCN) is probably the best choice as you get to know your camera. I recommend staying with Evaluative metering as you begin shooting with your PowerShot.

> **Tip**
>
> If you want to learn more about how to select and use the Evaluative, Center weighted averaging, and Spot AE point metering modes, jump to Chapter 5.

To change metering modes, switch to the P, Av, Tv, or M shooting mode and press the metering mode button, located on the back of the camera just southwest of the rear control dial. A screen pops up on the LCD offering three choices. Rotate the rear control dial until the choice you want is highlighted. Then press the metering mode button again to confirm your choice. The options are shown in Figure 2.7:

- **Evaluative metering.** The standard metering mode; the G1 X attempts to intelligently classify your image and choose the best exposure based on readings from several different zones in the frame. (Canon doesn't specify how many zones there are, or where they are located.) Use this mode for most scenes, especially when the most important areas are located outside the center of the frame.

- **Center weighted averaging metering.** The G1 X meters the entire scene, but gives the most emphasis to the central area of the frame. This mode is useful when the most important subject matter is in the middle of the frame.

- **Spot AE Point metering.** Exposure is calculated from a smaller spot. The metering frame is either the center of the LCD monitor or, when you're using the FlexiZone autofocus mode, the same position as the AF frame you've chosen. I'll show you how to set the autofocus mode and zone in Chapter 7. This metering mode is useful when there is a large difference between the brightness of your main subject and other areas of the photo, and you want to be able to zero in on a specific area.

Figure 2.7
Metering modes
(left to right)
Evaluative,
Center weighted
averaging, Spot
AE Point.

Choosing a Focus Mode

The Canon PowerShot G1 X offers both manual focus and automatic focus, and, when using autofocus (AF), you can choose *when* and *where* focus is calculated. *When*, in this case, means whether the camera continuously refocuses when your subject moves within the frame, or whether focus is locked down when you press the shutter release halfway. *Where*, on the other hand, determines what part of the frame is considered your main subject when the camera decides to lock in focus. You can select from three different types of "focus frames," including automatic detection of human faces using nine possible areas within the frame; automatic tracking of a moving subject that you choose; and FlexiZone, which allows you to choose what part of the image to focus on.

Tip
For more detail on selecting each of these focusing modes, and their advantages, jump to Chapter 6.

Manual Focus

You can manually focus the G1 X, either entirely by yourself if you want to set the focus point precisely or by using the Safety MF feature, which allows you to set the focus point manually, at which point the camera uses its autofocus features to fine-tune the focus for you. I'll explain all the manual focus options in Chapter 6. In this quick start, all you need to know is:

1. **Press the left cursor button on the thumbpad.** On the screen that appears, select Manual focus from among the Macro, Normal, and Manual Focus options that appear.

2. **Rotate the rear control dial to adjust the focus point.** A scale at the right side of the LCD (see Figure 2.8) shows you the approximate distance to the focus point as a guideline, and a magnified area in the center (it can be turned off as described later) provides an enlarged view of the center of the frame as you focus. When you focus down past the minimum marked distance on the scale, a new scale appears with focus milestones at the 50cm and 20cm marks.

3. **Fine-tune focus (optional).** If you're satisfied with the manual focus you've set, go ahead and take the picture. To use Safety MF to fine-tune, press the shutter button halfway or press the AF Frame Selector button (as described in the sidebar which follows). The camera will adjust the focus point using its autofocus feature.

Figure 2.8
Press the MF (left cursor) button to initiate manual focus.

4. **Turn off MF.** To turn off manual focus, press the MF (left cursor) button a second time and choose Macro or Normal focus.

> **Tip**
>
> Safety MF is easy to use. As noted in Step 3 above, you can activate Safety MF by pressing the shutter release halfway, or the AF Frame Selector/Single Image Erase (Trash) button, located above the rear control dial at roughly the 11 o'clock position. The G1 X will fine-tune your focus and beep. The Safety MF feature must be turned on through the Shooting menu, as described in Chapter 4. If it is not activated, pressing the button will still result in a beep, but the focus will not be fine-tuned. Also, note that pressing this button will not focus the image if it is badly out of focus; it will only fine-tune your manual focusing.

Other Settings

There are a few other settings you can make if you're feeling ambitious, but don't feel ashamed if you postpone using these features until you've racked up a little more experience with your PowerShot G1 X.

Adjusting White Balance and ISO

If you like, you can custom-tailor your white balance (color balance) and ISO sensitivity settings when you're using the non-automatic modes. To start out, it's best to set white balance (WB) to Auto, and ISO to ISO 100 or ISO 200 for daylight photos, and to ISO 400 for pictures in dimmer light.

To set the white balance quickly, press the FUNC./SET button in the center of the control dial (the directional pad) and use the up/down buttons to navigate to the White Balance entry near the top of the left-side menu. Then use the left/right buttons or rotate the rear control dial to select from among Auto, Daylight, Cloudy, Tungsten, Fluorescent (warm-white or cool-white), Fluorescent H (daylight fluorescent), Flash, Underwater, or Custom white balance. (See Figure 2.9.) I'll show you how to use each of these in Chapter 4, where you'll also learn how to tweak settings slightly by rotating the front control dial to adjust blue/amber bias, or pressing the MENU button to produce an adjustments screen.

ISO sensitivity is even easier to adjust. Just press the up button and rotate the rear control dial to the setting you want to use, from ISO 100 to 12800, or to the Auto position to allow the camera to choose an appropriate ISO setting for you in the range ISO 100–1600.

Figure 2.9
Choose the
white balance
setting you
want.

Using the Self-Timer

If you want a short delay before taking a picture—say, to allow the camera to steady itself, or to allow you to get in the shot, the built-in self-timer is at your beck and call. The self-timer is accessed by pressing the down cursor button.

You activate the self-timer by pressing the FUNC./SET button once; then press the down button again to move down to the self-timer row on the menu. If you want to change the time delay, turn the front dial (the wheel that falls under your right index finger on the front of the camera) to select from 0 to 30 seconds for the delay. (Don't ask me why a 0-second delay is available.) Use the left and right buttons to select the number of shots to be taken, from 1 to 10.

After you have made your selections, press the FUNC./SET button to exit the self-timer screen. A self-timer icon will remain on the screen. When the camera is set up (presumably on a tripod), press the shutter button to start the countdown. Once the countdown is started, it can be cancelled by pressing the down button again. Remember, there are other options similar to the self-timer, including the Smile, Wink, and Face detection triggers, which are discussed in Chapter 5 in connection with the Scene modes.

Using the Built-in Flash

Working with the G1 X's built-in flash (as well as external flash units like the Canon 580EX II) deserves a chapter of its own, and I'm providing one. (See Chapter 10.) But the built-in flash is easy enough to work with that you can begin using it right away, either to provide the main lighting of a scene or as supplementary illumination to fill in the shadows.

The G1 X will automatically balance the amount of light emitted from the flash so that it illuminates the shadows nicely, without overwhelming the highlights and producing a glaring "flash" look. (Think *Baywatch* when they're using too many reflectors on the lifeguards!)

Pop it up by pressing the flash button on the left side of the top panel of the camera. The small flash will elevate. Press the right cursor button, and choose either Flash Off (to disable the flash) or On (to enable it). There may be other flash options available, depending on what Shooting mode you've selected with the mode dial. They include Auto (to let the camera decide whether to fire it), and, Slow Synchro, which can be used to provide a balance between the ambient light and the flash, avoiding dark backgrounds. I'll explain the use of those modes, as well as the other flash options that appear when you press the MENU button while using this Flash menu, in Chapter 10. For now, all you need is On and Off.

Reviewing the Images You've Taken

The Canon PowerShot G1 X has a broad range of playback and image review options, including the ability to jump ahead by 10 or 100 images at a time, or to jump using other parameters, such as the dates pictures were taken. I'll cover the other options, including filtering and viewing images in the form of slide shows, in Chapter 3. For now, you'll want to learn just the basics.

- **View an image.** Press the Playback button (marked with a blue right-pointing triangle) to the right of the optical viewfinder to display the most recent image on the LCD.

- **Scroll among images.** Press the left cursor button to view a previous image. Press the right button to view the next image. You can also use the rear control dial to scroll through the images. If you turn the dial rapidly, you will see an iPod-like stream of smaller images. I'll discuss this feature further in Chapter 3. Movies will be differentiated from still images; press the SET button to view a movie.

■ **Zoom in and out.** Press the zoom lever toward the right to zoom in on an image. Press toward the left to zoom out. While zoomed in, you can use the cursor buttons to move the zoomed area around within the frame. You can also use the control dial to move to other images at the same enlargement factor.

■ **View index thumbnails.** From full-frame view, keep pressing the zoom lever toward the left to view four or nine thumbnails, and continue with presses of the lever to view 36 and 100 increasingly smaller thumbnail images. Use the cursor buttons to maneuver around the index images, and press the FUNC./SET button to view a highlighted thumbnail as a full-frame image.

Transferring Photos to Your Computer

The final step in your picture-taking session will be to transfer the photos you've taken to your computer for printing, further review, or image editing. Your G1 X allows you to print directly to PictBridge-compatible printers and to create print orders right in the camera, plus you can select which images to transfer to your computer. I'll outline those options in Chapter 4.

For now, you'll probably want to transfer your images either by using a cable transfer from the camera to the computer or by removing the memory card from the G1 X and transferring the images with a card reader. The latter option is the best, because it's usually much faster and doesn't deplete the battery of your camera. However, you can use a cable transfer when you have the cable and a computer, but no card reader (perhaps you're using the computer of a friend or colleague, or at an Internet café). Finally, if you like to use the latest cool technology, consider using an Eye-Fi card, which lets you transfer images to your computer over a Wi-Fi network.

To transfer images from the camera to a Mac or PC computer using the USB cable:

1. Turn off the camera.

2. Pull up the cover that protects the PowerShot's USB port on the right side of the camera (as you hold it in the shooting position), and plug the USB cable furnished with the camera into the USB port, the upper of the two openings. (See Figure 2.10.)

3. Connect the other end of the USB cable to a USB port on your computer.

4. Turn on the camera. Your installed software usually detects the camera and offers to transfer the pictures, or the camera appears on your desktop as a mass storage device, enabling you to drag and drop the files to your computer.

Figure 2.10
Images can be transferred to your computer using a USB cable plugged into this port.

To transfer images from a memory card to the computer using a card reader, as shown in Figure 2.11:

1. Turn off the camera.

2. Slide open the memory card/battery door on the bottom of the camera, and press on the card, which causes it to pop up so it can be removed from the slot.

3. Insert the memory card into your memory card reader. Your installed software detects the files on the card and offers to transfer them. The card can also appear as a mass storage device on your desktop, which you can open, and then drag and drop the files to your computer.

If you want to transfer your images using an Eye-Fi card, you will need to have a PC running Windows XP, Vista, or Windows 7, or a Macintosh running Mac OS X version 10.4 or later. You will also need access to a broadband Internet connection and a wireless (Wi-Fi) router. As for the Eye-Fi card itself, I recommend that you get a Pro X2 version or better with at least 8GB of capacity. (See Figure 2.12.) This variety of Eye-Fi card is capable of handling RAW files and video; lesser models can't deal with such large files.

Figure 2.11 A card reader is the fastest way to transfer photos.

Figure 2.12 An Eye-Fi card is the coolest way to transfer photos.

Once you have the card and the needed network connection, here are the basic steps to take:

1. With the Eye-Fi card inserted into the card reader that comes with it, connect the card reader to a USB port on your computer and allow the computer to recognize the card and reader.

2. Install the software that came with the card on your computer and follow the on-screen instructions.

3. When the software and network settings are properly configured, remove the card from the reader, leaving the reader plugged into the USB port. Insert the card into your PowerShot G1 X.

4. On the PowerShot G1 X, go into the Setup menu and select Eye-Fi settings. (Note: That option will not show up on the menu until an Eye-Fi card is inserted into the camera.) Make sure the Enable option is selected. If you have problems, select the Connection Info option from the Eye-Fi Settings menu to see the status of the connection of the card to the network.

5. Take a picture. If the software has been set up properly, a window should appear on your computer's screen showing a thumbnail of the image as it uploads to your computer. In a short while, the image will be available for viewing or editing in the folder that was designated during the setup process.

3

Canon PowerShot G1 X Roadmap

One of the reasons that the Canon PowerShot lineup of cameras has been popular with beginning snapshooters, avid photo hobbyists, and advanced photographers—including both amateurs and pros—is their easy access to features. The G1 X continues this combination with a rich set of functions that are quickly available with a well-designed array of controls and menus. Whether you're just learning to work with your PowerShot G1 X as your first advanced digital camera or you're a seasoned photographer looking for the kind of tools you expect from a sophisticated compact camera, you'll easily find what you need.

Whenever a camera manufacturer develops a new camera, there have to be tradeoffs among several design goals: easy access to controls, clarity of control functions, and simplicity. There's no perfect approach to the physical layout of the camera. If it bristles with dozens of buttons and wheels, the photographer can immediately get access to many functions, but may not intuitively understand which one to use for a particular purpose. On the other hand, a camera may be sleek and streamlined with few physical controls, but that design may require the user to master an obscure and deeply buried array of menu commands to carry out even the simplest of functions.

With the PowerShot G1 X, Canon has done a good job of providing ready access to the tools you need. Easily accessible dials and buttons simplify tasks like adding or subtracting exposure from the metered setting (exposure compensation) and switching among available shooting modes with the mode dial. However, as is the case with any camera as capable and sophisticated as this, the average user needs a clear guide to explain what each control does, and how to achieve the desired results using the various switches and dials.

Traditionally, there have been two ways of providing a roadmap to guide you through this maze of features. The most common approach, taken by Canon in the user's guide that ships with the PowerShot G1 X on CD, uses a few small black-and-white line drawings or photos that are peppered with dozens of labels or callouts keyed to the numbers of the pages in the book that tell you what these components do. (See, for example, pages 4 and 5 of the G1 X Camera User Guide.) Even if you can decipher these illustrations without viewing the PDF-only manual zoomed in on a large-screen monitor, getting the information you need from a miniature camera diagram is a lot like being presented with a world globe when what you really want to know is how to find the capital of Belgium.

I originated a more useful approach in my field guides, providing you with, instead of a long-range satellite view, a street-level map that includes close-up full-color photos of the camera from several angles (see Figure 3.1, for example), with a smaller number of labels clearly pointing to each individual feature. And, I don't force you to flip back and forth among dozens of pages to find out what a particular component does. Each photo is accompanied by a brief description that summarizes the controls available in that view, so you can begin using the features right away. Only when a particular function deserves a lengthy explanation do I direct you to a more detailed write-up later in the book.

Figure 3.1

So, if you're wondering what the ISO button does, I'll tell you the basics up front, rather than have you search the camera's user guide, which doesn't provide much information anyway. This book is not a scavenger hunt. But after I explain how to use the ISO button to change the sensitivity of the G1 X, I *will* provide a cross-reference to a longer explanation later in the book that clarifies noise reduction, ISO, and the effects of ISO on exposure.

It's really not possible to explain *everything* about *every* feature the first time that capability is mentioned. Many features of this PowerShot camera are interdependent. To really understand ISO sensitivity, you also need to understand how exposure works. So, to avoid having humongous 150-page chapters, I'll provide the key information you can use immediately up front, and use limited cross-references to direct you to the in-depth discussions you need to really understand a feature and all its options. I think this kind of organization works best for cameras as sophisticated as the PowerShot G1 X.

By the time you finish this chapter, you'll have a basic understanding of every control and what it does. I'm not going to delve into menu functions here—you'll find a discussion of your Setup, Shooting, and Playback menu options in Chapter 4. Everything here is devoted to the button pusher and dial twirler in you.

Front View

When we picture a given camera, we usually imagine the front view. That's the view that your subjects see as you snap away, and the aspect that's shown in product publicity and on the box. The frontal angle is, for all intents and purposes, the "face" of a camera like the PowerShot G1 X. But, not surprisingly, most of the "business" of operating the camera happens *behind* it, where the photographer resides. The front of the G1 X actually has very few controls and features to worry about. Nine front-located features are readily visible in Figures 3.2 and 3.3:

- **Hand grip.** This gently raised area has a lightly textured surface that provides a comfortable hand-hold, so the camera does not slip readily out of your grip.

- **Front dial.** This feature gives you ready access to various options within quick reach of your right index finger, and lets you use one dial to control shutter speed, with another to control aperture while in Manual exposure mode. Among the various tasks it carries out, the front control dial sets shutter speed when the camera is in Manual or Shutter priority mode, and it sets aperture when the camera is in Aperture priority mode. It also is used for some less critical roles, such as jumping to categories of images in Playback mode, making fine adjustments to white balance, and changing the time delay of the self-timer. In addition, as I'll discuss in Chapter 4, you can assign certain other functions to this dial using the Set Dial Functions option on the Shooting menu.

Figure 3.2

AV-Out/
compartment door

Front
control dial

Red-eye reduction/Self-
timer/Autofocus assist lamp

Viewfinder
window

DC power port   Hand grip

Figure 3.3

Pop-up flash

Neck strap
mount

Speaker

Lens ring release
button

- **Red-eye reduction/Self-timer/Autofocus assist lamp.** This LED provides a blip of light shortly before a flash exposure to cause the subjects' pupils to close down, reducing the effect of red-eye reflections off their retinas. When you're using the self-timer, this lamp also flashes to mark the countdown until the photo is taken. For its third trick, this versatile light beams into poorly illuminated areas in front of the camera to help the PowerShot's autofocus apparatus see what it's doing.

- **Viewfinder window.** This is the "eye" of the photographer when he or she is looking through the viewfinder, as opposed to using the LCD screen to compose a shot.

- **AV-Out/compartment door.** This little door on the right side of the camera (as you hold it to shoot) conceals the location of the ports or jacks that are used to connect your camera to a computer, TV set, or remote switch. The bottom port is for an optional HTC-100 mini-HDMI cable to connect the camera's video output to a high-definition TV set; the middle jack is for the optional remote switch; and the top one is a mini-USB port that accepts USB cables.

- **DC power port.** This door opens to allow the cord for the optional ACK-DC80 coupler (which replaces the battery when using AC power) to exit the battery chamber.

- **Built-in flash.** The PowerShot G1 X sports this very handy little pop-up flash tube that is always ready to fire at your command when elevated using the flash button on top of the camera. Of course, this flash is not nearly as powerful as the external units that can be connected to the camera's accessory shoe, but it serves a very useful purpose for general snapshooting and as a fill-in flash for some outdoor shots.

- **Speaker.** When you're playing back movies, the sound will emanate from the tiny speaker built into the side of the camera. It the sound is muted, move your hand!

- **Ring release button.** This inconspicuous little button is reminiscent of the lens release buttons found on dSLRs and other cameras that take interchangeable lenses. The difference is that this button does not release the lens; it just releases the ring around the lens, so you can install an adapter that is required when you are attaching certain accessories, filters, or a lens hood.

- **Neck strap mounts.** On both sides of the camera there are mounting brackets for the neck strap that's included with the camera. It's a good idea to install that strap (or an optional one of your own choosing, as discussed in Chapter 1) as one of your first steps after taking the camera out of the box, to give you some protection against dropping your new acquisition while getting acquainted with its features.

The LCD Screen: To Swivel or Not to Swivel

At this point in our tour of the PowerShot G1 X's real estate, before we embark on our perusal of the back yard, we need to pause for a close examination of one of the main features of the camera. I'm talking about the LCD screen—that marvelously informative rectangular expanse on the back of the camera that, depending on the context, shows you the shot you're composing, displays the scenes you've already captured, or provides you with detailed information about those images, as well as the camera's menus and settings. As you can see in Figure 3.4, the PowerShot G1 X has a swiveling display, consisting of a 3-inch LCD with a 922,000 pixel resolution and the ability to rotate on both vertical and horizontal axes.

The swiveling capability of the PowerShot G1 X's LCD screen is no small matter, and it is worth taking a few moments to discuss the benefits (and tradeoffs) that this enhancement brings to the camera. Let's discuss how the swiveling screen works, and what advantages that capability provides. When you first take the camera out of its box, you will find that the LCD screen is in its "closed" position (see Figure 3.5). In this position, the screen is folded in against the back of the camera, with its display surface hidden from view.

Figure 3.4

Figure 3.5

Why is this a useful configuration? For several reasons. First, it's a great way to protect the screen from damage, dirt, or the elements. Other cameras have their screens exposed to possible harm whenever they're out of their cases. The ability to fold the screen in provides a built-in screen protection system. In addition, in some situations you may want to take your pictures in as discreet a way as possible, such as at concerts or religious ceremonies, and you may not want to distract persons near you by having the LCD display showing. Of course, you can turn off the display of other digital cameras to save power, too—at least those that have optical viewfinders like the G1 X, so you won't be shooting blind. But it may be easier and more effective to just fold it in against the camera.

In practice, however, the only time I use the G1 X with the LCD reversed is when it is stored for traveling, and there is a possibility that the back of the camera will receive a sharp rap that might damage the screen. Most of the time I prefer to use a tempered glass protector on the LCD, such as the one offered by GGS, and available on Amazon and from other sources. That gives my LCD protection from scratches; the camera is always in a shooting configuration and, ironically, I don't have to worry about the back of the LCD receiving numerous scratches in everyday use.

Flip open the LCD on the PowerShot G1 X and take a look at what it has to offer in the way of photographic versatility. First, check out Figure 3.6. In this position, the screen is swiveled out to the left at various angles, allowing you to view your subject from one side, or even turn the display so you're looking around a corner. From here, you can swivel the screen vertically so it is aiming up at the sky, down toward the ground, or even turned all the way around to face in the same direction as the lens. These positions give you several options. With the screen swiveled out to the left and then flipped upward, you can easily hold the camera down at waist level and compose your image without bending over. In this way, you can compose a photograph that looks better when taken from a low angle, and you don't have to get down on your belly or crouch in a squat. On the other hand, if you flip the screen downward, you can hold the camera above your head to peer over the tops of crowds or physical obstructions,

Figure 3.6

Figure 3.7

and compose the image in the LCD, sort of like submarine commanders with their raised periscopes. I appreciate this mode at concerts, because I can raise the camera up over the heads of the multitude milling around in front of me. Finally, swivel the screen around to face the front, and you can indulge your narcissistic side by pointing the camera at yourself and taking a self-portrait that is nicely framed in the versatile LCD. (See Figure 3.7.)

The Canon PowerShot G1 X's Business End

The back panel of the PowerShot G1 X is dominated by the swiveling LCD screen, but the camera's designers also managed to find room for about a dozen different controls in the form of buttons and dials. That might seem like a lot of controls to learn, but I think you'll find, as I noted earlier, that it's usually a good deal easier to press a dedicated button or spin a dial than to navigate through a menu system every time you want to change a setting.

You can see the controls that populate the back of the G1 X in Figure 3.8. Because there are so many different controls, I've divided them into two illustrations. First, the controls on the upper half of the camera, as shown in Figure 3.9.

Figure 3.8

Shortcut/Print-share button · Diopter adjustment dial · Viewfinder eyepiece · Upper indicator LED · Lower indicator LED · Playback button · Movie Record button

Figure 3.9

The key controls and components and their functions are as follows:

- **Viewfinder eyepiece.** You can frame your composition by peering into the viewfinder. The PowerShot G1 X has no luxurious rubber eyecup or other frills; all you get is a small window to peer into and a view of the scene being viewed by your lens, at the current zoom factor. Unlike the situation with the typical dSLR camera, you get absolutely no information in the viewfinder other than an image of what the camera is pointing at.

  But you should be fairly happy with that view; there are quite a few cameras in this class that have no optical viewfinder at all, leaving you holding the unsteady camera out at arm's length, even in low-light situations where steadying the camera against your forehead might provide a more stable view. Or, without recourse to an optical viewfinder, you might be forced to squint at an LCD screen that can be washed out in bright sunlight. The viewfinder on the G1 X is not fancy, but it provides a very useful capability.

- **Diopter adjustment dial.** The little wheel just to the left of the viewfinder lets you adjust the viewfinder to correct for your eyesight, as described in Chapter 1.

- **Upper indicator light.** The G1 X is equipped with a set of two indicator lights just to the right of the viewfinder window. Because you can see them out of the corner of your eye, the information is available to you even when you're using the optical viewfinder. The upper indicator light provides these signals:

  - **Green.** Ready to shoot.

  - **Blinking green.** Low battery.

- **Lower indicator light.** This is an LED signal for focus conditions.

  - **Green.** Ready to shoot when flash is deactivated.

  - **Blinking green.** Image recording/reading/erasing/transfer underway. While that is happening, be careful not to turn off the camera, open the memory card door, or otherwise disturb the process. If you do, data could be lost or corrupted.

  - **Orange.** Ready to shoot when flash is activated.

  - **Blinking orange.** Distance warning or unable to focus (when flash is activated).

- **Set shortcut/Direct Print button.** This button, sitting away from its peers way up on the left side of the camera, is like a wildcard or programmable function button, giving you the chance to take one favorite action and assign it to this button for one-press access. To take advantage of this capability, go to the Shooting menu and select the Set Shortcut Button option, scroll to the function you want to assign to the button, and press FUNC./SET to confirm your selection. I'll explain use of the Shooting menu in more detail in Chapter 4.

  On the G1 X your choices are: Not Assigned, i-Contrast, White Balance, Custom White Balance 1, Custom White Balance 2, My Colors, Bracketing, Drive Mode, Flash Exposure Compensation/Flash Output, ND filter, Aspect Ratio, Select RAW or JPEG, Recording Pixels/Compression, Movie Quality, Servo AF, Red-Eye Correction, AF Lock, Digital Tele-Converter, and Display Off.

  What you do with this button depends on your own working habits. With the G1 X, Canon has added many more options to the list that this button can accommodate, so it's pretty likely you'll find one you like. Personally, I'm glad to see the addition of an option to select RAW or JPEG images.

  Finally, this button, like many of the others, has a second, completely unrelated function as the Direct Print button. If you connect the G1 X to a PictBridge-compatible printer, you can use this button to send images directly to the printer. I'll also describe this function in Chapter 4.

- **Playback button.** Pressing this button with the blue triangle displays the last picture taken (unless you use the menu system to change to showing the last picture viewed). Thereafter, you can move back and forth among the available images by pressing the left/right cursor buttons to advance or reverse one image at a time, using the control dial to move forward or back either image by image or using the front dial to move using a jump method you've selected. (See the section below for more on jumping.) To quit playback, press this button again. The G1 X also exits Playback mode automatically when you press the shutter button (so you'll never be prevented from taking a picture on the spur of the moment because you happened to be viewing an image).

■ **Movie Record button.** Press this button when the camera is set to any exposure mode (you don't need to rotate the mode dial to the Movie icon) to begin capturing video. Press a second time to stop recording. Rotating the mode dial to the Movie position gives you additional options during movie shooting, such as the ability to adjust exposure compensation (although, oddly, *not* with the Exposure Compensation dial, as I'll describe shortly).

PLAYBACK PAYBACK

There's one other convenient feature of the G1 X: when the camera is turned off, you can turn it back on with the Playback button, so you are immediately in playback mode. Press the Playback button again to turn it off. However, once you're in recording mode, pressing the Playback button toggles back and forth between recording and playback. You'll need to use the Power button to turn the camera off. The Playback on/Playback off trick works only if you remain in the Setup menu or use playback mode the whole time the camera is on, for example, simply to review images.

The right half of the PowerShot G1 X is dominated by a set of buttons that includes the cursor buttons, which serve as your directional controls for navigating around the screen and menus, and which do double-duty with other direct-access functions. The key controls shown in Figure 3.10 are as follows:

■ **Rear control dial.** This ridged dial that surrounds the array of cursor buttons and the FUNC./SET button is a workhorse that performs several functions. Canon simply calls it the "control dial" and applies a "front dial" moniker to its counterpart on the front of the camera. However, to avoid confusion, I'll use *rear control dial* and *front control dial* terminology.

In many cases, such as scrolling through the menu screens, you can use either the control dial or the cursor "buttons" to carry out the same operation. This dial also is used to move through your images in playback mode and to make settings for various functions, such as choosing among the options for metering mode and setting fine adjustments to white balance. In manual focus mode, you use the control dial to adjust the focus. In addition, this dial is used to set the aperture value in Manual exposure mode, while the front dial sets shutter speed. However, you can reverse these roles of the two dials using the Set Dial Functions item on the Shooting menu, and you can also set any one of several other functions to be performed by the control dial, including setting aspect ratio, white balance adjustments, and i-Contrast. I discuss these options in Chapter 4. In some cases, in Manual exposure mode, the control dial can have two different functions assigned to it at the same time. In that event, you can switch between the two settings by pressing the metering mode button, just above and to the right of the control dial. I discuss these options in Chapter 4.

Figure 3.10

AF frame selector/Single image erase button

Focus mode button

Directional buttons

Metering mode

AE lock-FE lock/ Jump button

ISO button

FUNC./SET button

Flash button

Rear control dial

DISP. button

MENU button

■ **Cursor buttons.** These "buttons" are an array of four directional controls that are actually just positions on the rear control dial at North, South, East, and West locations. They provide left/right/up/down movement to navigate menus, and are used to cycle among various options (usually with the left/right buttons) and to choose amounts (with the up/down buttons). The four cursor buttons also have secondary functions to select focus options, flash options, ISO settings, and display modes. (I'll describe these separately next.)

■ **Left cursor/Macro/Manual Focus button.** Press this button to engage Macro mode, Manual focus, or return to Normal focus mode. In Macro mode, the camera's focusing system is limited to close-up focusing. The distance range in Macro mode is about eight inches from the subject to the end of the lens, when the camera is zoomed out to the wide-angle setting. At the Manual focus setting, you can adjust the focus using the rear control dial. I'll supply more information about this procedure in Chapter 6.

■ **Top cursor/ISO button.** Press this button and a screen pops up that allows you to choose Auto ISO (sensitivity is set from ISO 100 to 1600 as appropriate), or fixed ISO settings from ISO 100 to 12800. When this screen is visible, you can press the MENU button to produce a second screen of adjustments specifically for the Auto ISO setting. You can change the *maximum* ISO setting the camera will select (from ISO 400 to 1600), and how quickly the G1 X responds to changing lighting conditions (choose Fast, Slow, or Standard). The Max ISO Speed option lets you retain the convenience of Auto ISO selection while putting the brakes on choosing a setting that might produce more visual noise than you'd find acceptable in a particular situation. The Rate of Change option can be used to adjust responsiveness, so that the camera can change ISO rapidly under lighting conditions that change (potentially producing widely varying noise levels in a series of shots). Or, you can set the camera to "stick" with one Auto ISO setting and change to another value only when lighting conditions change significantly.

- **Right cursor/Flash button.** This button gives you access to various functions associated with the built-in flash unit and any external flash that you attach and power up. If you press it lightly, each press moves to one of several options (depending on the shooting mode) for the flash setting: Automatic; Always on, Slow synchro; and Always off. If you hold down the button firmly, the camera displays the Flash Control menu, giving you access to additional flash settings. All of this is discussed more fully in Chapter 10.

- **Bottom cursor/DISP. button.** When pressed repeatedly in shooting mode, this button changes the amount of picture information displayed. In playback mode, pressing the DISP. button cycles among basic display of the image; a display with limited information, including battery life, image number, date, and time; a detailed display with a thumbnail of the image, shooting parameters, and a brightness histogram; and a display with two views of the image for checking focus. (I'll discuss that function later in this chapter.) It can also be used to switch off the LCD.

- **FUNC./SET button.** Push this button in to confirm a selection or activate a feature. It also provides direct access to the FUNC. menu, described in detail in Chapter 4. The FUNC. menu allows you to quickly access frequently changed settings, such as white balance and image size. As you'll see in Chapter 4, making those settings can be accomplished much faster in this way than by using the regular menu system, and you'll also find that less-used parameters are tucked away in the main menus.

- **MENU button.** Summons/exits the menu displayed on the LCD of the G1 X. When you're working with submenus, this button also serves to exit a submenu and return to the main menu.

■ **AF frame selector/Single image erase button.** This button's primary function is to let you perform certain functions in connection with the autofocus system, as described in the discussion of menu options in Chapter 4 and in the autofocus section in Chapter 6. This button's secondary function is to erase individual images. Press the button once when an image is displayed in playback mode, and the image will be erased if you confirm the operation with the navigation buttons and the FUNC./SET button.

■ **AE/FE (Autoexposure/Flash exposure) lock.** This button at the upper right of the camera's back, which is labeled with a star (*), has several functions, which differ depending on the AF point and metering mode. You can find more about these variations in Chapter 5.

In shooting mode, pressing this button locks the exposure or flash exposure that the camera sets when you partially depress the shutter button. The exposure lock will be released if you press another button after releasing the AE/FE lock button. When shooting movies with the mode dial set to the Movie position, this button allows applying Exposure Compensation (described in Chapter 5) in place of the Exposure Compensation dial (on top of the camera), used in still shooting modes.

When using flash, pressing the * button fires an extra pre-flash that allows the unit to calculate and lock exposure prior to taking the picture with the flash.

■ **Metering mode/Jump target button.** The primary job of this button is to let you select the exposure metering mode to be used by the camera, as described in Chapter 5.

  ■ In shooting mode, press the button, then turn the rear control dial to choose Evaluative (to base exposure on several different areas within the frame); Center weighted averaging (to emphasize the center area when calculating exposure); or Spot (to meter from a small area in the frame).

  ■ In Manual mode, if you have set the control dial to have two different functions at the same time, such as setting aperture and aspect ratio, using the Set Dial Functions option on the Shooting menu, you switch between the two functions using this button. Note, though, that pressing this button also activates the Metering Mode selection screen, so you will likely have to press this button a few times before it will switch the control dial's function to the one you are looking for. You will see a green circle representing the control dial next to the aperture or metering mode when it is controlling those functions; when it is controlling the third function, the green circle disappears from the screen.

  ■ When reviewing images, the button's third function is to let you specify the way the camera "jumps" between images when rotating the control dial. I'll talk more about this capability a little later in this chapter.

Going Topside

The top surface of the Canon PowerShot G1 X has a few frequently accessed controls of its own. The key controls, shown in Figure 3.11, are as follows:

- **Exposure compensation dial.** One of the very attractive features of the G1 X is the existence of this dial, which gives you instant access to adjust the exposure compensation, without having to immerse yourself in the menu system or embark on a series of button pushes. One quick twist of this knob, and you can dial in the amount of compensation you need, to account for backlighting or other challenging exposure conditions. This dial can't be used to adjust exposure compensation when shooting movies; you must switch the mode dial to the Movie icon and use the AE/FE lock button instead. I discuss exposure in more depth in Chapter 5.

- **Flash hot shoe.** Slide an electronic flash into this mount when you need a more powerful Speedlite. A dedicated flash unit, like those from Canon, can use the multiple contact points shown to communicate exposure, zoom setting, white balance information, and other data between the flash and the camera. There's more on using electronic flash in Chapter 10.

- **Mode dial.** This dial is used to select among the various shooting modes offered by the G1 X. I discuss the shooting modes in Chapter 5.

Figure 3.11

Microphones

Mode dial

Zoom lever

Shutter button

Flash button

Hot shoe

Exposure compensation dial

On/Off button

- **Microphones.** These record stereo sound during movie shooting. Be careful not to cover them with your fingers while capturing video.

- **Shutter release button.** Partially depress this button to lock in exposure and focus. Press all the way to take the picture. You can partially depress the shutter button to switch from playback mode to recording mode, also. You can also press this button halfway to wake the camera up from its sleep mode.

- **Zoom lever.** This control has quite a few functions. Its primary purpose is to change the focal length of the PowerShot G1 X's lens between its 28mm wide-angle setting and its full optical zoom length of 112mm. You can also use this lever to magnify the image beyond the optical zoom length, using the digital zoom feature, discussed in Chapter 4. In playback mode, discussed later, it changes views of your images, and when viewing menus, you can use this lever to switch from one menu system (Shooting, Playback, Setup) to another.

- **On/Off switch.** Press down to turn the PowerShot G1 X on, and press it again to turn the camera off. The green power light in the center of the button will illuminate while the power is on, and blinks when the battery is low.

Port-Side Terminals

When you're holding the PowerShot G1 X in your hands, the starboard (right) side of the camera is, oddly enough, the "port" side, where, underneath the terminal cover, you'll find three ports that let you connect the G1 X to the outside world. These connectors, shown in Figure 3.12, are as follows:

- **USB/Digital terminal.** This single connector has two purposes—to connect the camera to a computer or printer using the USB cable that is provided with the camera (or a generic equivalent), and also to connect the camera to a standard definition TV set, using the optional Stereo AV Cable AVC-DC400ST.

- **Remote terminal.** This small round jack accepts a wired remote switch, the Canon RS60-E3, which you can use to control the camera from a distance in the same way as the cable releases used on film cameras. There also are wireless remote switches available that are compatible with this connection.

- **HDMI connector.** This lower terminal accepts the optional Canon HDMI cable, model number HTC-100. You also can use any standard HDMI cable with a mini-HDMI connector at the camera end and a standard HDMI connector at the TV end. With the cable, you can connect the camera to a high-definition (HD) television set or monitor. If you're playing back images on an HDTV (or on a standard definition TV using the USB/Digital terminal), turning on the G1 X by pressing the Playback button instead of the Power button will activate the camera without extending the lens.

Figure 3.12

USB/Digital
terminal

Remote terminal

HDMI connector

LCD Panel Readouts

The PowerShot G1 X does not have a monochrome status LCD, like the one found on the top panel of many digital SLR cameras, and does not provide any display inside its viewfinder, as most dSLRs do. Lacking these auxiliary information displays, the G1 X uses the color LCD to show you everything you need to see, from images to a collection of informational data displays. When the camera is in shooting mode, the screen displays only basic information, including battery status, exposure mode, and a few values, including shutter speed and f/stop. Using the Custom Display option on the Recording menu, you can also set the camera to display grid lines, a histogram, and an electronic level, as I'll explain in Chapter 4.

When the camera is in playback mode, it can display your images accompanied by several different screens of information. Here's an overview of these displays, and how to access them.

Image Playback Displays

When the G1 X shows you a picture for review, you can select from among four different information overlays (three for movies). To switch among them, press the DISP. button while the image is on the screen. The LCD will cycle among:

- **Single image display,** which shows just the image that is on the memory card (or the initial frame of a movie); no other information is displayed (Figure 3.13).

- **Single image display with recording quality**, which also shows the image number, date, and time the image was taken. (Figure 3.14.) For movies, the information shown is slightly different.

- **Histogram display**, which shows basic shooting information such as shutter speed and aperture as well as a brightness histogram at bottom left (Figure 3.15). (I'll explain how to work with histograms in Chapter 5.)

- **Focus checking display.** A special screen designed to let you make a detailed assessment of the image's focus. This screen (shown in Figure 3.16) shows one view, on the left, of about normal size, with an orange frame showing where the camera's focus was set when the picture was taken. On the right is a smaller frame, enlarged. Move the zoom lever to the right to switch to the enlarged view, which then becomes highlighted. You can then change the magnification of this view with the zoom lever and scroll around it with the cross keys, to check the focus. This screen does not appear for movies.

Figure 3.13 Single image display.

Figure 3.14 Single image display with basic information.

Figure 3.15 Histogram display.

Figure 3.16 Focus checking display.

Jumping/Zooming Around

When you're ready to view the pictures you've taken, either on the camera's own LCD display or on a connected TV set, the PowerShot G1 X offers plenty of options for viewing them. You'll find more details about some of these functions later in this chapter or in other chapters that I point you to. Here is the must-know information.

- **Start review.** To begin reviewing your pictures, press the Playback button located above the LCD screen to the right of the viewfinder window. The image that shows up on the screen will be either the most recently viewed image or the most recently taken image, depending on your settings in the Playback menu. If the next item is a movie, press the FUNC./SET key to call up a VCR-like set of controls on the screen. Use the FUNC./SET key to operate those controls.

- **Cycle through information displays.** To view more or less information on the screen, press the DISP. button to move through the three (for movies) or four (for still images) different levels of items that show up on the screen. These displays can be invaluable in helping you to check composition, exposure, and focus, using tools such as the histogram and the focus check display.

- **View thumbnail images.** To change the view from a single image to 4, 9, 36, or 100 thumbnails, or to use the Jump button (just above the rear control dial, and marked with an asterisk) to move among shots by categories, dates, and other criteria, see the "Viewing Thumbnails" and "Jumping Around" sections that follow.

- **Zoom in and out.** To zoom in or out, press the zoom lever, following the instructions on "Zooming Around" in the next section.

- **Move back and forth.** To advance to the next image, press the right cursor button; to go back to a previous shot, press the left button. You can also use either the front dial or the control dial to move through your images. When you reach the first or last photo in your memory card's folder, the display "wraps around" to the next shot in the sequence.

- **Move back and forth rapidly using Scroll Display.** To advance through the images rapidly using the single image display, turn the control dial on the back of the camera quickly, and the images will scroll in a way similar to the "cover flow" scrolling on an iPod. When this Scroll Display feature is active, a pair of up and down arrows will appear on the screen, inviting you to select images by date; choose a date with the up/down cursor buttons. Go back to normal Playback display by pressing the DISP. button or the FUNC./SET button. You can disable this feature altogether using the Scroll Display option on the Playback menu; in that case, the control dial merely moves through your images normally.

- **Erase images.** To delete an image that's currently on the screen, press the Trash button, then move the highlight from Cancel to Erase on the screen, and press the FUNC./SET key to confirm the operation.

- **Cancel playback.** To cancel image review, press the Playback button again, or simply tap the shutter release button. (If you turned the camera on using the Playback button, pressing the button again will turn off the camera.)

Zooming Around

When an image is displayed in playback mode, press the zoom lever to the right (in the direction for zooming the lens) to fill the screen with a slightly magnified version of the image. You can keep pressing the zoom lever to magnify images up to about 10 times the normal size. Press the lever in the other direction as many times as needed to reduce the size to normal, or press the MENU button to reduce it to normal immediately. While the image is zoomed, you can scroll around in the zoomed image with the four cursor buttons. You can move to other images with the control dial while the images are zoomed.

Viewing Thumbnails

The PowerShot G1 X provides other options for reviewing images in addition to zooming in and out. You can switch between single image view and an index screen with 4 thumbnail images by moving the zoom lever to the left, toward the wide-angle view. Further pushes of the zoom lever take you to successive index screens with 9, 36, and 100 thumbnail images, assuming you have that many images stored on your memory card. One of the thumbnail images will be highlighted by a frame, and you can move to the other images on the screen one at a time with the cursor buttons or one row at a time with the control dial. Move the zoom lever back to the right to move back to screens with fewer thumbnails. When an individual image is highlighted on an index screen, you can erase it by pressing the Trash button and then confirming the action when prompted by the camera.

Jumping Around with Filtered Playback

The PowerShot G1 X has one more image-viewing trick up its sleeve, and a pretty powerful one at that. Some previous Canon models (not to mention models from other brands) have a Calendar function that lets you view images taken on a particular date. The G1 X can perform a similar feat, but with added punch—it will let you "jump" to other images not just by date, but also by category, first image in the folder, movies versus stills, 10-image jumps, and 100-image jumps. So, for example, if, like me, you use 16GB SDHC cards (which can hold thousands of images each) this is a welcome way to narrow down your search for images on a given card. Here's how to perform this sort of jump-search, which Canon calls Filtered Playback:

1. **Press the Playback button.** The camera enters playback mode.

2. **Press the Jump button.** That's the button above the right side of the control dial, marked with a * symbol. This action brings up a submenu on the left of the screen showing a line of icons. From top to bottom, these icons represent Favorites; date; category; still/movie; jump 10 images; and jump 100 images.

3. **Scroll to the desired search type.** Scroll down to highlight one of the above criteria you want to use to base your search on. If you're basing your search on the categories of images or on Favorites, see the discussions of those topics in Chapter 4.

4. **Select the filter data.** If there is more than one possibility for the search, such as with dates or categories, use the left/right cursor buttons to select the details of the search you want. For example, select the particular date you're searching for, or choose between stills and movies. If there's only one possibility for the search, such as jumping to Favorites, go directly to the next step below.

5. **Turn the rear control dial.** This is the step that actually takes you to the first image that meets the search factors you have chosen. Turn the dial to the right to select that first image of the search set, then keep turning it to continue displaying those images.

6. **Press the Jump button again.** Pressing the Jump button again will exit from this search mode.

Underneath Your PowerShot G1 X

There's not a lot going on with the bottom panel of your PowerShot G1 X. Besides the door to the battery and memory card compartment, you'll find a tripod socket, which secures the camera to a tripod, or to certain optional accessories, such as the BKT-DC1 bracket, which is used to mount a macro ring flash unit and other external flash units. Figure 3.17 shows the underside view of the camera.

Figure 3.17

Setting Up Your Canon PowerShot G1 X

For a highly portable "point-and-shoot" camera, the PowerShot G1 X provides you with an impressive collection of options and settings that let you customize the way your camera operates. Not only can you change shooting settings used at the time the picture is taken, but you can adjust the way your camera behaves. Indeed, if your G1 X doesn't operate in exactly the way you'd like, chances are you can make an adjustment in the Shooting menu, the Playback menu, or the Setup menu to tweak the camera's behavior to your liking. If you don't like the organization of the menus themselves, you can create a customized mini-menu system of your own by gathering your favorite functions using the My Menu feature. In addition, you can get virtually instant access to several of the most important choices for setting up your shots through the FUNC. menu, which is summoned with one press of your finger.

This chapter will help you sort out the settings for all the G1 X's menus. These include the aforementioned Shooting, FUNC., and Playback menus, which determine how the G1 X uses many of its shooting features to take a photo and how it displays images on review. In addition, I'll show you how to use the Setup menu to adjust items such as power-saving timers, screen brightness, and others.

As I've mentioned before, this book isn't intended to replace the manual you received with your G1 X, nor have I any interest in rehashing the contents of the Canon user's guide. The owner's manual is useful as a standby reference that lists every possible option in exhaustive (if excruciating) detail—without really telling you how to use those options to take better pictures. There is, however, some unavoidable duplication between the Canon manual and this chapter, because I'm going to explain all the key menu choices and the options you may have in using them. You should find, though, that I will give you the information you need in a much more helpful format, with plenty of detail on why you should make some settings that are particularly difficult to understand.

I'm not going to waste a lot of space on some of the more obvious menu choices in these chapters. For example, you can probably figure out, even without my help, that the Sound Options item on the PowerShot G1 X's Setup menu deals with the solid-state sound chip in your camera that produces electronic chirps and beeps during various activities (such as the self-timer countdown). In this chapter, I'll devote no more than a sentence or two to the blatantly obvious settings and concentrate on the more confusing aspects of G1 X Setup, such as autofocus. I'll start with an overview of using the G1 X's menus themselves.

Anatomy of the PowerShot G1 X's Menus

The main menu system of the PowerShot G1 X should seem quite familiar to anyone who has used a similar-sized digital camera, especially another PowerShot, within the past few years. After all, given the profusion of features found on modern cameras, there are only so many ways that engineers can organize menu items for all of those features in a logical and user-friendly manner.

The designers of the PowerShot G1 X menu system have succeeded quite well in the user-friendliness arena. To make use of the system, just press the MENU button, located to the right of the viewfinder, and use either the left/right cursor buttons or the zoom lever (surrounding the shutter button) to highlight the menu tab you want to access—Shooting or Playback, depending on the mode the camera is in, or Setup, which is accessible from either shooting or playback mode. (There's also a printing menu, for functions relating to printing images directly from the camera, and the My Menu tab, which lets you set up a customized menu.) Then, scroll up and down within a menu with the up/down cursor buttons or by spinning the rear control dial.

Here's a shortcut: If you happen to get stuck one or more screens down in the options of one of the menus, you can quickly switch back to either of the other menus by moving the zoom lever to the right or left. That way, you don't have to scroll all the way back up to the top of one menu system before switching to another one, as you otherwise would. One more tip: when you get to the bottom (or top) of a menu, you can wrap around by continuing in that direction. For example, if you're on the top item of a long menu and want to get to the bottom item, or to an item that's closer to the bottom than to the top, your quickest route will be to scroll up beyond the top item, which will take you straight to the last item, from which you can then scroll up to the neighboring items. This technique can save lots of time when you need to navigate the menus in a hurry.

On the PowerShot G1 X, pressing the MENU button brings up a typical menu screen like the one shown in Figure 4.1. (If the camera goes to "sleep" while you're reviewing a menu, you may need to wake it up again by tapping the shutter release button or the MENU button.) There are three menu tabs visible while the camera is set to shooting mode: Shooting, Setup, and My Menu. (When the camera is in playback mode, the three menu choices are Playback, Printing, and Setup. We'll discuss those later.)

The tabs are labeled with icons: a camera for the Shooting menu, a wrench and hammer for the Setup menu, and a star for the My Menu tab. (The Playback menu is represented by a right-pointing triangle, and the Printing menu by a printer icon. Neither is shown in the view presented in Figure 4.1; you'll work with them later in this chapter.) The currently selected menu's icon is highlighted in orange. Here are the things to watch for as you navigate the menus:

■ **Menu tabs.** In the top row of the menu screen, the menu that is currently active will be highlighted as described earlier. Just remember that the camera icon stands for shooting options; the right-pointing triangle represents playback options; the wrench/hammer icon stands for Setup options; and the star stands for personalized menus.

■ **Selected menu item.** The currently selected menu item will be highlighted by an orange-colored bar.

Figure 4.1
The PowerShot G1 X's menus are arranged in a series of tabs.

■ **Other menu choices.** The other menu items visible on the screen will have a dark gray background. With the PowerShot G1 X, you won't always see "grayed out" menu lines for items that are not available in a particular mode. Instead, in some cases, those items just will not appear on the menu if they are not available. For example, when the camera's shooting mode is set to Auto, several Shooting menu options, such as AF Frame, Servo AF, and certain Flash Control options are not available, and simply do not show up—they are left out of the menu list. However, there are other situations in which the camera *does* use the "grayed out" approach. If you remain in a particular shooting mode but select an option that renders some menu selections unusable, those selections will be "grayed out." For example, if you are in Program mode, most of the menu options are available. But if you then select manual focus by pressing the MF button on the back of the camera, Presto! No more AF options are available on the menu; they are "grayed out."

■ **Current setting.** The current settings for visible menu items are shown in the right-hand column. Unlike some other cameras' menu systems, in most cases, the full screen of the G1 X menu stays visible on the camera's display while you select the value for a particular menu item. (With some other cameras, when you select a menu item, it takes up the whole screen, and all other menu items disappear until that item's value has been selected.)

When you've used the up/down cursor buttons (or the rear control dial) to move the menu highlight bar to the menu item you want to work with, press the left/right cursor button to select the desired value for the item. Many of the items can be set only to On or Off, but others can have one of several values. For example, the Review function, which determines how long a new image stays on the screen for review, can be set to a time from 2 to 10 seconds, to hold indefinitely, or to be off altogether—a total of 11 separate choices, plus Off, any of which can be selected by moving the left and right cursor buttons.

In a few cases, such as Flash Control, once you've highlighted the menu item, you need to press the FUNC./SET key to get access to a submenu with further options (see Figure 4.2). Such menu items have three dots after their names, to indicate that more details are available by pressing FUNC./SET. In most cases, though, you can make all your selections for the various menu items without leaving the main menu screen. This system makes it clean and easy to make your settings without having to go through a lot of extra button pushes or to go into and out of a series of submenus.

In order to select your desired menu option, you ordinarily only have to highlight it; you don't have to press the FUNC./SET key to select it. Once your selection is highlighted, just press the MENU key or press halfway down on the shutter button to exit the menu system, and you're ready to shoot with the newly selected option activated.

Figure 4.2
The Flash Control item on the Shooting menu leads to this submenu with numerous options, in some shooting modes. In the more automatic modes, fewer options appear on this list.

Shooting Menu Options

The various settings that are controlled directly by buttons and dials on the top and back panels of the camera, including ISO sensitivity, metering mode, exposure compensation (EV), self-timer, and flash, are likely to be the most common settings you make, with changes during a particular session fairly common. You'll probably find that the Shooting menu options, along with the FUNC. menu options, which I'll discuss later, are those that you access second-most frequently. You might make such adjustments as you begin a shooting session, or when you move from photographing one type of subject to another. Canon makes accessing these changes very easy.

This section explains the options of the Shooting menu and how to use them. As noted earlier, the G1 X sometimes changes its list of visible menu options according to the current context, such as whether the camera is set to Auto shooting mode. This system is good in that it eliminates the need to scroll through a series of options that you can't select, but it has the negative aspect of making it somewhat confusing to discuss the options that are available, because some of them will be invisible to you if the camera is set to a mode in which you can't make certain selections. (If you would like to go through the Shooting menu and see almost all of the available options, set the camera to Aperture priority mode by turning the mode dial to the Av setting; that mode has more Shooting menu options available than any other mode, as you can see from the chart at pages 226–235 of the camera's User Guide.)

With that caveat, then, the options you'll find in the Shooting menu, at least in some shooting modes, are the following:

- AF Frame
- Digital Zoom
- AF-Point Zoom
- Servo AF
- Continuous AF
- AF-Assist Beam
- MF-Point Zoom
- Safety MF
- Flash Control

- ISO Auto Settings
- High ISO NR
- Hg Lamp Corr.
- Spot AE Point
- Safety Shift
- Wind Filter
- Review
- Review Info
- Blink Detection

- Custom Display
- Reverse Display
- IS Settings
- Date Stamp
- Set Dial Functions
- Set Shortcut button
- Save Settings

AF Frame

The first choice presented to you in the Shooting menu is AF Frame, which gives you three options for the behavior of the autofocus frame. The first choice is Face AiAF, which I am going to venture to translate as "artificial intelligence autofocus." With this option, the camera attempts to find a human face in the scene before the camera. When it has found one or more likely candidates, it puts a white frame on what seems to be the main subject, as shown in Figure 4.3, and places gray frames on up to two other faces. If it finds no apparent faces, or no apparent main face, once you press the shutter button halfway, the camera will set up to nine green frames to show the points it will use for autofocus.

The second option on this menu is Tracking AF. When you choose this option, the focus area on the screen becomes a small white box with four little lines sticking out in each direction. Place this box over your subject (such as a fidgety child or pet), and press the AF Frame/Trash button, to the upper left above the rear control dial. The camera will then attempt to keep your chosen subject in its crosshairs, even as it (or the camera) moves. When you're ready to take the picture, press the shutter button halfway to calculate focus and exposure; the camera will continue to adjust focus and exposure on your subject until you press the shutter button all the way to take the picture.

Your third option here is FlexiZone, which I personally find preferable to the others for most ordinary shooting, when I don't need to track a moving subject. With FlexiZone, you work with a single AF frame, whose size and position you can change, so you can focus on a particular area of the scene in question to achieve a fairly precise level of control over your composition. Once you have selected this AF method, press the AF Frame/Trash button, and the AF frame will turn orange. The frame then becomes movable. Move it around the screen quickly with the rear control dial or the front

Figure 4.3
Face AiAF can locate faces in a frame, and lock in focus.

control dial, or in smaller steps with the cursor buttons. If you press the DISP. button, you can then change the size of the frame between normal and small. Fix the frame's location and size by pressing the FUNC./SET button or by pressing the shutter button halfway to focus.

If you do a lot of photography involving groups of people and the face detection works for you, that's great. For me, though, the FlexiZone system offers an excellent approach to achieving sharp focus. Decide what part of the image you want to be in the sharpest focus, select FlexiZone, and place a small-sized AF frame over that area while the lens is zoomed in. (If focus is sharp when the lens is zoomed in, it's sure to be sharp when zoomed back also.) Then zoom the lens back out if that's the view you want, and take the picture. Your focus should be right on the mark.

I'll discuss your focus options in more detail in Chapter 6.

Digital Zoom

Digital zoom, quite frankly, is not a feature to get particularly excited about. The PowerShot G1 X, like most compact digital cameras, has a nice "optical zoom" capability, going from 28mm (wide angle) to 112mm (telephoto), using the standard 35mm-equivalent ratings of focal length. That means that the camera's lens zooms in to a focal length that makes objects look four times larger than at the shortest focal length. That capability can be called a "real" zoom capability, because the image is magnified as with binoculars or a telescope; in other words, you actually get more information through the viewfinder and in your final image than without the zoom. This feature is the first one listed on the second page of the Shooting menu as you scroll down. (See Figure 4.4.)

With the "digital zoom," on the other hand, you really don't get any more picture information for your final image. What happens is that the camera electronically magnifies a portion of the image that the lens sees, in the same way that you can blow up the image on your computer to enlarge a small part of it. Just as on a computer, the enlarged part becomes blocky, or pixilated, and you don't really see any more information than without the enlargement. That's not to say that digital zoom has no useful purpose at all. When the camera magnifies your view like this, then the exposure metering can be limited to a small part of the image, and you may be able to compose your shot better by zooming in digitally. But don't expect to get the benefit of a real enlargement of the image, as with optical zoom.

If you want to turn Digital Zoom on, the aspect ratio (see later discussion in this chapter) has to be set to 4:3. In any other aspect ratio, the Digital Zoom option will be dimmed on the menu and cannot be selected. Your choices in the menu system are to leave it off, or turn it on at a zoom factor of 1.5 or 1.9, or at a setting of Standard, which gives you the whole zoom range, up to 16 times the normal view, with a highly pixilated

Figure 4.4
Digital Zoom is the first entry on the second page of the Shooting menu.

image at the 16X range. I recommend leaving Digital Zoom turned off, unless you're faced with a situation in which it may be of some advantage to have your image electronically enlarged for purposes of exposure or composition.

If you do choose to use Digital Zoom, you can tell when it's active by looking at the numbers that show up near the top of the LCD to report the magnification level of your zoom, such as 5.0X, or 16X. If those numbers are blue rather than white, that means that Digital Zoom is being used to achieve that magnification level. Also note that Digital Zoom is not available, and will be grayed out on the menu, when you are using RAW quality (or RAW+JPEG).

AF-Point Zoom

This is a handy little feature that gives you the option of having a magnified autofocus frame. The only option is to turn it on or off. When it's on, if the AF Frame is set to FlexiZone or a face is detected in Face AiAF mode, the AF frame will be magnified when you press the shutter button down halfway to check the focus. This system lets you check to make sure the autofocus has locked on and focused properly. If you find the magnified frame distracting, turn it off, but I find it quite useful and reassuring to be able to see the focus point more clearly. Note that the feature does not function in all situations, such as when the AF Frame is set to Tracking AF or to Face AiAF and no faces are detected. It also cannot function if Servo AF is activated or Digital Zoom is set to 1.4X or 2.3X (a Standard setting is fine). (If you find that AF-Point Zoom is grayed out on the menu, check to see if Digital Zoom or Servo AF is interfering; if so, deactivate the offending setting and AF-Point Zoom will become available again.)

Servo AF

Ordinarily, when you press the shutter button down halfway, the focus and exposure are locked in. If you keep the shutter button halfway down and move the camera, you will keep the same settings until you press the shutter all the way in. If you have a digital SLR, that function is often called Single Servo AF, or AF-S. With the G1 X, the Servo AF setting on the Shooting menu is the equivalent of Continuous Servo AF (AF-C) on a digital SLR. In Servo AF mode, the G1 X readjusts focus as required. So, when you press the shutter halfway, the focus and exposure will continuously adjust as the subject or camera moves, or as lighting conditions change. You will hear the camera make a continuous whirring or clicking sound as the focus mechanism keeps adjusting. This feature is great if you are tracking a moving subject and want to have the focus and exposure ready for the instant when you finally snap the picture. As you might guess, the downside is that you may run through batteries faster than you would like. I'll discuss the uses of this feature in more detail in Chapter 6.

Continuous AF

This feature, which has a name that's similar to that of the continuous servo feature found in digital SLRs, is similar to Servo AF, but in a different context. Normally, when this feature is off, the camera autofocuses on your subject only when you press the shutter button halfway. If you turn this feature on, then the camera constantly alters its focus as you move the focus frame over different subjects, without the need to partially depress the shutter release. In other words, this feature controls whether the camera constantly focuses before you press the shutter halfway, and the Servo AF feature controls whether the camera constantly focuses after you have pressed the shutter halfway. Of course, this feature, like the previous one, has a good side and a bad side: it can help you achieve sharp focus quickly, but it also can drain your battery quite rapidly. More about this feature in Chapter 6.

AF-Assist Beam

The autofocus mechanism sometimes needs some extra light in order to figure out whether the scene before the camera is in sharp focus. Without that light, the shape in question might be too indistinct for the camera to find the straight lines that can help it determine focus. If you're shooting at a religious ceremony or in another environment in which you don't want to send out beams of light, or you believe your focus will be adequate without that help, go ahead and set this feature to Off in the menu system. Be warned, though, that you may still see the same beam of light, because the camera also sends out a similar beam to reduce the red-eye effect. So, unless you have Red-eye reduction and AF-Assist Beam turned off, beware the light beams!

MF-Point Zoom

When you set the camera to manual focus using the MF button, ordinarily the focus area in the center of the LCD screen is magnified so you can fine-tune the focusing by turning the rear control dial. If for some reason you prefer not to have that enlarged area appear (maybe you find it distracting from the composition), you can turn off the enlarging effect with this menu option.

Safety MF

This is another feature that works in conjunction with manual focus. Ordinarily, even when you are using manual focus, you have the option of fine-tuning the focus to full sharpness, after first focusing roughly with the rear control dial, by pressing the shutter button halfway, or pressing the AF Frame/Trash button. This feature is called Safety MF. If you want to disable this feature, you can do so with this menu option. You might want to disable it if you have a tricky manual focusing situation, and you don't want the camera to change your manual focus when you press the shutter button down to take the picture.

Flash Control

This menu item, on the next page of the Shooting menu (see Figure 4.5), is one of those that lead to several other options; it's not just an On or Off feature. I'll be talking about the use of flash in more detail in Chapter 10, but I'll discuss the main options of the Flash Control menu here for reference. After highlighting the Flash Control line on the Shooting menu, press the FUNC./SET button to bring up the submenu with the options discussed below.

Flash Mode

This option, available only in the Shutter priority and Aperture priority shooting modes, can be set to either Auto or Manual. It lets you control the flash output in those modes. When this option is set to Manual, the Flash Output option becomes available so you can control the intensity of the flash. When it is set to Auto, the Flash Exposure Compensation option is available instead of Flash Output.

Flash Output

As discussed in connection with Flash mode, above, this option becomes available when the camera is set to Shutter priority or Aperture priority shooting mode and the Flash mode is set to Manual. In those circumstances, you can set the intensity of the flash

Figure 4.5
Flash Control is the first entry on the next page of the Shooting menu.

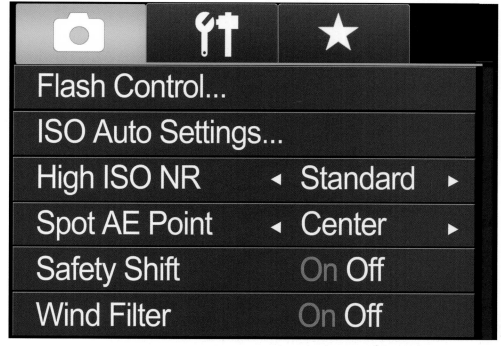

manually using this feature. You can also use this feature when the shooting mode is set to Manual. This is one of those menu entries that is invisible until its prerequisites (Tv or Av exposure; Manual flash mode) are met.

Flash Exposure Compensation

This entry is a way to set flash exposure compensation (that is, raising or lowering the normal flash output) as an alternative to doing so through the FUNC. menu. To set this value using the Shooting menu, highlight this option, then dial in the amount of flash EV compensation you want using the left/right cursor buttons. Press the MENU button to exit. This setting works for both the built-in flash and for a compatible external flash that's inserted in the camera's hot shot, such as the Canon Speedlite 430EX II or 580EX II. However, there are differences in the operation of this feature, depending on what flash is being used. You can adjust the flash output up to plus or minus 2 EV with the built-in flash; with some external units, you can adjust it up to 3 EV in either direction. In addition, with the built-in flash, you can make the adjustment by pressing the Flash key (right cursor button) and then immediately turning the front control dial; that method is not available with an external flash unit. If the camera is set to Manual exposure mode, the same adjustment can be made, but it is then considered Flash Output rather than Flash Exposure Compensation, and the adjustment units are shown differently, but the effect is the same.

Shutter Sync

You can choose 1st Curtain sync, which fires the flash as soon as the shutter is completely open (this is the default mode). Alternatively, you can select 2nd Curtain sync, which fires a pre-flash used to measure exposure as soon as the shutter release is pressed down all the way, but before the shutter opens, and then triggers a second flash at the end of the exposure, just before the shutter starts to close. This action allows photographing a blurred trail of light from moving objects with sharp flash exposures at the beginning and the end of the exposure. I'll explain how it works in Chapter 10.

Red-Eye Correction

You're probably familiar with the red-eye effect that populates snapshots at parties with people looking as if they wandered off the set of a *Twilight* movie. The problem is that electronic flash (or, rarely, illumination from other sources) bounces off the retinas of the subjects, with the red from retinal blood vessels adding the unwanted coloration to the eyes. The PowerShot G1 X attacks this problem with two distinct approaches, which are very different even though they both are housed on the Flash Control menu. The camera uses both correction and reduction. Reduction involves shining a light at the subject's eyes to narrow the pupils, thereby reducing the chance of reflections from the retinas. We'll return to that approach in a moment; it's the next menu choice. For now, the topic is red-eye correction.

The first arrow in the G1 X's quiver of anti-red-eye measures is digital correction. Put simply, this means that the camera's circuitry looks for unnaturally red areas in or near people's eyes, and attempts to de-redden them digitally. This system is not perfect; this correction technique may take effect when someone has red makeup applied near the eyes, so don't rely on it too heavily to fix red-eye. This feature can be turned either On or Off.

Red-Eye Lamp

This is the second way the G1 X combats the scourge of red-eyed photos. If this feature is turned on, the camera lets loose a beam of light toward the subject before the flash fires for taking the picture, in order to narrow his or her pupils, as discussed above. (You may have to ask the subject to look straight at the camera to gain maximum effect.) Actually, the best way to truly eliminate red-eye is to use an external flash and raise it up off the camera so its illumination approaches the eye from an angle that won't reflect directly back to the retina and into the lens. That alone is a good reason for using an external flash. If you're working with your G1 Xs's built-in pop-up flash, your only recourse may be to use the two red-eye-reduction strategies discussed here. Figure 4.6 shows the effects of wider pupils (left) and those that have been contracted using the G1 X's Red-Eye Lamp feature.

Figure 4.6
Red-eye is blatant (left), but tamed (right) thanks to the PowerShot G1 X's Red-eye reduction lamp.

Safety FE

This final option on the Flash Control menu is a safety mechanism programmed into the camera. When this feature is activated (as it is by default), the camera automatically adjusts the aperture and shutter speed when the flash fires, to prevent a situation in which the shot is overexposed by an overly powerful flash discharge. If you turn this feature off, the camera will let the chips fall where they may, and your highlights may be blown if the flash turns out to be too bright for the conditions. This setting is not available in Manual exposure mode or in other modes when Flash mode is set to Manual. You can turn this option off if you have a particular need to let the flash over-expose the image, but it's generally a useful feature to leave in place, to minimize the chance of pictures that are completely washed out by excessive brightness from the flash.

ISO Auto Settings

This menu option gives you the ability to change the way the ISO Auto setting works. There are two settings available in P and Av exposure modes: Maximum ISO Speed and Rate of Change. The Maximum ISO can be set to 400, 500, 640, 800, 1000, 1250, or 1600. You might want to set a number lower than 1600 if you're using the Auto ISO setting and you want to make sure that the camera does not set ISO high enough to introduce noticeable noise into your images. The Rate of Change option can be set to Standard, Fast, or Slow. This setting regulates how quickly the camera will change its ISO setting when ISO Auto is active. You might want to set it to one of the slower speeds to avoid having unwanted shifts in ISO during a shooting session. However, if you are shooting in a rapidly changing environment (such as an area where clouds are periodically blocking the sunlight), you might want to set the Rate of Change to High so the camera can keep up with the changing lighting conditions. Rate of Change is not available in Tv mode (only Max ISO Speed is available), and the ISO Auto Settings entry disappears entirely if you switch to Manual exposure mode.

High ISO NR

This menu option lets you specify how much noise reduction will be applied to images shot at elevated ISO settings (above ISO 800). Choose from Standard, High, or Low. As noise reduction reduces the amount of detail that's visible as it removes visual noise artifacts, you might want to minimize it with the Low setting if you don't mind a little grain or plan to apply noise reduction in your image editor. I think it's unfortunate that Canon doesn't give you the option of turning high ISO NR off entirely, especially if you have access to a more advanced software noise reduction like Noise Ninja.

Hg Lamp Corr.

Turn On to tell the G1 X to automatically counter the greenish cast found in evening scenes when mercury vapor lamps are the primary source of illumination. Set to Off if you don't want such correction, say, because the tinge adds a particular mood to your image.

Spot AE Point

This feature has one very specific purpose—to link the exposure frame to the focus frame when you have the camera set for both FlexiZone autofocus and Spot metering, so you can choose a particular spot for the camera to set both focus and exposure. Here are the steps to follow:

1. Using the Metering Mode button and the rear control dial, select Spot as the metering method.

2. Set the AF Frame option on the Shooting menu to FlexiZone.

3. Select Spot AE Point on the Shooting menu, and set the option to AF Point (as opposed to Center).

4. In the center of the LCD screen, you will see a double set of brackets enclosed within a rectangle, indicating that both the focus and the exposure are being determined by this small area in the middle of the screen (see Figure 4.7). (The brackets look slightly different if you set the AF Frame to its smaller size.)

Figure 4.7
The FlexiZone focus frame is linked to the Spot metering frame using the Spot AE Point feature.

Now, since the camera is set to the FlexiZone focusing mode, you can press the AF Frame button and then move or resize the focus frame as you wish. You may notice dramatic changes in exposure of the scene as you move the small exposure and focus area to different parts of the scene before you, because of the effect of the Spot metering. You won't want to use this technique without a good reason, but if you know your exposure and focus should both be determined by the same small area of the scene, it's a good item for your photographic toolkit.

Safety Shift

This feature is another one with a very limited purpose. This menu option appears only when the shooting mode is set to Aperture priority or Shutter priority. When you activate Safety Shift in one of those shooting modes with the flash turned off, the camera will automatically shift the setting you made (for aperture or shutter speed) if proper exposure cannot be obtained using that setting. For example, let's say you're using Shutter priority mode and have set the shutter speed to 1/2,000th of a second in a dimly lit room with the flash turned off. With Safety Shift off, if you take the picture at these settings, you can enter the result into a contest for photos of coal-bin interiors with a good chance of victory. With Safety Shift turned on, the camera is quite likely to switch your shutter speed to something like 1/6th of a second, and you will now have a reasonably visible representation of your dimly lit room. With this option, the camera will raise the ISO setting to a certain extent to achieve a correct exposure, but it will likely still shift your setting in order to avoid raising the ISO too high. Of course, if the shutter speed is shifted to a slow value, such as 1/6th of a second, you will have to hold the camera very steady or use a tripod.

Wind Filter

I'm discussing this feature here in the interest of covering all items on the Shooting menu, even though this one applies only to movies, and not to stills. With this feature activated, the camera will attempt to suppress wind noise coming into its tiny microphone. It may or may not help, and it may result in unnatural-sounding audio if there is no wind, so experiment and see if it's useful before you activate this feature for important footage in any particular environment.

Review

This menu option, the first on the next page of the Shooting menu (see Figure 4.8), controls how long an image displays on the LCD screen after it has just been recorded. You can set the review time to any value from 2 to 10 seconds; to hold on the screen until the shutter button is pressed halfway; or not to display at all. Keeping the review time short is one good way to preserve your battery's charge.

Figure 4.8
The Review
function is the
first entry on
the next page of
the Shooting
menu.

Review Info

This menu option works in conjunction with the Review function, discussed above, to set how images display on the screen right after they've been shot. Therefore, this option is available only if the Review function is turned on with the previous menu option. The choices for Review Info are Off, Detailed, and Focus Check. With Off, there's no information displayed, just the image. With Detailed, the screen provides details about the exposure as well as a histogram showing the brightness values graphically. With Focus Check, the camera displays a special screen that lets you enlarge various portions of the image for closer inspection of the image's focus. I discuss histograms in Chapter 5.

Blink Detection

With this setting turned on, the camera will display a frame with a little blinky-eyed face if it detects that an image you have taken has a person with his or her eyes shut. This option may seem at first blush to be a bit Big Brotherish, but it actually could be useful, because it can be pretty hard for you as the photographer to check your subject's eyes during a shooting session.

Custom Display

This menu option lets you customize the information that is shown on the LCD screen when you are in Shooting mode. Once you have selected this option, you are presented with a matrix containing the three screens that can be shown with successive presses of the DISP. button (see Figure 4.9). In the first two columns of this matrix, you can choose among four items to be displayed on the two screens summoned by the DISP. button: (1) shooting info, which includes things such as battery life, quality and image size settings, and general settings such as i-Contrast and the like; (2) grid lines, a set of intersecting lines that can help with composition; (3) electronic level, a bar with a pointer that centers and turns green when the camera is being held level; and (4) histogram. The third column lets you choose whether to have a blank screen display in the cycle of screens summoned by the DISP. button. If you want to have a blank (dark) screen available, navigate to the top of the second column, then move right to the third column, and press the FUNC./SET button to put a check mark in that column. In daily use, you may want to have your first screen uncluttered with much of this information, and your next screen (summoned by the DISP. button) to show just grid lines. It's all a matter of how you use the information on the screen. The electronic level is a nice feature, and I like to include it on both information screens.

Figure 4.9
The Custom Display menu option lets you specify what information appears on the detailed shooting information display and lets you decide whether to have a blank screen appear as one option when the DISP. button is pressed.

Reverse Display

Here's another menu item that was created to address a very specific issue, which arises because of the PowerShot G1 X's swiveling screen. If you fold the LCD screen out to the side and then flip it vertically (on its horizontal axis), the screen will be facing you if you are staring at the lens. With the Reverse Display setting turned on, you will see a mirror image in the screen, rather than the normal image that the camera's lens sees. This is done largely so you can take a self-portrait; in other words, the LCD shows you a mirror image of what it's aimed at, though, if you then take the picture, when you view it later it will be oriented correctly, not a mirror image. If you don't want the image in the LCD screen reversed when the screen is flipped around to the front, you can turn this setting off.

IS (Image Stabilization) Settings

The PowerShot G1 X is equipped with a very capable image-stabilization system, which detects camera motion and uses electronic circuitry to counteract it, thus reducing the chances your shots will be marred by blurring if the camera shakes while you're taking pictures. With image stabilization engaged (set to Continuous on this menu), you can hand-hold the camera at slower shutter speeds without ending up with ruined images, so it's a very useful feature. The problem is that it eats up battery life, so if you're out in the field without access to batteries or chargers, you may want to minimize the use of this feature. One way to do so is by the use of a tripod, which is a good idea for any situation in which you can use one. There is nothing like a good, solid tripod for contributing to strong, clear photographs. If you do use a tripod, you should set this option to Off, even if battery life is not an issue, because the feature is not needed in that situation, and possibly could degrade the image slightly in some way. If turning stabilization completely off is not a viable option, you can use this menu item to switch it to Shoot Only, which means stabilization will be applied only when the shutter is pressed.

The final option is Powered IS, which can be turned On or Off. When activated, Powered IS reduces the kind of mild (but annoying) camera shake you get from shooting movies at a telephoto setting, and your hand tends to wander a bit. Turn this On to counter that. This fine-tuning of normal image stabilization will not counter the more severe camera vibrations produced when you're capturing video from a moving car, while walking, or when you're panning the camera to follow a subject. If you have that type of video clip in mind, turn Powered IS off.

Date Stamp

When you turn this menu option on (by setting it to Date or Date and Time, as opposed to Off), the PowerShot G1 X will display the date (or date and time) in the lower-right corner of each image taken while the option is activated. The word Date will be shown in the lower-right corner as you are shooting to remind you that this function is set. You need to be sure you want to do this before you set the function, because the information is permanently embedded in the image, and cannot be removed unless you crop it out of the picture or otherwise alter the image. Your images will always have the date information recorded in the file anyway, so you can tell when the image was taken (assuming the date and time were set correctly). The Date Stamp function does not work with RAW images.

Set Dial Functions

One of the very welcome features of the PowerShot G1 X is the front control dial, which gives you one dial to adjust aperture and an additional one to adjust shutter speed when in Manual exposure mode. Of course, as I have already discussed throughout this book, both the front control dial and the rear-located control dial have numerous other functions as well. The Set Dial Functions menu option gives you the ability to make certain choices about what duties these two dials carry out.

There are two main things you can accomplish with this menu option. First, you can change the roles of the two dials for controlling shutter speed and aperture. By default, the front control dial adjusts shutter speed in Tv and M modes, it adjusts aperture in Av mode, and the rear control dial adjusts aperture in M mode. If you select this menu option and press the FUNC./SET button, you will see an orange block that says either Front Dial 1, Front Dial 2, or Control Dial. Scroll through those three choices using the left/right cursor buttons. If you leave this option set at its default setting of Front Dial 1, shutter speed and aperture are handled as noted above. If you set this block to Front Dial 2, the roles of the two dials are reversed: the front control dial controls aperture, and the rear control dial controls shutter speed. If you set the orange block to Control Dial, then the rear control dial controls both shutter speed and aperture; in Manual mode, you need to alternate between the two settings by pressing the metering mode button. (I presume the rear control dial setting is for people who got used to this system on previous PowerShot G-series models, which had only the single dial.)

In addition, no matter which of the three main settings you select (Front Dial 1, Front Dial 2, or Control Dial), you have the option of making some other assignments of functions to either or both dials. For example, if you have chosen Control Dial as the main setting, then you can assign a function to the front control dial for each of the relevant shooting modes: M, Av, Tv, and P. There are only five settings you can assign: Step Zoom, Aspect Ratio, White Balance fine adjustments, i-Contrast, and Not Assigned. In some cases, you can assign one of these three settings to a dial that already is handling either aperture or shutter speed. In that case, you alternate between those functions for the dial by pressing the Metering Mode button. Changing dial functions can cause confusion, so if you want to return to the original settings, you can reset them if necessary.

Confused yet? Canon's description in its manual is even more cryptic. I'm going to step you through each of the three main settings so you can see exactly what your options are.

Front Dial 1/2

It's best to think of Front Dial 1, Front Dial 2, and Control Dial as Option 1, Option 2, and Option 3, because you can choose only one of them. When you select the Front Dial 1 option, the screen will look like Figure 4.10. The four columns to the right are labeled M, Av, Tv, and P. Here's what they mean:

- **M.** In Manual exposure mode, the front control dial adjusts the shutter speed, and the rear control dial adjusts the aperture.

- **Av.** In Aperture priority mode, the front control dial adjusts the aperture, and the rear control dial adjusts a second function, currently undefined (as indicated by the dash). I'll show you how to choose a second function shortly.

- **Tv.** In Shutter priority mode, the front control dial adjusts the shutter speed, and the rear control dial adjusts a second function, also currently undefined.

- **P.** In Program exposure mode, the camera adjusts both the shutter speed and aperture, so the front and rear control dials are shown as undefined.

Figure 4.10
Front Dial 1
option settings.

If you choose Front Dial 2 instead, the screen will look almost exactly like Figure 4.10, except that in the M column, the Tv and Av settings will be reversed. Rotating the front control dial adjusts the aperture, and rotating the rear control dial adjusts the shutter speed.

To assign a function to one of the unassigned settings, just follow these steps:

1. **Access unassigned settings.** Press the up/down buttons to activate access to the unassigned settings. Orange highlighting will appear in one of the unassigned boxes.

2. **Choose setting to change.** Rotate the rear control dial to move the highlighting to one of the free settings. You can select rear control dial for Manual, Av, Tv, or P modes, plus front control dial for P mode.

3. **Assign a function.** When any of the four available boxes is highlighted, rotate the front control dial to cycle among the options. These include Aspect Ratio Switching, White Balance Correction, Step Zoom, i-Contrast control, or Not Assigned. Note that you can select different functions for each of the four modes, or assign the same function to a particular dial for all four.

4. **Confirm choice.** Press the FUNC./SET button to confirm your choice, and then the MENU button to back out of the FUNC./SET screen.

To use these new assignments, just make sure that Front Dial 1 or Front Dial 2 is selected in this menu; after that, the front and rear control dials will function as you have assigned them.

> **Tip**
>
> If you have assigned a second function to the rear control dial in Manual exposure mode, the rear dial will continue to adjust the aperture by default. To switch to that second function in Manual mode, press the Metering Mode button twice to activate the additional function. Press it again to return the rear control dial to its aperture adjustment function. (Pressing the Metering Mode button once accesses the metering mode function.)

Control Dial

If you choose Control Dial as your dial options selection, things get interesting. The front control dial loses all its pre-assigned definitions, so you can select any of the four functions to that dial. The rear control dial assumes all the aperture/shutter speed functions, and only in Program mode can an additional functions be assigned. Figure 4.11 shows what the screen looks like when the control dial is specified.

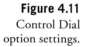

Figure 4.11
Control Dial
option settings.

The four columns to the right are labeled M, Av, Tv, and P. Here's what they mean in this mode:

- **M.** In Manual exposure mode, the rear control dial adjusts the shutter speed *and* the aperture. Rotate the dial to change shutter speed; press the Metering Mode button to cycle between aperture and metering mode options. This option is best when you're shooting in Manual exposure mode and want to adjust only the shutter speed *or* the aperture and prefer to use a single dial for either. Spin the rear control dial to adjust shutter speed, say, or press the Metering Mode button to switch so that the same dial adjusts the aperture instead. You can ignore the front control dial, or assign it to one of the other four functions.

- **Av.** In Aperture priority mode, the rear control dial adjusts the aperture, and the front control dial is either unassigned or operates the function you've specified. I showed you how to choose the second function previously.

- **Tv.** In Shutter priority mode, the rear control dial adjusts the shutter speed, and the front control dial is either unassigned or operates the function you've specified.

- **P.** In Program exposure mode, the camera adjusts both the shutter speed and aperture, so the front and rear control dials are shown as undefined.

Set Shortcut Button

This menu option lets you set the Shortcut button, at the upper left of the camera's back, to carry out one function that you want to be able to activate quickly, without going through menu options. When you choose this item on the Shooting menu, you are presented with a screen showing the possible selections: Not Assigned, i-Contrast, White Balance, Custom White Balance 1, Custom White Balance 2, My Colors, Drive mode, Self-Timer, ND filter, Aspect Ratio, Select RAW or JPEG, Servo AF, Powered IS, AF Lock, Digital Tele-Converter, and Display Off. Just choose the one option you're most likely to want at your fingertips, and select it with this menu option. Of course, you can easily change to a different option whenever you want to.

Save Settings

This is a very useful, well-designed function. When you choose Save Settings from the Shooting menu, you are presented with a very simple, but powerful pair of options—you can save your current settings to one of two locations in the camera, either C1 or C2 (see Figure 4.12). If you look at the mode dial on top of the camera, you will see those two settings, right along with Program, Shutter priority, Aperture priority, and

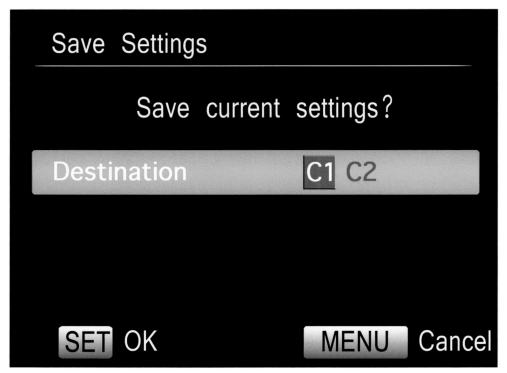

Figure 4.12
Use the Save Settings option on the Shooting menu to save a set of your favorite shooting settings to the C1 or C2 location on the mode dial.

the rest. So, in effect, you can design your own two custom Shooting modes through this very simple option. When you choose to save your current settings to either of these slots, here is what is saved: your Shooting mode (P, Tv, Av, or M); all of the items that you have set for that mode, such as shutter speed, aperture, exposure compensation, and the like; all of the items you have set through the Shooting menu; the zoom position of the lens; the manual focus position; and the inclusion of any items in the My Menu settings. You can reset either the C1 or the C2 slot to the default settings by choosing Reset All from the Setup menu. Once you are comfortable with the camera's settings, you may well find some good uses for this capability. Many cameras will let you save some settings in this way, but the G1 X is unusually flexible in this area, and you may find it very helpful to be able to twirl the mode dial slightly and instantly have the camera set up with your favorite settings, including the amount of zoom.

Playback Menu Options

The Playback menu is where you select options related to the display, review, transfer, and printing of the photos you've taken (see Figure 4.13). You can view the Playback menu when you press the MENU button while viewing any image on your memory card.

Figure 4.13
The Playback menu includes options for viewing, printing, and transferring images.

The choices you'll find are as follows:

- Movie Digest Playback
- Smart Shuffle
- Slideshow
- Erase
- Protect
- Rotate

- Favorites
- My Category
- i-Contrast
- Red-Eye Correction
- Trimming
- Resize

- My Colors
- Scroll Display
- Group Images
- Auto Rotate
- Resume
- Transition

Movie Digest Playback

As I described in Chapter 2, the Auto Clip Recording or Movie Digest scene mode (selectable from the Function menu when the mode dial is in the SCN position), captures a series of 2–4 second video clips each time you take a still picture, and appends them onto a single file of all the clips captured on a given day.

If the camera is powered down, you can quickly turn it on in Playback mode by pressing the Playback button. The lens will not extract from the body. When viewing this menu item, choose a date from among those available, and press the FUNC./SET button to begin playback. If you have many dates with movie digests recorded, you can press the Jump button (it's marked with an asterisk) from single image viewing mode, and choose to filter by Favorites, a specific Shot Date, My Category, Stills/Movies/Movie Digests, or Jump by 10 or 100 images. Select Movie Digests as your filter, and you can rotate the rear control dial to choose from among only those files that match your condition. (Printing and Setup menus are also available in this mode.)

Smart Shuffle

This option is basically a way to entertain yourself (or your friends) with a random sampling of your images. If you have at least 50 images shot with this camera on your memory card, select this option and the camera will display one image at random, with thumbnails of four others arranged in each direction. Use the cursor buttons to choose one direction, and the next image will be selected from that side of the first image. The process can continue as long as you want it to. To exit from Smart Shuffle, press the MENU button.

Slideshow

The Slideshow option is a convenient way to review images one after another, without the need to manually switch between them. To activate this feature, just choose Slideshow from the Playback menu. During playback, you can press the FUNC./SET button to pause and then restart the "slideshow" (in case you want to examine an image more closely). You also can use the left and right cursor buttons or the rear control dial during playback to move the show along. You can hold down the left/right cursor button to fast forward or fast reverse through the images. For example, you might want to review a set of images to judge the exposure of the group of pictures. It's important to note that the Slideshow option does not include any mechanism for selecting what images to include in the show. To make that selection, you need to use the My Category option, discussed later in this section. To set up your slideshow, follow these steps:

1. **Begin setup.** Choose Slideshow from the Playback menu, pressing FUNC./SET to display the screen shown in Figure 4.14.

2. **Choose Repeat options, Play time, and Effect.** Navigate to highlight Repeat and select On or Off, to determine whether the show will repeat after it ends. Move down to Play Time and select a time for each image to display, from 3 to 10, or 15 or 30 seconds. Then move to Effect, and select one of the transition effects listed.

3. **Start the show.** Highlight Start and press FUNC./SET to begin your show. (If you'd rather cancel the show you've just set up, press MENU instead.)

4. **Use show options during display.** Press FUNC./SET to pause/restart; left and right cursor buttons or the rear control dial to speed through the images; and MENU to stop the show.

Figure 4.14
Set up your slideshow using this screen.

Erase

As I discussed earlier, one way to delete images from the memory card in the camera is to press the AF Frame/Trash button while a single image is displayed, and then confirm the operation using the navigation keys and the FUNC./SET key. If you need to erase more than just one or two images at a time, though, you're probably better off using the Erase option on the Playback menu. Choose this menu entry and you'll be given three choices: Select, Select Range, and All Images (see Figure 4.15).

- **Select.** The first option displays the most recent image. Press the left/right cursor buttons or use the rear control dial to navigate through the images, and mark or unmark various images for deletion using the FUNC./SET key (a check mark will appear in a box in the upper-left corner when an image is marked for deletion). If you try to mark a protected image for deletion, the warning Protected appears on the screen. When finished marking pictures, press the MENU button, and you'll see a screen that says Erase? with two options, Stop and OK. Highlight OK, then press the SET button to erase the images, or select Cancel and press the SET button to return to the selection screen. Press the MENU button to leave your selections marked and return to the display of marked images.

Figure 4.15
The Playback menu's Erase menu item on the PowerShot G1 X gives you options for what images to erase.

- **Select Range.** To speed things up, you can select a range of images rather than marking them individually. After choosing the Select Range option, navigate to the first image in the range to be deleted, and select it with the FUNC./SET key. Then navigate to the last picture in the range (which must be higher numbered than the first one), and press FUNC./SET again. Confirm your selections as with the first option.

- **All Images.** If you're ready to part with all images on your memory card, choose the All Images option and confirm with the FUNC./SET key when prompted by the menu system. This choice removes all the pictures on the card, except for those you've marked with the Protect command, and does not reformat the memory card. If you have categorized your images using the My Category option (described later), you can display images in a particular category, and use the All Images option to erase just the images from that category. If you want to erase all images on the card and don't need to preserve any protected ones, your best bet is to use the Format command, which not only removes the images but also prepares the card for reuse with a new file system.

Protect

If you want to keep an image from being accidentally erased (either with the Erase button or by using the Erase menu option that we just discussed), you can mark that image for protection. To protect one or more images, enter Playback mode, press the MENU button, and choose Protect. Then either select individual images or a range of images, in the same way as with the Erase procedure described above. A key icon will appear in the lower-left corner on each image when it is marked as protected, and when that image is reviewed later. To remove protection, repeat the process and use the FUNC./SET key to remove the protection from individual images or a range of images. You can also protect all images on the card, using the All Images selection. In addition, if you have used the My Category function to place images in categories, you can display images from a given category, and then use the All Images selection to protect all images in that category. Image protection will not save your images from removal when the card is reformatted.

Rotate

The PowerShot G1 X will automatically rotate images that you take while holding the camera in the vertical position, so they will display vertically on the horizontal screen during playback. You can rotate the camera to the vertical position, and the camera will rotate the image to suit, so it's always shown in its correct orientation. You can't turn this automatic rotation function off, but you can manually rotate an image during playback using this menu selection, so it will display as originally oriented. Select Rotate from the Playback menu, use the left/right cursor buttons to page through the available images on your memory card until the one you want to rotate appears, then press FUNC./SET. The image will appear on the screen rotated 90 degrees, as shown in Figure 4.16. Press FUNC./SET again, and the image will be rotated another 90 degrees. You can keep rotating it until you achieve the desired orientation, including returning it to its original position.

When rotating an image, viewing a vertical image in correct orientation when holding the camera horizontally means that the longest dimension of the image is shown using the shortest dimension of the LCD, so the picture is reduced in size.

Figure 4.16
An image can be manually rotated in 90-degree increments using the Rotate function on the Playback menu.

Favorites

This menu option is similar in its functioning to the Erase and Protect functions discussed above. After selecting this menu option, navigate through your images and mark/unmark them as Favorites using the FUNC./SET button. A star will appear in the lower-left corner of each image marked as a favorite. You can then use the Jump function, discussed in Chapter 3, to filter your images by the Favorites classification, and delete or protect all images in that classification, for example.

My Category

This menu option is quite powerful and useful. It permits you to organize your images in the camera into several categories that are predefined for you. Choose My Category from the Playback menu and press the FUNC./SET button. Press the up/down cursor buttons or turn the rear control dial to choose either Select or Select Range and press the FUNC./SET button again to make your choice. If you choose Select, you are presented with a screen displaying your first image, with a list of categories on the left, each one having a selection box beside it. The categories are: People, Scenery, Events, Category 1, Category 2, Category 3, and To Do. For each image, you can scroll down through this list of categories and use the FUNC./SET button to check the box for one or more categories. Then move to the next image and continue the process until you have placed any or all of your images into as many categories as you want. If you prefer, you can use the Select Range option, which lets you assign a range of images to a category (or to multiple categories).

Once you are done assigning your images to categories, you can then perform any of the following operations on all the images in a given category at once: viewing slideshows; protecting images; erasing images; and choosing images for printing directly to a printer. You can also view your images by category, using the filtered playback procedure with the Metering Mode/Jump button. The PowerShot G1 X also automatically places some images into one of three categories (People, Scenery, or Events) when they are shot, basing its decisions on various factors, such as whether a face was detected, whether a scenic setting such as Beach or Fireworks was used, and the like. However, you can manually unassign images from any of those categories.

i-Contrast

This option gives you an opportunity to let the camera bring out additional detail in an image by tweaking the contrast or brightness in particular areas, such as faces. Select this option from the Playback menu, then scroll through your images to choose an image to be adjusted. Once your chosen image is displayed, press FUNC./SET to confirm your choice of image and then use the left/right cursor buttons or the rear control dial to select Auto and let the camera make the adjustment, or choose a Low, Medium, or High amount of adjustment, and then press FUNC./SET again to apply the desired correction. The changed image will be saved as a new file, and the original image will still be present on the memory card. Note that you cannot make this adjustment to a RAW image. (You shouldn't need to, because RAW images are intended to be subjected to considerable post-processing through software in any event.) The i-Contrast settings are also available while shooting pictures, as discussed later in this chapter in the section on the FUNC. menu.

Red-Eye Correction

This menu item is an old friend that we saw earlier on the Shooting menu. This option lets you apply digital correction to an image of a person with the red-eyed vampire stare. Just as with its counterpart on the other menu system, this procedure does not come with a guarantee of success, or even of improvement of the image, but it is worth a try. Scroll through your images until you find one that appears to need correction, then press FUNC./SET to apply it. If the camera detects red-eye it will attempt to correct it. When the correction has been applied, you have the choice of saving the new version to a new file, or overwriting the original image with the altered one. As with i-Contrast, this procedure cannot be performed on a RAW image.

Trimming

This is another one of the procedures available through the G1 X's menu system that gives you the ability to alter the images you have already taken. In this case, you can crop an image to remove unwanted parts or to emphasize certain subjects by altering the composition. Since I use software such as Adobe Photoshop, Photoshop Elements, or similar programs to perform post-processing actions like cropping, I tend to view features of this sort as not having that much value. However, there could be situations in which a photographer out in the field needs to create a slideshow quickly, without access to a computer. In such a case, this Trimming function could be a lifesaver. To use it, highlight this option on the Playback menu, then use the left/right cursor buttons or the rear control dial to display the image to be trimmed and select it by pressing the FUNC./SET button. Then, follow the prompts given by the camera to change the size and location of the trimming frame. Use the zoom lever to change the size of the frame, the four cursor buttons to move it, and the DISP. button to change it between vertical and horizontal. Use the rear control dial to switch between gray frames, which the camera will display to indicate faces in the image. (Those frames can be used for trimming.) Once you have the trimming frame set the way you want it, press FUNC./SET to make the crop. The trimmed image will be saved as a new image file. This function cannot be performed on RAW images or on Small images.

Resize

This procedure lets you change the image size of a picture that is already saved on the camera's memory card. Note that "resize" is used here in a very specific sense; you can't really change the apparent size of the image; all you can do is cause the camera to save a new copy of the original image with a smaller file size. Here again, this is something I ordinarily would do using a computer, but there probably are situations in which it could be useful to do this in-camera. After you've selected this option from the Playback menu, navigate to the image in question, then follow the camera's prompts to select the new size, and press FUNC./SET to save the new, smaller file. As with the Trimming function, this procedure cannot be used with RAW images or those that are already of the smallest possible size.

My Colors

This operation allows you to perform another sort of post-processing in the camera on your saved images by applying one of the camera's several built-in color settings to alter the general appearance of the picture. These are the same color settings you can apply when taking pictures using the FUNC. menu, as discussed later in this chapter. In this case, you select My Colors from the Playback menu, and then use the left/right cursor buttons or the rear control dial to highlight the image to be changed, then press the FUNC./SET button to select it. You can then use the left/right cursor buttons or the rear control dial to select whichever of the available color settings you want to apply: Vivid; Neutral; Sepia; Black and White; Positive Film; Lighter Skin Tone; Darker Skin Tone; Vivid Blue; Vivid Green; and Vivid Red. This transformation cannot be done with RAW images. The My Colors settings are discussed in more detail in the section later in this chapter describing the features of the FUNC. menu.

Scroll Display

This menu option lets you turn on and off the Scroll Display feature. If this feature is enabled (as it is by default), then, when the camera is in Playback mode, if you spin the rear control dial on the back of the camera rapidly enough, the images will display in a horizontal stream, in which you can see the images before and after the current one as they scroll by (see Figure 4.17). In addition, the camera displays the date of the image, with arrows beside the date to let you quickly change it using the up and down cursor buttons, thereby switching the display to select images from that date. A gray "thermometer" scroll bar appears below the images to let you know where you are in the stack. You might want to disable this feature if you would find it distracting to have the display suddenly switch from a conventional progression through your images to a more rapid scrolling with date selection that you don't need. In addition, the scrolling display shows the images at a slightly reduced size in order to accommodate the multiple pictures and the date selection area, so you might want to disable the feature in order to keep the images displayed at their normal sizes.

Figure 4.17
When the Scroll Display feature is enabled, turning the rear control dial causes the images to display in a continuous stream.

Group Images

This menu is useful when you're using the High Speed Burst HQ mode, described in Chapter 5. Ordinarily, the G1 X will group all the images shot in each burst together, and display only the first one in the group on picture review. You can see the others in the group by pressing the FUNC./SET button. If you'd prefer the camera to not "stack" the images together in this way and always display them individually, change from the default On value to Off.

Auto Rotate

Tells the camera to automatically rotate images shot with a vertical orientation during picture review, so that you can view them upright without turning the camera 90 degrees. Vertical images will be smaller in this mode, as the longest dimension of the image is shown using the shortest dimension of the LCD, leaving wasted black space to the right and left of the picture area.

Resume

This menu option is quite simple and straightforward. Its only purpose is to give you the option of which image will be displayed on the camera's screen when you go into playback mode—either the last image you had viewed previously or the last image that was shot. Select Last seen or Last shot, and you're done with this option.

Transition

Use this selection on the Playback menu to choose from the three possible effects that are available to mark the transition from one image to the next when you are viewing single images on the camera's display. The three choices are Fade, Scroll, and Slide. Or, you can choose Off, and the images will appear with simple "cuts" from one to the next, with no transitions between them.

Print Menu Options

When the PowerShot G1 X is set to playback mode, there are three menus displayed at the top of the menu screen. We've already talked about one of them—Playback—and will move quickly on to the Setup menu next. The additional menu, likely to be the least-used of the three, is the Print menu, tucked between the Playback and Setup menus in playback mode (and not visible at all when you're using shooting mode).

The options in this menu are of use only when you have connected the camera directly to a PictBridge-compatible printer and are preparing to send images straight from the camera to the printer. I'm not going to spend a lot of time discussing these menu options, because they're essentially self-explanatory. Your choices are as follows:

- **Print.** Use this choice to begin printing once you have selected the images using the other entries in the Print menu.

- **Select Images & Qty.** This entry allows you to scroll through the images on your memory card using the left/right cursor buttons or rear dial. Press the FUNC./SET button to activate the up/down cursor buttons and specify the number of prints for each image. (Leave the quantity at zero if you don't want to make any prints of a given photo.) Press the MENU button when you've finished to return to the Print menu.

- **Select Range.** As with the Erase command, to speed things up, you can select a range of images rather than marking them individually. After choosing the Select Range option, navigate to the first image in the range to be printed, and select it with the FUNC./SET key. Then navigate to the last picture in the range (which must be higher-numbered than the first one), and press FUNC./SET again.

- **Select All Images.** Use this to mark all the images on your card.

- **Clear All Selections.** This entry allows you to unmark all images and start your selection process over again.

- **Print Settings.** Choose whether to print thumbnail images (using the Index option), full-size images (using the Standard option), or both; and decide whether to include the dates and file numbers with the images.

To print in PictBridge mode:

1. **Connect camera.** First link the camera to the printer, using the mini-USB cable that comes with the camera. Plug it into the top connector inside the door on the right side of the camera, then connect it to the printer.

2. **Choose images to print.** Go into the Print menu, and you will find options for selecting the images to print, either by marking them individually using the FUNC./SET button or by selecting a range, in the same way as with the Erase and Protect functions discussed earlier.

3. **Specify print format.** When you have the images selected, choose Print Settings and specify how you want the images printed.

4. **Print selected images.** When all your choices are made, select Print, and sit back while the printer does its work.

Setup Menu Options

The Setup menu (shown in Figure 4.18 as it's accessed while in Shooting mode, where its tab is located in the middle) provides the opportunity to make adjustments on how your camera behaves during your shooting session, as differentiated from the Shooting menu (discussed later in this chapter), which adjusts how the pictures are actually taken, and the Playback menu, which adjusts how images are viewed. Your choices on the Setup menu include:

■ Mute	■ File Numbering	■ Electronic Level
■ Volume	■ Create Folder	■ Video System
■ Sound Options	■ Lens Retract	■ Ctrl via HDMI
■ Hints & Tips	■ Power Saving	■ Eye-Fi Settings
■ LCD Brightness	■ Time Zone	■ Copyright Info
■ Start-up Image	■ Date/Time	■ Language
■ Format	■ Distance Units	■ Reset All

Figure 4.18
The Setup menu gives you access to many options for controlling the camera's operations.

Mute

This first option on the Setup menu is a simple on-off selection—you can set the camera either to mute all electronic sounds or set them to be heard. Obviously, this option can be of use if you're at a school play or other event where it's best to keep your auditory footprint to a minimum. If you set Mute to On, then the camera will not emit an electronic sound when the shutter is released, and there won't be any beeps when you move from one image to another on the screen or press a navigation key. This is not to say the camera will be so silent that you could sneak through a secret laboratory and photograph the plans of the next doomsday device without being detected; the camera still will emit some clicks and other sounds from its purely mechanical operations. But you will cut down on the general cacophony of electronic chatter.

Volume

This option allows you to control individually the volume of four operational sounds the camera makes. This menu item will be grayed out and unavailable if you have turned the Mute feature On. If Mute is Off, then you can choose to set the volume from level 1 to 5 in each of four categories: the camera's Start-up Volume; its Operation Volume (essentially, beeps as you press buttons); Self-timer Volume; and Shutter Volume.

Sound Options

Now that we have covered how to mute the camera's operational sounds and how to adjust their volume, here is the menu option on the PowerShot G1 X that lets you select which three sounds are assigned to each of the four categories we discussed in connection with the Volume setting. I don't know that there's a very good way to describe these sounds in words; you just have to sample each one and decide which type of high-tech beepy or chirpy noise you like the best for each category.

Hints & Tips

With this setting, which is turned on by default, as you scroll through the lines of a menu, including the FUNC. menu, a line or two of explanation shows up at the bottom of the LCD screen to give a little extra information about the item that is highlighted. I personally find this feature quite useful. One nice point is that this feature is somewhat context sensitive. So, for example, if you have Mute set to On, and highlight the Mute line, the hint at the bottom of the screen will say: Turns on camera sounds. If you have Mute set to Off, the hint line will say: Turns off camera sounds. The reason to turn this feature Off would be to regain one line of screen real estate; in other words, if Hints & Tips is turned Off, one more line of the menu has room to display, so you don't have to scroll quite as much to get through the menus.

LCD Brightness

This menu option lets you adjust the brightness of the LCD display screen within a five-point range. This setting will remain in effect even after the camera is turned off and then on again.

Start-up Image

With this setting, you can select from three preset start-up screen images supplied by Canon, or you can choose to have no start-up image. The preset screens show the Canon logo or the PowerShot G1 X logo. If you want, you also have the option of choosing one of the images on your memory card in the camera as the start-up image. In order to do this, you have to have the camera in playback mode, and access the Setup menu while in that mode. Then, select option number 3 on the Start-up Image menu item, and press FUNC./SET. Scroll through your images until you find the one you want to use as the start-up image, and press FUNC./SET again. The camera will ask if you want to "register" that image; choose OK if you do, and that image will now appear briefly whenever you power up the camera.

Format

Use this menu option to erase everything on your memory card and set up a fresh file system ready for use. When you select Format, you'll see a display like Figure 4.19, showing the capacity of the card, how much of that space is currently in use, and two choices at the bottom of the screen to Cancel or OK (proceed with the format). A bar appears on the screen to show the progress of the formatting step. You also are presented with the option to perform a Low Level Format, which is a slower, but more thorough reformatting that can help restore a memory card that has picked up some bad sectors that aren't locked out by the normal Format step.

Figure 4.19
You must confirm the format step before the camera will erase a memory card.

File Numbering

The PowerShot G1 X will automatically apply a file number to each picture you take, using consecutive numbering for all your photos over a long period of time, spanning many different memory cards, starting over from scratch when you insert a new card, or when you manually reset the numbers. Numbers are applied from 0001 to 9999, at which time the camera creates a new folder on the card (100, 101, 102, and so forth), so you can have 0001 to 9999 in folder 100, then numbering will start over in folder 101. A given folder can hold only 2000 images, but, as discussed below, the numbering of images in a folder can still go as high as 9999.

The camera keeps track of the last number used in its internal memory. That can lead to a few quirks you should be aware of. For example, if you insert a memory card that had been used with a different camera, the G1 X may start numbering with the next number after the highest number used by the previous camera. (I once had a brand new camera start numbering files in the 8000 range.) I'll explain how this can happen next.

On the surface, the numbering system seems simple enough: In the menu, you can choose Continuous or Automatic Reset. Here is how each works:

- **Continuous.** If you're using a blank/reformatted memory card, the G1 X will apply a number that is one greater than the number stored in the camera's internal memory. If the card is not blank and contains images, then the next number will be one greater than the highest number on the card *or* in internal memory. (In other words, if you want to use continuous file numbering consistently, you must always use a card that is blank or freshly formatted.) Here are some examples.

  - You've taken 4,235 shots with the camera, and you insert a blank/reformatted memory card. The next number assigned will be 4236, based on the value stored in internal memory.

  - You've taken 4,235 shots with the camera, and you insert a memory card with a picture numbered 2728. The next picture will be numbered 4236.

  - You've taken 4,235 shots with the camera, and you insert a memory card with a picture numbered 8281. The next picture will be numbered 8282, and that value will be stored in the camera's menu as the "high" shot number (and will be applied when you next insert a blank card).

- **Automatic Reset.** If you're using a blank/reformatted memory card, the next photo taken will be numbered 0001. If you use a card that is not blank, the next number will be one greater than the highest number found on the memory card. Each time you insert a memory card, the next number will either be 0001 or one higher than the highest already on the card.

Create Folder

By default, the PowerShot G1 X creates new folders each month. With this option in the Setup menu, you can change this so the camera creates a new folder for each new shooting date. Just change the setting for this menu item from Monthly to Daily to accomplish this result.

Lens Retract

By default, when you're in shooting mode and you then switch to playback mode, the camera's lens retracts back into its housing about one minute after you press the Playback button, because it appears that you won't be needing the lens for a while, and it's a good idea for it to be pulled back away from sources of possible scratches or damage. You can change this setting to zero seconds, in which case the lens will retract almost immediately after you push the Playback button while the lens is out. If you're likely to go back and forth between shooting and playback modes, I suggest sticking with the normal one-minute wait time, to avoid overstraining the motor with the motions of a frantic turtle. This setting does not affect lens retraction when the camera is turned off while in shooting mode.

Power Saving

This entry in the Setup menu allows you to determine whether the PowerShot G1 X powers itself off after not being used for about three minutes in shooting mode, and after about five minutes in playback mode. Your only options here are to turn the feature on or off; you don't get to select how long the camera waits before powering down (see Figure 4.20). If you leave this feature turned on, the camera will turn itself completely off after the three minutes, and you then will have to press the power button to

Figure 4.20
The Power Saving menu option controls whether the camera powers off after a few minutes and how soon the display goes dark when not in use.

turn it back on. If you leave this feature off, you have to be careful to turn the camera off when you're done with it, or you'll drain the battery before you know it.

This menu item also has a second option that involves turning off just the display screen after a certain amount of time. In this case, you do get to select the timing—you can choose to have the screen turn off automatically after 10, 20, or 30 seconds, or 1, 2, or 3 minutes. The screen power-off feature is available even if the general power-saving feature is turned off.

SAVING POWER WITH THE POWERSHOT G1 X

There are three settings and several techniques you can use to help you stretch the longevity of your G1 X's battery. The first setting is the Review option described earlier in this chapter under the Shooting menu. The large LCD uses a lot of juice, so reducing the amount of time it is used (either for automatic review or for manually playing back your images) can boost the effectiveness of your battery. Second, Power Saving turns off the camera and/or the LCD screen after defined intervals, depending on your settings. The third setting is the LCD Brightness adjustment on the Setup menu, described above. If you're willing to shade the LCD with your hand, you can often get away with lower brightness settings outdoors, which will further increase the useful life of your battery. The techniques? Use the internal flash as little as possible; no flash at all or fill flash use less power than a full blast. Turn off image stabilization if you're using a tripod or if you just feel you don't need it. When transferring pictures from your G1 X to your computer, use a card reader instead of the USB cable. Linking your camera to your computer and transferring images using the cable takes longer and uses a lot more power.

Time Zone

Using this entry in the Setup menu, you can set your home time zone. Then, when you travel to another time zone, you can set the camera to a travel time zone, so the images will be recorded with the correct local time. To set your Home Time Zone, follow the camera's prompts, and, using the FUNC./SET button and the left/right cursor buttons, move the yellow highlight over the world map to select your home base. To set the destination time zone for a trip, follow a similar procedure, highlighting the airplane symbol instead of the home symbol. Then, when you are leaving on your trip, go into this menu option and highlight the airplane symbol, and it will then appear on the Setup menu's Time Zone line, indicating that the camera will be using the destination time zone until you reset it back to Home.

Date/Time

Use this option to set the date and time, which will be embedded in the image file along with exposure information and other data. Having this information recorded accurately will also let you select your images for viewing by date. I showed you how to set the date and time in Chapter 1. Note that setting the date and time does not embed them visibly in your images; if for some reason you need to do that, you have to use the Date Stamp function on the Recording menu, discussed above.

Distance Units

Use this option to select feet and inches or meters and centimeters, according to your preference. The camera will then display distances in your preferred system of notation.

Electronic Level

As I noted earlier, one of the nice new features provided with the PowerShot G1 X is the option to display an electronic level on the LCD screen while you're shooting images. When you turn this option on using the Custom Display item on the Shooting menu, the camera shows a small black bar with a pointer that moves left and right of center to indicate whether the camera is level, when you are shooting still images (not movies). The Electronic Level item on the Setup menu lets you calibrate the level. Make sure the camera is solidly positioned and completely level, and select Calibrate from the submenu; when the operation is done, the level will be calibrated to provide an accurate leveling readout. If for some reason you have second thoughts about your current calibration, you can select Reset and set the level back to its previous calibration.

Video System

This setting controls the output of the G1 X through the supplied AV cable when you're displaying images on an external monitor. You can select either NTSC, used in the United States, Canada, Mexico, many Central, South American, and Caribbean countries, much of Asia, and other countries; or PAL, which is used in the UK, much of Europe, Africa, India, China, and parts of the Middle East.

Ctrl via HDMI

This option has just two settings—Enable or Disable. Choose Enable if you are connecting the G1 X to an HDTV and you want to control the camera using the TV's remote control. This setup may not work with all types of HDTVs, but this setting may help the two devices speak the same electronic language.

VIEWING ON A TELEVISION

Canon makes it quite easy to view your images on a standard television screen with the PowerShot G1 X, and not much more difficult on a high-definition television (HDTV). (You have to buy a separate cable for each; one is not supplied in the box.) For regular TV, obtain the optional Video Cable AVC-DC400ST, and open the port cover on the right side of the camera, plug the small connector on the cable supplied with the camera into the socket labeled AV Out, and connect the other ends to the yellow VIDEO RCA composite jack and the red and white audio jacks (for movies) on your television or monitor.

For HDTV display on the G1 X, purchase the optional HDMI Cable HTC-100 (or a generic equivalent) and connect it to the mini-HDMI terminal above the standard video terminal on the right side of the camera. Connect the other end to an HDMI input port on your television or monitor (my 42-inch HDTV has three of them; my 26-inch monitor has just two). Then turn on the camera and press the Playback button. The image will appear on the external TV/HDTV/monitor and will not be displayed on the camera's LCD. HDTV systems automatically show your images at the appropriate resolution for that set.

If you plug in the HD cable, be aware that you cannot also plug in the Remote cable, which goes into an adjacent port; trying to plug them both in at the same time could result in damage to the camera or the cables.

Eye-Fi Settings

This menu option does not appear at all unless you have installed an Eye-Fi card into the camera. This type of card, as described in Chapter 1, has a tiny transmitter that sends your images wirelessly to your computer over a Wi-Fi network. This menu option has two subitems that may help this process work properly. The first item lets you choose Enable to help ensure that the Eye-Fi card's transmitter is functioning. The other item, Connection Info, provides information about what Wi-Fi access point, if any, the card is connected to. If you are having trouble getting your Eye-Fi card to transmit images, use these menu settings to help correct the problem. Also, if you are using an Eye-Fi card for image storage but have no network available at a given time, you can choose Disable on this menu so the camera does not waste its power in trying to help the Eye-Fi card connection when no connection is available.

Copyright Info

This option makes it easy to embed your name and other copyright information in each and every image file you capture.

Its menu has four entries:

- **Display Copyright Info.** This choice shows you the currently entered copyright information that will be added to the data included in your image file.

- **Enter Author's Name.** Produces a screen where you can input the name you want included in the image file. Uppercase and lowercase letters from A to z are included, along with a selection of symbols. Use the cursor keys to move from one character to another, and press FUNC./SET to add it to the text. The Trash button will remove a highlighted character. When you're satisfied with the entry, press MENU to return to the Copyright Info screen.

- **Enter Copyright Details.** A screen for entering copyright information, such as date or e-mail address. Use parentheses and a lowercase c as a copyright symbol: (c) 2013, for example. Navigate around the available characters as just described and press MENU to confirm your entry and return to the Copyright Info screen.

- **Delete Copyright Info.** Deletes all the existing information you've entered, giving you a blank slate.

Language

Choose from 27 languages for menu display, rotating the rear control dial or using the cursor buttons until the language you want to select is highlighted. Press the SET button to activate. Your choices include English, German, French, Dutch, Danish, Finnish, Italian, Norwegian, Swedish, Spanish, Simplified/Traditional Chinese, Japanese, Russian, Portuguese, Korean, Greek, Polish, Czech, Hungarian, Turkish, Thai, Arabic, Romanian, Ukrainian, Farsi, and Hindi.

If you accidentally set a language you don't read and find yourself with incomprehensible menus, don't panic. Just choose the second option from the bottom of the Setup menu, and select the idioma, sprache, langue, or kieli of your choice. Also, if you want to bypass the Setup menu, just push the Play button to enter playback mode, then, while pressing and holding the FUNC./SET button, press the MENU button; this action will bring up the language-selection screen.

Reset All

This is a very handy function to have available if you've been fooling around with the camera's settings for hours and don't want to have to retrace all your steps to get things back to normal. Just go into the Setup menu and select this option; your only choices are to confirm the reset or cancel. This action will put most settings back to their defaults, but note that there are certain settings that will not be reset. These include Date/Time; Language; Video System; and a few others.

My Menu

The Canon PowerShot G1 X has a great feature that allows you to define your own menu, with just the items listed that you want. You can set up My Menu to include only the items you use most often, and jump to those items quickly by pressing the MENU button. To create your own My Menu set of options, you just have to select the menu items you want to include. To do so, follow these steps while using Shooting mode:

1. Press the MENU button and use the left/right cursor buttons or the zoom lever to highlight the My Menu tab, marked by a star. When you first begin, the personalized menu will be empty except for the My Menu settings entry. Highlight this line and press the FUNC./SET button to select it. You'll then see a screen like the one shown in Figure 4.21.

2. Use the up/down cursor buttons to highlight Select Items, then press the FUNC./SET button.

3. Use the up/down cursor buttons or the rear control dial to scroll down through the continuous list of all menu entries that can be selected to find one you would like to add. Press FUNC./SET to set a check mark beside that item.

4. Continue to select up to five of the listed menu entries for your My Menu set; press FUNC./SET for each one.

5. When you're finished, press the MENU button twice to return to the My Menu screen to see your customized menu, which might look like Figure 4.22.

In addition to selecting menu items, you can perform other functions at the My Menu settings screen:

- **Changing the order.** Choose Sort to reorder the items in My Menu. Select the menu item to be moved and press the SET button. Press the up/down cursor buttons to move the item up and down within the menu list. When you've placed it where you'd like it, press the MENU button to lock in your selection and return to the previous screen.

- **Set Default View.** Ordinarily, when you press the MENU button, the G1 X displays the menu system with the Shooting menu highlighted. However, if you enable the Set Default View option, pressing the MENU button will *always* display My Menu first. You are free to switch to another menu tab if you like, but the next time you press the MENU button, My Menu will come up again. Use this option if you work with My Menu a great deal and make settings with other menu items less frequently.

Figure 4.21
The My Menu settings screen gives you access to the ability to select various menu items to include on your personalized My Menu list.

Figure 4.22
A typical set of options added to the My Menu list might include items such as those shown here.

FUNC. Menu

We have now discussed all of the "official" menus that are present in the PowerShot G1 X: Shooting, Playback, Setup, Printing, and My Menu. Those are the only menus in the camera that look and act like traditional menus—that is, menus that take up the whole screen and present you with lines of items that you scroll through to choose various options. But we're not done yet with the menu system of this camera. The G1 X comes equipped with another, different sort of menu system, used only to select shooting options, which Canon calls the FUNC. menu, because it is invoked with a press of the FUNC./SET key.

The FUNC. menu is very convenient to use once you get the hang of it, but it may take a little practice to get a feel for it. Here is how it works. When you're in shooting mode, just press the FUNC./SET key in firmly, and at the left and bottom of the LCD screen you will see two lines of symbols. The vertical list on the left, reading from top to bottom, represents the categories of settings that you can change with this system: Dynamic Range Correction/i-Contrast; White Balance; My Colors; Bracketing; Drive Mode; Self-Timer; Flash Control; Neutral-Density Filter; Aspect Ratio; Image Quality; Image Size; and Movie Size. These categories include some of the most important settings you can make.

i-Contrast

When you first press the FUNC./SET button to get access to the FUNC. menu, the i-Contrast symbol will be highlighted at the top of the vertical list and its four possible settings will be arrayed at the bottom of the screen in a horizontal list. This setting, which we encountered earlier on the Playback menu, is also available when shooting your images. This setting essentially is used to increase the dynamic range of your images. That is, the camera's digital sensor does not have the wide range of adaptability to varying intensities of light that the human eye does. As a result, a given image may be properly exposed for items that are in sunlight, but badly underexposed and muddy in the areas that are in the shade. With the varying levels of the i-Contrast settings, the G1 X will attempt to pull some details out of the overly dark areas of an image and vary the contrast to reduce blown highlights. There are two components to be adjusted: Dynamic Range Correction, or DR Correction, which reduces blown highlights, and Shadow Correct, which pulls detail out of dark areas of the image.

With the i-Contrast option selected at the top of the left-side vertical menu, scroll across the bottom menu to highlight the degree of correction you want for DR Correction: Off, Auto, 200%, or 400%. Then press the MENU button to bring up the options for Shadow Correct, which has only two settings: Off or Auto. Experiment with these settings to see how they help when you are taking photographs in challenging environments with bright and shadowy areas. These settings are not available when image quality is set to RAW or RAW + JPEG, and the i-Contrast icon will be grayed out in those cases. You can read more about i-Contrast in Chapter 5.

White Balance

When you press the FUNC./SET button to get access to the FUNC. menu, the AWB symbol will be at the next-to-top place on the vertical list and at the left of the horizontal list, assuming you have not previously changed the white balance setting (and assuming you're not in Auto shooting mode, in which case you won't be able to change the white balance setting) (see Figure 4.23). AWB stands for Automatic White Balance. In many cases, you can leave this setting alone and let the G1 X assess the lighting situation and set the white balance for you. If you would prefer to set the white balance to one of the predefined settings, use the right cursor button or the rear control dial to scroll through the list at the bottom of the screen until you find the one you want, then press FUNC./SET to select it, and the lists will disappear, leaving your setting in place. The choices are: Automatic White Balance; Daylight; Cloudy; Tungsten; Fluorescent (cool-white/warm-white); Fluorescent H (daylight); Flash; Underwater; and Custom 1 and Custom 2. If you select Custom 1 or Custom 2, you need to follow the instructions below to establish a value for that setting. That value will be retained permanently for that Custom slot until you go back and reset the value to something else.

Figure 4.23
The FUNC. menu is called up by a press of the FUNC./ SET key. Here, the white balance item is set to AWB, for Automatic White Balance.

To use the Custom settings to set the white balance to an appropriate color temperature under the current ambient lighting conditions:

1. Press the FUNC./SET key

2. Use the up/down cursor buttons to highlight the top icon on the list at the left of the screen, for white balance.

3. Use the right cursor button or the rear control dial to scroll over to Custom 1 or Custom 2 on the list at the bottom of the screen. (Or use the left cursor button and wrap around to the left to reach the Custom settings a bit quicker.)

4. Aim the camera so the screen (or viewfinder) is filled with the white (or gray) color you are using as a standard.

5. Press the Metering Mode key. The camera will evaluate the correct white balance for the current lighting conditions and store that value under the Custom 1 or Custom 2 setting. The screen will briefly darken to indicate that a reading is taking place.

6. Press the FUNC./SET button to exit back to shooting mode.

7. Set the white balance to that saved setting again whenever you need to shoot under those same lighting conditions.

You can adjust the white balance setting even further, if you want. Regardless of which setting you have used for white balance, that is, Daylight, Cloudy, Tungsten, or a Custom one, you can go on to make manual adjustments. Just follow these steps:

1. With the current white balance setting on the screen, rotate the front control dial to make the image "colder" or "warmer" in tone by specifying a value along a scale that ranges from B9 (blue) at the left to 0 (neutral) to A9 (amber) at the right.

2. For additional fine-tuning options, press the MENU button to view the screen shown in Figure 4.24. You can then move the white balance point around to any position on the "map" seen at left. Rotate the front control dial to adjust along the blue-amber axis, and/or the rear control dial to tweak along the green-magenta axis. You can use either or both controls for precise color correction.

3. If you want to cancel your changes in the white balance map, press the Metering Mode button to Reset the values to 0,0.

4. Press the MENU button when finished.

Figure 4.24
On the PowerShot G1 X, it is possible to fine-tune any white balance setting by using the four cursor buttons and the camera's two dials to adjust the levels of blue, green, amber, and magenta.

My Colors

This option gives you the opportunity to exercise a bit of color-oriented creativity when you're shooting your images. Select this third option down from the top of the FUNC. menu's vertical list, and the horizontal list at the bottom of the screen will give you 11 options for altering the color cast of your images: Vivid, Neutral, Sepia, B/W (Black & White), Positive Film, Lighter Skin Tone, Darker Skin Tone, Vivid Blue, Vivid Green, Vivid Red, and Custom Color. Or, of course, you can also set this feature to Off. Most of these choices are self-explanatory; the Vivid choices emphasize the given color; Positive Film combines the effects of having all three Vivid colors together. Neutral tones down all colors. You may want to play around with these and see which ones yield results that meet your needs. Note that this feature is not available and can't be selected when shooting RAW images, because you can tweak your RAW images to produce the same effects when importing your photos into your image editor.

Although the My Colors feature is not as powerful or flexible as the Picture Styles feature introduced to the Canon EOS camera line with the Canon EOS 30D back in February 2006, it does offer considerable benefits. Canon has set the parameters for the ten predefined selections to suit the needs of most photographers. Unlike the situation with Picture Styles, you cannot adjust the settings for those predefined selections. However, you can use the Custom Color option to create one brand-new selection that is all your own. If you want rich, bright colors to emulate Velvia film or the work of legendary photographer Pete Turner, you can build your own color-soaked style. If you want soft, muted colors and less sharpness to create a romantic look, you can do that, too. Perhaps you'd like a setting with extra contrast for shooting outdoors on hazy or cloudy days.

To make use of Custom Color, highlight that final option in the list of My Colors choices. (This is a good opportunity to wrap around by using the left cursor button.) Then press the MENU button. You will then see the word Contrast on the screen (see Figure 4.25). Use the left/right cursor buttons or the rear control dial to adjust the amount of contrast up or down, then use the up/down cursor buttons to highlight the other parameters (Sharpness, Saturation, Red, Green, Blue, and Skin Tone, discussed next). Make your desired adjustments to each of them. When you are finished adjusting all of the parameters to your liking, press the MENU key again and then the FUNC./ SET key to exit the My Colors screen.

The parameters that you can adjust with the My Colors option are as follows:

- **Contrast.** Adjust this slider to change the number of middle tones between the deepest blacks and brightest whites. Low contrast settings produce a flatter-looking photo, whereas high contrast adjustments may improve the tonal rendition while possibly losing detail in the shadows or highlights.

Figure 4.25
The My Colors option lets you adjust several parameters for each setting: contrast, sharpness, saturation, red, green, blue, and skin tone. On the screen shown here, contrast can be adjusted with the left/right cursor buttons or the rear control dial.

■ **Sharpness.** This parameter determines the apparent contrast between the outlines or edges in an image, which we perceive as image sharpness. When adjusting sharpness, remember that more is not always a good thing. A little softness is necessary to reduce or eliminate the moiré effects that can result when details in your image form a pattern that is too close to the pattern, or frequency, of the sensor itself. The default (0) level sharpening was chosen by Canon to allow most moiré interference to be safely blurred to invisibility, at the cost of a little sharpness. As you boost sharpness, moiré can become a problem, plus, you may end up with those noxious "halos" that appear around the edges of images that have been oversharpened. Use this adjustment with care.

■ **Saturation.** This parameter controls the richness of the color, making, say, a red tone appear to be deeper and fuller when you increase saturation, and tend more toward lighter, pinkish hues when you decrease saturation of the reds. Boosting the saturation too much can mean that detail may be lost in one or more of the color channels, producing what is called "clipping."

■ **Red.** Adjusts amount of red.

■ **Green.** Adjusts amount of green.

■ **Blue.** Adjusts amount of blue.

■ **Skin Tone.** This adjustment has the most effect on skin tones, making them either redder or yellower.

Bracketing

Bracketing is a method for shooting several consecutive exposures using different settings, as a way of improving the odds that one of them will be exactly right, or for use in Photoshop or another application to merge images with a larger range of dark-to-bright tones. Many cameras have the ability to bracket exposures at different settings, and some cameras also can bracket other settings, such as white balance. The PowerShot G1 X provides bracketing for two settings: exposure and focus, through the FUNC. menu.

Navigate one icon below My Colors on the FUNC. menu and you arrive at the Bracketing option. Highlight that icon, and the list at the bottom of the screen shows three choices: Off, AEB, and Focus-BKT (see Figure 4.26). The default selection is Off. Following are descriptions of the other two choices, each of which sets the camera up to automatically shoot a sequence of three images, one at the chosen setting, and one each at settings greater and lesser than that setting, with the goal of having one of those three images be right on the mark with its results.

Figure 4.26
The Bracketing option on the FUNC. menu gives you access to Auto Exposure Bracketing and Focus Bracketing.

Auto Exposure Bracketing

The AEB setting produces a series of shots as follows: standard exposure, underexposure, and overexposure. To use this option, follow these steps:

1. **Turn off the flash.** Exposure bracketing won't work if the flash fires. To turn it off, press the Flash key (right cursor button) repeatedly until you see the Flash Off icon.

2. **Select Bracketing from the FUNC. menu.** Press the FUNC./SET key and navigate down to the Bracketing option.

3. **Select AEB.** Move the highlight to the AEB icon at the bottom of the screen to select Auto Exposure Bracketing.

4. **Press the MENU button.** This gives you access to the bracketing scale (see Figure 4.27).

Figure 4.27

The Auto Exposure Bracketing option can be set to take exposures at intervals from 1/3 EV to 2 EV.

5. **Set the interval for the three exposures.** Use the left/right cursor buttons or the rear control dial to move the little orange markers to the desired intervals on the scale for exposure bracketing. You can select an interval of up to 2 Exposure Value (EV) units, in increments of 1/3 EV. If you have dialed in any exposure compensation, that will be reflected in these settings, so be sure to check the exposure compensation dial before setting the exposure bracketing interval. When you've made your choice of interval, press FUNC./SET to lock in the choice.

6. **Take the pictures.** Aim at your subject and hold the camera steady while it makes its three successive exposures. If you've made good choices, one of those exposures should be right on the money.

Focus Bracketing

Focus Bracketing sets up the camera to take three images: one at the manual focus position, one nearer, and one farther. The steps to take are just like those for Auto Exposure Bracketing. Again, the flash must be forced to Off. Also, of course, the camera must be set to Manual focus. Select Bracketing from the FUNC. menu and scroll over to the third icon at the bottom of the screen to select Focus Bracketing. As with Auto Exposure Bracketing, use the MENU button to get access to the bracketing scale, then move the orange markers to indicate how far apart the three focus settings should be. Press FUNC./SET to lock in those settings, and press the shutter button to take the three bracketed images.

Drive Mode

This next option on the FUNC. menu gives you access to the continuous shooting capabilities of the PowerShot G1 X. When you turn on one of the options for multiple shots, the G1 X will fire off a stream of shots as long as you hold your finger on the shutter button, but with some limitations. For one thing, there is no continuous shooting available in Auto mode or in several of the Scene modes. Also, depending on the camera's settings, such as whether a slow shutter speed is set or flash is being used, the shooting may slow down or come to a stop. Despite its limitations, this is a very useful feature to have available, especially now in the digital age, when you don't have to run through 100 feet of expensive film (plus processing) to capture the fleeting expressions of portrait subjects or the fast-breaking events of a sporting contest.

To turn continuous shooting on, select the fifth icon down on the FUNC. menu's list at the left of the screen—the icon that looks like a rectangle or stack of rectangles, depending on what mode is currently in effect. Then move the highlight to the icon you want at the bottom of the screen. The three choices are the default, Single Shot; Continuous; and Continuous AF. With Continuous shooting, you can take about two images per second. The focus and exposure are locked as soon as the first image is taken, and they won't change after that, even if conditions change. If you choose Continuous AF, the camera autofocuses for every shot, and the speed is reduced to about 0.7 images per second. In certain modes, though, such as when the camera is set to Manual focus, Continuous AF will be changed to Continuous LV, and the camera will not autofocus. If you want to speed things up, you can set the mode dial to the Low Light shooting mode, in which case the continuous shooting speeds up considerably, to about four images per second, though the quality of your images is reduced, as is always the case with that shooting mode.

Flash Exposure Compensation

In this case, unlike the other options on the FUNC. menu discussed above, the FUNC. menu provides an alternate way to accomplish something that is available from the "regular" menu system. In certain shooting modes, Flash Exposure Compensation can be selected from the Shooting menu, under the Flash Control setting. But, if you want to get quicker access to that setting, the FUNC. menu is a good way to do so. Press FUNC./SET to bring up the lists of options, then select the sixth icon down on the left side—the lightning bolt with a plus and minus sign. With this setting, the scale you need is displayed immediately; all you have to do next is to use the left/right cursor buttons or the rear control dial to select as much positive or negative flash exposure compensation as you want, in 1/3-stop increments. (Depending on the Shooting mode, the available option may be Flash Output instead of Flash Exposure Compensation.) Oh, and in case you thought that having two distinct ways to choose this option were not enough, here are two more: press the Flash key, then the MENU button, or just hold down the Flash button, until the Flash Exposure Compensation scale appears. These work with both internal and external flash. Somebody at Canon really likes this feature.

Neutral-Density Filter

This next option down the list on the FUNC. menu gives you the choice of using a neutral-density (ND) filter. With film cameras, and with digital cameras for that matter, you can use a physical ND filter in front of the lens, which is essentially a dark piece of glass that cuts down the light reaching the film, for use when light conditions are too bright, or for when you need to use a slow shutter speed or large aperture for some reason. With the PowerShot G1 X, the built-in filter reduces the light reaching the sensor to one-eighth of its actual value, resulting in an exposure setting that needs to be three f/stops greater. (For example, if you were shooting with your aperture at f/8.0, you could change it to f/2.8 to reduce depth-of-field for selective focus with the ND turned on.) This option is easy to set. Select the ND icon on the list at the left, then move the highlight on the bottom list to ND, and you're done. See Figure 4.28, which illustrates

Figure 4.28
Dial in the neutral-density filter if you want to use longer exposures than normally available with a minimum ISO setting of ISO 100 and an f/8 minimum aperture.

how a neutral-density filter allows using a 1/2-second exposure that normally wouldn't be available even under overcast conditions, with an ISO setting of 100 and a minimum aperture of f/8.

Aspect Ratio

The next option down the list on the FUNC. menu, Aspect Ratio, lets you choose the shape of the image recorded by the G1 X. There are five available options, each one expressed as a ratio of the width of the image to its height: 16:9, 3:2, 4:3, 1:1, and 4:5. Each of these has its merits and uses. The 16:9 ratio is often called "widescreen"; it is the ratio used by most widescreen TV sets. The 3:2 ratio is a very common one; it is the same ratio as that for 35mm film and for the 6-inch by 4-inch prints that are the most widely used size for photographic prints in the United States. The 4:3 ratio also is a very familiar one, being the same shape as the camera's LCD screen. The 1:1 ratio, of course, represents a square. It has the advantage of being perfectly symmetrical, not favoring one dimension over the other. Finally, the 4:5 ratio is the only one in which the image is taller than it is wide. It can be useful for taking portraits or images of thin or vertically oriented subjects. For RAW images, the aspect ratio is fixed at 4:3. Of course, though, with any image, you can alter the aspect ratio through cropping in your photo-editing software, so, if you plan to process your photos on your computer, you don't need to be too concerned about shooting in a particular aspect ratio. If you want to use the digital zoom feature, you have to set the aspect ratio to 4:3; otherwise, digital zoom is not available.

Image Quality and Size

The final three options on the FUNC. menu, and three of the most important, are the ones at the bottom of the menu's list, which give you choices for three significant attributes of your shots: Image Type, Image Quality, and Image Size (for both stills and movies). Although these are separate selections on the menu, they are so closely related that it makes sense to discuss them together. After pressing the FUNC./SET key to call up the menu, move the highlight all the way down the list on the left, just below the Aspect Ratio item. This action takes you to the selection area for these choices. Before I describe the details of making your selections, this topic needs some background.

The bottom entry, Movie Size, is the easiest. You get just three options: 1920, 1280, and 640:

- **1920.** With this choice, your video is captured in Full HD format, with a resolution of 1920 × 1080. You'll often see this size referred to by the number of vertical lines in the clip, as *1080p*. With the G1 X, the number of frames captured per second in this format is 24 fps.

- **1280.** With this choice, your video is captured in Standard HD format, with a resolution of 1280 × 720. You'll often see this size referred to by the number of vertical lines in the clip, too, as *720p*. With the G1 X, the number of frames captured per second in this format is 30 fps.

- **640.** With this choice, your video is captured in VGA format, or 640 × 480, also at 30 fps.

For still images, the choices are a tad more complicated, but still easy to understand. There are three separate decisions you need to make when selecting your image size and quality. Your first is whether to shoot everything as RAW files, which provide the best possible quality and most post-processing options, but which take up considerably more space on your memory card than JPEG files. You'll sometimes be told that RAW files are the "unprocessed" image information your camera produces, before it's been modified. That's nonsense. RAW files are no more unprocessed than your camera film is after it's been through the chemicals to produce a negative or transparency. A lot can happen in the developer that can affect the quality of a film image—positively and negatively—and, similarly, your digital image undergoes a significant amount of processing before it is saved as a RAW file. Canon even applies a name (DIGIC 5) to the digital image processing (DIP) chip used to perform this magic in the PowerShot G1 X.

A RAW file is more similar to a film camera's processed negative. It contains all the information, captured in 14-bit channels per color (and stored in a 16-bit space), with no compression, no sharpening, no application of any special filters or other settings you might have specified when you took the picture. Those settings are stored with the RAW file so they can be applied when the image is converted to a form compatible with your favorite image editor. However, using RAW conversion software such as Adobe Camera Raw or Canon's Digital Photo Professional, you can override those settings and apply settings of your own. You can select essentially the same changes there that you might have specified in your camera's picture-taking options.

RAW exists because sometimes we want to have access to all the information captured by the camera, before the camera's internal logic has processed it and converted the image to a standard file format. RAW doesn't save as much space as JPEG. What it does do is preserve all the information captured by your camera after it's been converted from analog to digital form.

So, why don't we always use RAW? Although some photographers do save only in RAW format, it's more common to use either RAW plus the JPEG option or just shoot JPEG and eschew RAW altogether. While RAW is overwhelmingly helpful when an image needs to be fine-tuned, in other situations working with a RAW file can slow you down significantly. RAW images take longer to store on the memory card, and require more post-processing effort, whether you elect to go with the default settings in force when the picture was taken, or make minor adjustments.

As a result, those who depend on speedy access to images or who shoot large numbers of photos at once may prefer JPEG over RAW. Wedding photographers, for example, might expose several thousand photos during a bridal affair and offer hundreds to clients as electronic proofs for inclusion in an album. Wedding shooters take the time to make sure that their in-camera settings are correct, minimizing the need to post-process photos after the event. Given that their JPEGs are so good, there is little need to get bogged down shooting RAW. Sports photographers also eschew RAW files for similar reasons.

JPEG was invented as a more compact file format that can store most of the information in a digital image, but in a much smaller size. JPEG predates most digital cameras and was initially used to squeeze down files for transmission over slow dial-up connections. Even if you were using an early digital camera with 1.3 megapixel files for news photography, you didn't want to send them back to the office over a modem at 1,200 bps.

But, as I noted, JPEG provides smaller files by compressing the information in a way that loses some image data. JPEG remains a viable alternative because it offers several different quality levels. At the highest quality Fine level, you might not be able to tell the difference between the original RAW file and the JPEG version, even though the RAW file occupies, by Canon's estimate, about 15MB on your memory card, while the Large, Fine JPEG takes up about 2.5MB of space. You've squeezed the image by five-sixths without losing much visual information at all. If you don't mind losing some quality, you can use more aggressive Normal compression with Large JPEG to cut the size in half again, to about 1.2MB.

So, using the above considerations, first decide whether to use RAW (or RAW plus JPEG) for all your shooting. If you go that route, you don't need to spend too much time thinking about other decisions regarding image quality and size, because all RAW files on this camera are of the same size and quality.

If you decide to shoot in one of the JPEG formats, though, you have some more decisions to make: First, what image size to select, and, second, what amount of JPEG compression to choose. Here are your choices of image size, showing the figures for an aspect ratio of 4:3; other aspect ratios have smaller numbers of pixels, except the 16:9 ratio, which has more:

- L (14.3 megapixels or 4352 × 3264 pixels)
- M1 (7 megapixels or 3072 × 2304 pixels)
- M2 (2 megapixels or 1600 × 1200 pixels)
- S (0.3 megapixels or 640 × 480 pixels)
- RAW (14.3 megapixels or 4352 × 3264 pixels)
- RAW+L JPEG.

Now let's look at the second choice you need to make from the FUNC. menu—the amount of compression to be used for your JPEG images, which directly affects their quality. To reduce the size of your image files and allow more photos to be stored on a given memory card, the G1 X uses JPEG compression to squeeze these images down to a smaller size. This compacting reduces the image quality a little, so you're offered your choice of various levels of compression.

The G1 X provides just two levels of compression: Fine and Normal. The choice of Fine compression is represented on the camera's screen by a smooth quarter-circle. That level of compression provides the smoothest results, while Normal compression, signified on the screen by a stair-step icon, provides lower-quality, "jaggier" images.

Image size, quality, and compression go hand-in-hand to determine the overall quality of your images, so the PowerShot G1 X provides you with the ability to make these three choices together in the same menu system. On the G1 X, the quality choice (JPEG, RAW, or RAW+JPEG) is made on the next-to-bottom level of the FUNC. menu's list of icons; the image size choice (L, M1, M2, S) and the compression choice are both made on the bottom level.

After pressing the FUNC./SET button, navigate with the up/down cursor buttons to the next-to-bottom icon on the left side of the screen, then use the rear control dial or the cursor buttons to select JPEG, RAW, or RAW+JPEG. If you select RAW, you're done; no other choices need to be (or can be) made, and you can exit the menu by pressing the FUNC./SET button again.

If you selected JPEG or RAW+JPEG, you still need to select the size and compression level for the JPEG images. Navigate down to the bottom item on the FUNC. menu, then move the highlight across the menu on the bottom of the screen to select L, M1, M2, or S for the image size. As you are making this choice, you will see the MENU icon on the screen. Without exiting from the image size screen, press the MENU button and you'll be shown a pair of icons representing the two choices of image compression: the smooth quarter-circle and the jagged stair-step shape. At this point, move the highlight to select either the quarter-circle (Fine) or the stair-step shape (Normal), then press the FUNC./SET key to confirm the selection.

In practice, you'll probably want to use only the Fine compression and the L (Large) or RAW selections for your serious photography. There are some limited advantages to using the M (Medium) and S (Small) resolution settings, and Normal JPEG compression setting. They all allow stretching the capacity of your memory card so you can shoehorn quite a few more pictures onto a single memory card. That can be useful when you're on vacation and running out of storage, or when you're shooting non-critical work that doesn't require full resolution (such as photos taken for real estate listings, web page display, photo ID cards, or similar applications). Some photographers like to record RAW+JPEG Fine so they'll have a JPEG file for review, while retaining access to the original RAW file for serious editing.

For most work, using lower resolution and extra compression is false economy. You never know when you might actually need that extra bit of picture detail. Your best bet is to have enough memory cards to handle all the shooting you want to do until you have the chance to transfer your photos to your computer or a personal storage device.

MANAGING LOTS OF FILES

The only long-term drawback to shooting everything in RAW+JPEG is that it's easy to fill up your computer's hard drive if you are a prolific photographer. Here's what I do. My most recent photos are stored on my working hard drive in a numbered folder, say G1 X -01, with subfolders named after the shooting session, such as 101201Trees, for pictures of trees taken on September 1, 2012. An automatic utility (TrueImage Home) copies new and modified photos to a different hard drive for temporary backup four times daily.

When the top-level folder accumulates about 30GB of images, I back it up to DVDs and then move the folder to a 1.5TB (1500GB) drive dedicated solely for storage of folders that have already been backed up onto DVD. Then I start a new folder, such as G1 X -02, on the working hard drive and repeat the process. I always have at least one backup of every image taken, either on another hard drive or on a DVD.

Part II

Getting the Most from Your Canon PowerShot G1 X

This part consists of three chapters designed to help you get the most out of your Canon PowerShot G1 X, now that you've mastered the basic controls and features of the camera. After all, if all you wanted to do was point-and-shoot, you would have purchased a less versatile camera. If you, like the majority of G1 X owners, belong to the point-*think*-shoot crowd, you'll want to read each of the following chapters so you can get the most from the capabilities at your fingertips.

At the beginning of this book, I promised not to throw you off the dock into deep water and expect you to learn how to swim before you went under for the third time. Instead, I've helped you learn all the basic strokes, in preparation for Part Two, in which, I trust, you'll master the techniques that will transform you from a dog paddler to a championship swimmer.

As with Part One, you can start with any of the three chapters that follow, depending on your interests and skill level:

- **If you want to learn how to capture a full range of tonal values, every time, read:** *Chapter 5: Fine-Tuning Exposure.* This chapter will show you how to handle tricky situations, such as backlighting, how to create silhouette images, how to choose from among the G1 X's exposure and metering modes, and techniques for optimizing exposure using tools like histograms.

- **If you want to explore ways to use selective focus or deep focus, jump to:** *Chapter 6:Mastering the Mysteries of Autofocus.* Here, I'll show you exactly how your G1 X's autofocus system works, and help you understand how to apply focus creatively.

- **If you know that producing compelling videos involves more than just pointing the camera and pressing the Movie button, you'll want to go to:** *Chapter 7: Movie-Making with Your Canon PowerShot G1 X.* I'll explain all your camera's movie options and offer tips on planning, shooting, and editing your clips.

5

Fine-Tuning Exposure

The Canon PowerShot G1 X offers the best of two worlds when it comes to capturing exactly the right exposure—a picture with the optimum balance of tones and colors that are neither too light nor too dark to reveal all the detail in the original subject. You can select one of the numerous predefined shooting modes suitable for your subject matter—such as portrait, landscape, underwater, sports, or beach—and the camera will do an excellent job of calculating the right settings to give you an outstanding picture with little input on your part beyond the initial mode dial selection. If you can't decide for yourself which of those specific shooting modes is best, you can select the green Auto icon instead, and the PowerShot G1 X will still do a fine job.

So, why do I include an entire chapter titled "Fine-Tuning Exposure" in all my Canon books? As you learn to use your PowerShot G1 X creatively, you're going to find that the right settings—as determined by the camera's exposure meter and intelligence—need to be *adjusted* to account for your creative decisions or special situations.

For example, when you shoot with the main light source behind the subject, you end up with *backlighting*, which results in an overexposed background and/or an underexposed subject. The PowerShot G1 X recognizes backlit situations nicely, and can properly base exposure on the main subject, producing a decent photo. A feature like i-Contrast (introduced in Chapter 4) can fine-tune exposure to preserve detail in the highlights and shadows.

But what if you *want* to underexpose the subject, to produce a silhouette effect? Or, perhaps, you might want to make use of the camera's built-in flash unit to fill in the shadows on your subject. The more you know about how to use your PowerShot G1 X, the more you'll run into situations where you want to creatively tweak the exposure to provide a different look than you'd get with a straight shot.

This chapter shows you the fundamentals of exposure, so you'll be better equipped to override the PowerShot G1 X's default settings when you want to, or need to. After all, correct exposure is one of the foundations of good photography, along with accurate focus and sharpness, appropriate color balance, freedom from unwanted noise and excessive contrast, as well as pleasing composition.

Understanding Exposure

Exposure determines the look, feel, and tone of an image, in more ways than one. Incorrect exposure can impair even the best-composed image by cloaking important tones in darkness, or by washing them out so they become featureless to the eye. On the other hand, correct exposure brings out the detail in the areas you want to picture, and provides the range of tones and colors you need to create the desired image. However, getting the perfect exposure can be tricky, because digital sensors can't capture all the tones we are able to see. If the range of tones in an image is extensive, embracing both inky black shadows and bright highlights, the sensor may not be able to capture them all. Sometimes, we must settle for an exposure that renders most of those tones—but not all—in a way that best suits the photo we want to produce. You'll often need to make choices about which details are important, and which are not, so that you can grab the tones that truly matter in your image. That's part of the creativity you bring to bear in realizing your photographic vision.

For example, look at the two typical tourist snapshots presented side by side in Figure 5.1. The camera was mounted on a tripod for both, so the only way you can really see that they are two different images is by examining the differences in the way the water flows over the rocks. However, the pair of pictures does vary in exposure. The version on the left was underexposed, which helps bring out detail in the ridges and sky in the background, but makes the water and foreground look murky and dark. The overexposed version on the right offers better exposure for the foreground area, but now the ridges and sky are too light.

With digital camera sensors, it's tricky to capture detail in both highlights and shadows in a single image, because the number of tones, the *dynamic range,* of the sensor is limited. The solution, in this particular case, was to resort to a technique called High Dynamic Range (HDR) photography, in which the two exposures from Figure 5.1 were combined in an image editor such as Photoshop, or a specialized HDR software program. The resulting shot is shown in Figure 5.2. I'll explain more about HDR photography later in this chapter, including instructions for using the G1 X's own HDR mode. For now, though, I'm going to concentrate on showing you how to get the best exposures possible without resorting to such tools, using only the features of your Canon PowerShot G1 X.

Figure 5.1
At left, the image is exposed for the background highlights, losing shadow detail. At right, the exposure captures detail in the shadows, but the background highlights are washed out.

Figure 5.2
Combining the two exposures produces the best compromise image.

rstand exposure, you need to understand the six aspects of light that combine to produce an image. Start with a light source—the sun, an interior lamp, or the glow from a campfire—and trace its path to your camera, through the lens, and finally to the sensor that captures the illumination. Here's a brief review of the things within our control that affect exposure.

- **Light at its source.** Our eyes and our cameras—film or digital—are most sensitive to that portion of the electromagnetic spectrum we call *visible light*. That light has several important aspects that are relevant to photography, such as color, and harshness (which is determined primarily by the apparent size of the light source as it illuminates a subject). But, in terms of exposure, the important attribute of a light source is its *intensity*. We may have direct control over intensity, which might be the case with an interior light that can be brightened or dimmed. Or, we might have only indirect control over intensity, as with sunlight, which can be made to appear dimmer by introducing translucent light-absorbing or reflective materials in its path.

- **Light's duration.** We tend to think of most light sources as continuous. But, as you'll learn in Chapter 10, the duration of light can change quickly enough to modify the exposure, as when the main illumination in a photograph comes from an intermittent source, such as an electronic flash.

- **Light reflected, transmitted, or emitted.** Once light is produced by its source, either continuously or in a brief burst, we are able to see and photograph objects by the light that is reflected from our subjects toward the camera lens; transmitted (say, from translucent objects that are lit from behind); or emitted (by a candle or television screen). When more or less light reaches the lens from the subject, we need to adjust the exposure. This part of the equation is under our control to the extent we can increase the amount of light falling on or passing through the subject (by adding extra light sources or using reflectors), or by pumping up the light that's emitted (by increasing the brightness of the glowing object).

- **Light passed by the lens.** Not all the illumination that reaches the front of the lens makes it all the way through. Filters can remove some of the light before it enters the lens. Inside the lens barrel is a variable-sized diaphragm called an *aperture* that dilates and contracts to control the amount of light that enters the lens. You, or the PowerShot G1 X's autoexposure system, can control exposure by varying the size of the aperture. The relative size of the aperture is called the *f/stop*.

- **Light passing through the shutter.** Once light passes through the lens, the amount of time the sensor receives it is determined by the PowerShot G1 X's shutter, which can remain open for as long as 60 seconds or as briefly as 1/4,000th second.

■ **Light captured by the sensor.** Not all the light falling onto the sensor is captured. If the number of photons reaching a particular photosite don't pass a set threshold, no information is recorded. Similarly, if too much light illuminates a pixel in the sensor, then the excess isn't recorded or, worse, spills over to contaminate adjacent pixels. We can modify the minimum and maximum number of pixels that contribute to image detail by adjusting the ISO setting. At higher ISOs, the incoming light is amplified to boost the effective sensitivity of the sensor.

These factors—the quantity of light produced by the light source; the amount reflected or transmitted toward the camera; the light passed by the lens; the amount of time the shutter is open; and the sensitivity of the sensor—all work proportionately and reciprocally to produce an exposure. That is, if you double the amount of light that's available, increase the aperture by one stop, make the shutter speed twice as long, or boost the ISO setting 2X, you'll get twice as much exposure. Similarly, you can increase any of these factors while decreasing one of the others by a similar amount to keep the same exposure.

F/STOPS AND SHUTTER SPEEDS

If you're *really* new to more advanced cameras, you might need to know that the lens aperture, or f/stop, is a ratio, much like a fraction, which is why f/2.8 is larger than f/5.6, just as 1/2 is larger than 1/4. However, f/2.8 is actually *four times* as large as f/5.6. (If you remember your high school geometry, you'll know that to double the area of a circle, you multiply its diameter by the square root of two: 1.4.)

Apertures in digital cameras are usually marked with intermediate f/stops that represent a size that's twice as much/half as much as the previous aperture. So, a lens might be marked: f/2.8, f/4, f/5.6, f/8, with each larger number representing an aperture that admits half as much light as the one before, as shown in Figure 5.3, which is a graphic illustration of f/stops, and not an actual photograph of your G1 X's lens apertures.

Shutter speeds are actual fractions (of a second), but in some cameras' displays the numerator is omitted, so that 60, 125, 250, 500, 1000, and so forth represent 1/60th, 1/125th, 1/250th, 1/500th, and 1/1000th second. In the PowerShot G1 X, Canon actually found room to include the numerators. However, to avoid all chance of confusion, Canon uses quotation marks to signify longer exposures: For example, 0"5, 2", and 4" represent 0.5, 2.0, and 4.0 second exposures, respectively.

Figure 5.3
Top row (left to right): f/2.8, f/4; bottom row, f/5.6, f/8.

Most commonly, exposure settings are made using the aperture and shutter speed, followed by adjusting the ISO sensitivity if it's not possible to get the preferred exposure (that is, the one that uses the "best" f/stop or shutter speed for the depth-of-field or action-stopping we want). Table 5.1 shows equivalent exposure settings using various shutter speeds and f/stops.

When the PowerShot G1 X is set for P mode, the metering system selects the correct exposure for you automatically. However, you can change quickly to an equivalent exposure by holding down the shutter release button halfway and pressing the * button ("locking" the current exposure), and then spinning the control dial (on the back of the camera) until the desired equivalent exposure combination is displayed. The equivalent exposures appear as a pairing of shutter speeds and f/stops on the LCD, which you can change using the control dial. This Program Shift feature does not work when you're using flash.

Table 5.1 Equivalent Exposures

Shutter speed	f/stop	Shutter speed	f/stop
1/250th second	f/8	1/1000th second	f/4
1/500th second	f/5.6	1/2000th second	f/2.8

In Aperture priority (Av) and Shutter priority (Tv) modes, you can change to an equivalent exposure, but only by adjusting either the aperture (the camera chooses the shutter speed) or shutter speed (the camera selects the aperture). I'll cover all these exposure modes later in the chapter.

How the PowerShot G1 X Calculates Exposure

Your G1 X calculates exposure by measuring the light that reaches the sensor, based on the assumption that each area being measured reflects about the same amount of light as a neutral gray card that reflects a "middle" gray of about 12 to 18 percent reflectance. (The photographic "gray cards" you buy at a camera store have an 18 percent gray tone; your camera is calibrated to interpret a somewhat darker 12 percent gray; I'll explain more about this later.) That "average" 12 to 18 percent gray assumption is necessary, because different subjects reflect different amounts of light. In a photo containing, say, a white cat and a dark gray cat, the white cat might reflect five times as much light as the gray cat. An exposure based on the white cat will cause the gray cat to appear to be black, while an exposure based only on the gray cat will make the white cat washed out.

This is more easily understood if you look at some photos of subjects that are dark (they reflect little light), those that have predominantly middle tones, and subjects that are highly reflective. The next few figures show some images of actual cats (actually, the *same* cat rendered in black, gray, and white varieties through the magic of Photoshop), with each of the three strips exposed using a different cat for reference.

Correctly Exposed

The three pictures shown in Figure 5.4 represent how the black, gray, and white cats would appear if the exposure were calculated by measuring the light reflecting from the middle, gray cat, which, for the sake of illustration, we'll assume reflects approximately 12 to 18 percent of the light that strikes it. The exposure meter sees an object that it thinks is a middle gray, calculates an exposure based on that, and the feline in the center of the strip is rendered at its proper tonal value. Best of all, because the

Figure 5.4
When exposure is calculated based on the gray cat in the center, the black and white cats are rendered accurately, too.

resulting exposure is correct, the black cat at left and white cat at right are rendered properly as well.

When you're shooting pictures with your G1 X, and the meter happens to base its exposure on a subject that averages that "ideal" middle gray, then you'll end up with similar (accurate) results. The camera's exposure algorithms are concocted to ensure this kind of result as often as possible, barring any unusual subjects (that is, those that are backlit, or have uneven illumination). The G1 X has several metering modes (described next), plus Scene modes, each of which is equipped to handle certain types of unusual subjects, as I'll outline.

Overexposed

The strip of three images in Figure 5.5 show what would happen if the exposure were calculated based on metering the leftmost, black cat. The light meter sees less light reflecting from the black cat than it would see from a gray middle-tone subject, and so figures, "Aha! I need to add exposure to brighten this subject up to a middle gray!" That lightens the black cat, so it now appears to be gray.

But now the cat in the middle that was *originally* middle gray is overexposed and becomes light gray. And the white cat at right is now seriously overexposed, and loses detail in the highlights, which have become a featureless white.

Figure 5.5
When exposure is calculated based on the black cat at the left, the black cat looks gray, the gray cat appears to be a light gray, and the white cat is seriously overexposed.

Underexposed

The third possibility in this simplified scenario is that the light meter might measure the illumination bouncing off the white cat, and try to render that feline as a middle gray. A lot of light is reflected by the white kitty, so the exposure is *reduced*, bringing that cat closer to a middle gray tone. The cats that were originally gray and black are now rendered too dark. Clearly, measuring the gray cat—or a substitute that reflects about the same amount of light, is the only way to ensure that the exposure is precisely correct. (See Figure 5.6.)

As you can see, the ideal way to measure exposure is to meter from a subject that reflects 12 to 18 percent of the light that reaches it. If you want the most precise exposure calculations, if you don't have a gray cat handy, the solution is to use a stand-in, such as

Figure 5.6
When exposure is calculated based on the white cat on the right, the other two cats are underexposed.

the evenly illuminated gray card I mentioned earlier. But, because the standard Kodak gray card reflects 18 percent of the light that reaches it and, as I said, your camera is calibrated for a somewhat darker 12 percent tone, you would need to add about one-half stop *more* exposure than the value metered from the card.

Another substitute for a gray card is the palm of a human hand (the backside of the hand is too variable). But a human palm, regardless of ethnic group, is even brighter than a standard gray card, so instead of one-half stop more exposure, you need to add one additional stop. That is, if your meter reading is 1/500th of a second at f/8, use 1/500th second at f/5.6 or 1/250th second at f/8 instead. (Both exposures are equivalent.)

WHY THE GRAY CARD CONFUSION?

Why are so many photographers under the impression that cameras and meters are calibrated to the 18-percent "standard," rather than the true value, which may be 12 to 14 percent, depending on the vendor? You'll find this misinformation in an alarming number of places. I've seen the 18-percent "myth" taught in camera classes; I've found it in books, and even been given this wrong information from the technical staff of camera vendors. (They should know better—the same vendors' engineers who design and calibrate the cameras have the right figure.)

The most common explanation is that during a revision of Kodak's instructions for its gray cards in the 1970s, the advice to open up an extra half stop was omitted, and a whole generation of shooters grew up thinking that a measurement off a gray card could be used as-is. The proviso returned to the instructions by 1987, it's said, but by then it was too late. Next to me is a ©2006 version of the instructions for KODAK Gray Cards, Publication R-27Q, and the current directions read (with a bit of paraphrasing from me in italics):

■ For subjects of normal reflectance increase the indicated exposure by 1/2 stop.

■ For light subjects use the indicated exposure; for very light subjects, decrease the exposure by 1/2 stop. (*That is, you're measuring a cat that's lighter than middle gray.*)

■ If the subject is dark to very dark, increase the indicated exposure by 1 to 1-1/2 stops. (*You're shooting a black cat.*)

lly wanted to use a gray card, place it in your frame near your main subject, facing the camera, and with the exact same even illumination falling on it that is falling on your subject. Then, use the Spot metering function (described in the next section) to calculate exposure. Of course, in most situations, it's not necessary to do this. Your camera's light meter will do a good job of calculating the right exposure, especially if you use the exposure tips in the next section. But, I felt that explaining exactly what is going on during exposure calculation would help you understand how your G1 X's metering system works.

In serious photography using creative shooting modes such as A, P, or S, you'll want to choose both the *metering mode* (the pattern that determines how brightness is evaluated) and *exposure method* (more accurately called the operating mode that determines how the appropriate shutter speed and aperture is set).

Choosing a Metering Method

The PowerShot G1 X has three different schemes for evaluating the light received by its exposure sensors—Evaluative, Center weighted, and Spot. You can choose among them by pressing the Metering Mode button (southwest of the cursor pad) and rotating the rear control dial until the mode you want is selected. (In this case, you can't use the left/right cursor buttons to make the selection, because pressing those keys in this context will activate their other functions—selecting Macro/manual focus shooting or Flash.)

- **Evaluative.** The PowerShot G1 X slices up the frame into various different zones. (As is typical with its non-dSLR cameras, Canon doesn't reveal how many zones there are, or exactly where they are located.) The camera evaluates the measurements, paying special attention to the metering zones that appear to include certain levels of brightness or features such as human faces, to make an educated guess about what kind of picture you're taking, based on examination of thousands of different real-world photos. For example, if the top sections of a picture are much lighter than the bottom portions, the algorithm can assume that the scene is a landscape photo with lots of sky. This mode is the best all-purpose metering method for most pictures. It's the mode used when the camera is set to Auto shooting. A typical scene best measured by Evaluative metering is shown in Figure 5.7.

- **Spot AE Point.** This mode confines the reading to a limited (and non-specified) area in the center of the viewfinder, making up only a small percent of the image. This mode is useful when you want to base exposure on a single, limited area in the frame. If that area is in the center of the frame, so much the better. If not, you'll have to take steps to make sure the reading is accurate. One way is to make your meter reading by placing the center spot over the main part of the subject and then locking exposure by pressing the shutter release halfway, or by pressing the AE lock button, before moving the camera back into position for taking the picture. Another

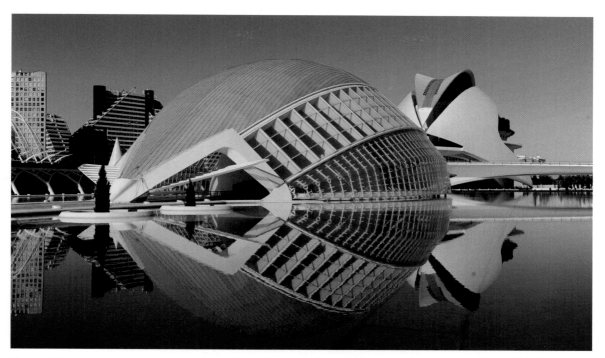

Figure 5.7 Evaluative metering can assess a complex scene like this one and provide the correct exposure.

way is to use the FlexiZone focusing capability, discussed in Chapter 6, which lets you move the autofocus bracket around the screen. Using the Spot AE Point option on the Shooting menu, as discussed in Chapter 4, you can link the Spot AE Point to the AF Point. Then, when you move the FlexiZone AF Frame around the screen, you will be moving the Spot AE Point at the same time, so you can choose precisely what area of the scene is measured for your exposure. The Spot AE Point Frame and AF Frame are moved around using the cursor buttons or the dials after you press the frame selector button (just east of the LCD). The frame turns orange and can be changed in size using the DISP. button. A typical scene suitable for this type of metering is shown in Figure 5.8.

■ **Center weighted averaging.** In this mode, the exposure meter emphasizes a zone located roughly in the center of the frame to calculate exposure, on the theory that, for most pictures, the main subject will be located in the center. Center weighting works best for portraits, architectural photos, and other pictures in which the most important subject is located in the middle of the frame. As the name suggests, the light reading is *weighted* toward the central portion, but information is also used from the rest of the frame. If your main subject is surrounded by very bright or very dark areas, the exposure might not be exactly right. However, this scheme works well in many situations if you don't want to use one of the other modes, such as the scene shown in Figure 5.9.

Figure 5.8
If you want to meter from a specific point in a scene, such as the musician's face, use Spot AE Point metering.

Figure 5.9
Scenes in which the center portion of the image is important work well with Center weighted averaging metering.

Choosing an Exposure Method

If you set the PowerShot G1 X's shooting mode dial to Auto or SCN modes, the camera will take care of choosing an exposure method (Evaluative) and calculating the exposure for you. But if you're inclined to exercise more control over the exposure decision, you'll find three semi-automated methods—Program, Aperture priority, and Shutter priority—plus the Manual mode for choosing the appropriate shutter speed and aperture. Just spin the mode dial to choose the method you want to use. Your choice of which is best for a given shooting situation will depend on things like your need for lots of (or less) depth-of-field, a desire to freeze action or allow motion blur, or how much noise you find acceptable in an image. Each of the PowerShot G1 X's non-automatic exposure methods emphasizes one aspect of image capture or another. This section introduces you to all four. I'll cover the SCN modes later in the chapter.

Aperture Priority

In Av (the letters stand for Aperture value) mode, you specify the lens opening used, and the PowerShot G1 X selects the shutter speed. Aperture priority is especially good when you want to use a particular lens opening to achieve a desired effect. Perhaps you'd like to use the smallest f/stop possible to maximize depth-of-field in a close-up picture. Or, you might want to use a large f/stop to throw everything except your main subject out of focus, as in Figure 5.10. Maybe you'd just like to "lock in" a particular f/stop because it's the sharpest available aperture. Or, you might prefer to use, say, f/4, even though the G1 X's lens has a maximum aperture of f/2.8, because you want the best compromise between speed and sharpness.

Aperture priority can even be used to specify a *range* of shutter speeds you want to use under varying lighting conditions, which seems almost contradictory. But think about it. You're shooting a soccer game outdoors with a telephoto zoom setting and want a relatively high shutter speed, but you don't care if the speed changes a little should the sun duck behind a cloud. Set your PowerShot G1 X to Av, and adjust the aperture until a shutter speed of, say, 1/1000th second is selected at your current ISO setting. (In bright sunlight at ISO 200, that aperture is likely to be around f/8.) Then, go ahead and shoot, knowing that your camera will maintain that f/8 aperture (for sufficient depth-of-field as the soccer players move about the field), but will drop down to 1/800th or 1/500th second if necessary should the lighting change a little.

A shutter speed displaying in orange (rather than white) on the LCD indicates that the PowerShot G1 X is unable to select an appropriate shutter speed at the selected aperture, and that over- or underexposure will occur at the current ISO setting (see Figure 5.11). That's the major pitfall of using Av: you might select an f/stop that is too small or too large to allow an optimal exposure with the available shutter speeds. For example, if you choose f/2.8 as your aperture and the illumination is quite bright (say, at the beach or in snow), even your camera's fastest shutter speed might not be able to cut down the

Figure 5.10
Use Aperture priority mode to "lock in" a large f/stop when you want to blur the background.

Figure 5.11
When the PowerShot G1 X cannot achieve proper exposure in Av mode, the shutter speed will turn orange.

amount of light reaching the sensor to provide the right exposure. Or, if you select f/8 in a dimly lit room, you might find yourself shooting with a very slow shutter speed that can cause blurring from subject movement or camera shake. (However, you can minimize this risk by turning on the Safety Shift feature through the Shooting menu, as described in Chapter 4.) In general, Aperture priority is best used by those with a bit of experience in choosing settings. Many seasoned photographers leave their cameras set on Av all the time.

Note that there may be situations in which the expected aperture cannot be set. This can happen when the built-in flash is turned on, because, on the PowerShot G1 X, the fastest shutter speed available when using the built-in flash is 1/2000. So, for example, if you are photographing in bright conditions and set a wide aperture such as f/2.8, and the appropriate shutter speed would be 1/4000, the G1 X will reset the aperture to a value such as f/5.6, so the shutter speed can be reset to a slower speed.

Finally, note that, with the G1 X, as you zoom the lens in beyond its wide-angle setting of 28mm, some apertures become unavailable. For example, when the lens is zoomed all the way in to its 112mm telephoto value, the widest aperture available is f/5.8. That's because the *effective* aperture of the f/2.8 lens becomes f/5.8 at the maximum zoom position.

Shutter Priority

Shutter priority (Tv, for Time value) is the inverse of Aperture priority: you choose the shutter speed you'd like to use, and the camera's metering system selects the appropriate f/stop. Perhaps you're shooting action photos and you want to use the absolute fastest shutter speed available with your camera; in other cases, you might want to use a slow shutter speed to add some blur to a sports photo that would be mundane if the action were completely frozen. Or, you might want to give a feeling of motion, as with the image by Cleveland photographer Kris Bosworth of an antique auto cruising down the parkway at dozens of miles per hour. (See Figure 5.12.) Shutter priority mode gives you some control over how much action-freezing capability your digital camera brings to bear in a particular situation.

You'll also encounter the same problem as with Aperture priority when you select a shutter speed that's too long or too short for correct exposure under some conditions. I've shot outdoor soccer games on sunny fall evenings and used Shutter priority mode to lock in a 1/1000th second shutter speed, only to find my camera indicated an incorrect exposure when the sun dipped behind some trees and there was no longer enough light to shoot at that speed, even with the lens wide open.

Figure 5.12 Lock the shutter at a slow speed to introduce blur, as with this panned image of an antique automobile.

Figure 5.13
A minimum or maximum aperture displayed in orange means the camera cannot achieve a correct exposure in Shutter priority mode.

As with Av mode, it's possible to choose an inappropriate shutter speed using Tv mode. If that's the case, 2.8, the maximum aperture of your lens (to indicate underexposure) or 8.0, the minimum aperture (to indicate overexposure) will show up as orange on the LCD display (see Figure 5.13). Again, as with Av mode, you can avoid this problem by turning on Safety Shift through the Shooting menu.

Note that, just as with aperture settings, there may be times when you think you've set a particular shutter speed—say, 1/4000, but the camera seems to ignore your setting and changes it to 1/2000 or 1/250. Here's why this happens. As noted above, the fastest shutter speed the G1 X can use with the built-in flash in Tv mode is 1/2000, and it will reset itself to that shutter speed when the flash is activated, even though it will let you set a faster speed of 1/2500, 1/3200, or 1/4000 initially. However, if you have a compatible external flash attached, then the fastest shutter speed the camera will let you set is 1/250th second. In that situation, if you set a faster shutter speed, the camera will reset it to no faster than 1/250th second.

Program Mode

Program mode (P) uses the PowerShot G1 X's built-in smarts to select the correct f/stop and shutter speed using a database of picture information that tells it which combination of shutter speed and aperture will work best for a particular photo. If the correct exposure cannot be achieved at the current ISO setting, the shutter speed and aperture indicators in the viewfinder will *both* display in orange at their extreme settings, showing 1" and 2.8 to indicate underexposure or 1/4000 and 8.0 to indicate overexposure. You can then boost or reduce the ISO to increase or decrease sensitivity.

The PowerShot G1 X's recommended exposure can be overridden if you want. Use the exposure compensation feature (described later, because it also applies to Tv and Av modes) to add or subtract exposure from the metered value. And, as I mentioned earlier in this chapter, you can change from the recommended setting to an equivalent setting (as shown earlier in Table 5.1) that produces the same exposure, but with a different combination of f/stop and shutter speed. To accomplish this, use the Program Shift feature as follows:

1. **Disable flash.** Make sure the flash is forced off by pressing the Flash button and highlighting the icon showing the lightning bolt with a line through it.

2. **Lock exposure.** Press the shutter release halfway to lock in the current base exposure, and press the AE lock button (*) on the back of the camera (in which case the * indicator will be displayed on the screen to show that the exposure has been locked).

3. **Choose exposure combination.** A pair of slide-rule-like dials will immediately appear on the screen, with the apertures on top, and the corresponding shutter speeds below them. Spin the control dial to move the pairings of shutter speed and aperture in tandem until you find the combination you want.

4. **Take photo.** Press the shutter button to grab your shot.

Your adjustment remains in force for a single exposure; if you want to change from the recommended settings for the next exposure, you'll need to repeat those steps.

Making EV Changes

Sometimes you'll want more or less exposure than indicated by the PowerShot G1 X's metering system. Perhaps you want to underexpose to create a silhouette effect, or overexpose to produce a high key look. It's easy to use the camera's exposure compensation system to override the exposure recommendations, as long as you're using the Program, Aperture priority, or Shutter priority shooting mode.

Exposure Compensation with the PowerShot G1 X

One of the great features of the PowerShot G1 X is the presence of a dial dedicated to exposure compensation. This is one of the functions that serious photographers really appreciate—the ability to tweak the camera's automatic exposure setting according to conditions, and, more importantly, according to the photographer's vision of how the image should look. With the addition of this dedicated dial, you have immediate access to this adjustment. So, the instructions for using this feature on the G1 X are quite brief—turn the exposure compensation dial to the desired value: into the + area to lighten the image, and into the − area to darken it. (See Figure 5.14.)

Figure 5.14
If your image is too bright (top), rotate the exposure compensation dial to −1 to produce a version that's better exposed (middle). Don't go too far: −2 exposure compensation (bottom) creates an image that's too dark.

When using exposure compensation, it's important to remember that any adjustment you make to that value will remain in place even after the camera has been turned off and back on again; you have to be sure to move the exposure compensation dial back to zero when you no longer need the adjustment. The adjustment is not available in Manual or Auto shooting mode. However, if you turn the dial while in one of those modes, the adjustment will take effect if you later switch to a shooting mode that does permit exposure compensation.

Manual Exposure

Part of being an experienced photographer comes from knowing when to rely on your PowerShot G1 X's automation (including Auto mode, P mode, and other automated settings), when to go semi-automatic (with Tv or Av), and when to set exposure manually (using M). Some photographers actually prefer to set their exposure manually, but that doesn't leave you completely on your own; the PowerShot G1 X provides an analog exposure scale on the LCD to indicate when its metering system judges your manual settings provide the proper exposure.

Manual exposure can come in handy in some situations. You might be taking a silhouette photo and find that none of the exposure modes or EV correction features give you exactly the effect you want. For example, when I shot the dancer in Figure 5.15 in front of a mostly dark background highlighted by an illuminated curtain off to the right, there was no way any of my camera's exposure modes would be able to interpret the scene the way I wanted to shoot it. So, I took a couple test exposures, and set the exposure manually, using the exact shutter speed and f/stop I needed. Or, you might need to set the aperture manually when working with non-dedicated flash units, and your camera's exposure meter can't interpret the flash exposure at all.

Although, depending on your proclivities, you might not need to set exposure manually very often, you should still make sure you understand how it works. Fortunately, the PowerShot G1 X makes setting exposure manually quite easy. Here are the steps to take:

1. **Choose Manual exposure.** Set the mode dial to M.

2. **Set shutter speed and aperture.** Rotate the front control dial to set your desired shutter speed, and rotate the rear control dial to select the f/stop you want. (Those are the standard functions of those dials by default. As discussed in Chapter 4, you can use the Set Dial Functions menu item to change the roles of the dials, if you want.)

3. **Check metered exposure.** Press the shutter release halfway and the camera will determine what the metered exposure should be. Look at the vertical scale with tick marks at the right of the screen; it will have a white marker on the right side of the scale that moves up and down as the manual exposure setting changes. (See Figure 5.16.)

Figure 5.15
The only way to expose this shot of a dancer correctly was to use Manual exposure.

Figure 5.16
When setting exposure manually, an exposure scale shows the difference between your settings and the metered exposure.

corrections, if desired. If that marker goes above the mid-point on the that means the camera considers the manual exposure setting to be too ___ ; if the marker goes below the mid-point, the camera believes the exposure setting is too dark. If the difference becomes greater than 2 EV in either direction, the white marker on the right turns orange. Change shutter speed and/or aperture, as described in Steps 2 and 3, until the exposure you want is set. The LCD display will change in brightness in response to your EV corrections.

5. **Or, let the camera correct your manual exposure settings.** If you prefer to let the camera set the exposure, you can press the AE lock (*) and the camera will attempt to change your manual exposure setting to its own metered setting by adjusting either the aperture or the shutter speed. (If the manual settings are both too far away from the metered settings, the camera will not be able to achieve a proper exposure setting by adjusting shutter speed or aperture. You'll have to do it manually.)

6. **Take your photo.** Once you have adjusted the shutter speed and aperture to your liking, and checked them against the vertical scale on the right of the screen, press the shutter button to take the picture.

Correcting Brightness with i-Contrast

The i-Contrast feature locates extra-bright and extra-dark portions of your images, including faces or background areas, and adjusts the exposure to counter washed-out highlights or murky shadows. You can select from several different correction methods, two for dynamic range, and one for shadow correction, plus Auto settings for each of these. This feature operates when shooting JPEG format (only). It is not available when using RAW or RAW+JPEG file formats.

■ **Dynamic Range Correction.** Adjusts for images that have extended ranges of tones that cannot be captured with the default settings. Press the FUNC./SET button and select DR Correction (each DR setting is preceded by a down-arrow icon). The default setting is ↓Off, but you can choose ↓Auto (fixes overexposed areas), ↓200% (adjusts dynamic range 200 percent), ↓400% (expands dynamic range by 400 percent). Note that with the ↓200% and ↓400% settings, ISO settings higher than ISO 1600 cannot be selected or used. In addition, with the ↓200% and ↓400% settings, ISOs lower than ISO 200 and ISO 400 (respectively) cannot be selected.

■ **Shadow Correct.** Press the FUNC./SET button and select DR Correction. Then press the MENU button to switch to Shadow Correction mode. Each Shadow Correction setting is preceded by an up-arrow icon. You can choose ↑Off to turn off Shadow Correction, or ↑Auto to brighten shadow areas.

Automatic and Scene Modes

Other important tools in your exposure repertoire are the numerous automatic and scene-oriented shooting modes, which can automatically make all the basic settings needed for certain types of shooting situations, such as portraits, landscapes, sports, fireworks, underwater pictures, and others. These "autopilot" modes are especially useful when you suddenly encounter a picture-taking opportunity and don't have time to decide exactly which of the more advanced shooting modes you want to use. Instead, you can spin the mode dial to select the appropriate automatic mode and fire away, knowing that at least you have a fighting chance of getting a good or usable photo.

These modes are also helpful when you're just learning to use your PowerShot G1 X. Once you've learned how to operate your camera, you'll probably prefer one of the advanced modes that provide more control over shooting options. The automatic or Scene modes may give you few options or none at all. In some cases, the AF mode, drive mode, or metering mode will be set for you, or your options for selecting those items may be sharply limited.

Auto Mode

First, we need to mention Auto mode, because it occupies its own separate place on the mode dial. Turn the dial to that setting, and most of the time you are likely to be pleased with the results of your shots, because the camera will use its electronic intelligence to make reasonably good judgments about shutter speed, aperture, backlighting, and other factors. This is the mode to use when you hand your camera to a total stranger and ask him or her to take your picture posing in front of the Eiffel Tower. All the photographer has to do is look through the viewfinder and press the shutter release button. Just about every other decision is made by the camera's electronics. You can still set image size and quality (but you can't shoot in RAW quality), and you can control exposure compensation, aspect ratio, and a few other items, but enough basic decisions are made by the camera to result in a usable image virtually every time. However, you should be aware that, perhaps because the PowerShot G1 X is intended for use by more experienced photographers, the camera does not (always) treat you like a dummy—it will let you change settings that you might not expect. For example, in Landscape mode, although the flash is set to Off initially, you still have the option of turning it back on if you want to for some reason. In Fireworks mode, though, the camera *does* treat you like a dummy, and won't let you turn the flash on. However, in most SCN modes, you can choose to have the flash on, off, or automatically selected when needed. In Auto mode, you can choose to turn the flash on or off. You also have the option to turn on Tracking AF by pressing the Metering Mode button (which is available for this unusual purpose because it can't be used to select the metering mode in the Auto shooting mode).

Scene Modes

Next, we come to the impressive array of specific shooting modes that Canon's engineers have devised to help you cope with the ever-changing environment that you're confronted with in the varied activities of your life. To get access to these modes, set the mode dial to the SCN setting, press the FUNC./SET button, and then turn the rear control dial to move to the specific scene type you want to select. As you rotate the rear control dial, the camera displays the name of each scene type on the screen (for example, "Foliage") so you're not left guessing what the sometimes-cryptic icons represent. And, the camera goes so far as to display a short phrase on the screen explaining what the selected mode is designed for (for example, "shoot foliage in vivid colors"). One important note: None of these settings is available if you're shooting with RAW quality. I'll provide some brief points about each of these scene modes in the list below.

- **Movie Digest.** Strictly speaking, this is not a scene mode but, rather, a way of telling the G1 X to record a video "diary" of two- to four-second long clips to accompany the still photos you shoot in a given day, all appended to a single movie file you can review later at your leisure.

- **Portrait.** This mode tends to use wider f/stops and faster shutter speeds, providing blurred backgrounds and images with no camera shake. If you want, you can turn on continuous shooting using the FUNC. menu, as discussed in Chapter 4. Then, if you hold down the shutter release, the PowerShot G1 X will take a continuous sequence of photos, which can be useful in capturing fleeting expressions in portrait situations.

- **Landscape.** The camera tries to use smaller f/stops for more depth-of-field, and boosts saturation slightly for richer colors.

- **Kids & Pets.** An "action" scene mode for capturing fast-moving pets and children without subject blur and with continuous focusing.

- **Sports.** In this mode, the camera tries to use high shutter speeds to freeze action, switches to continuous drive to allow taking a quick sequence of pictures with one press of the shutter release, and uses Continuous AF to continually refocus as your subjects move around in the frame. You can find more information on autofocus options in Chapters 4 and 6.

- **Smart Shutter.** Although this setting is bunched in with Portrait, Landscape, and other subject-specific Scene types, it is really designed to set the camera's automatic face-detection features for any type of scene involving people—whether at a party, on the beach, or in a business or school environment. After you select this setting, press the DISP. button. This action pops up a small menu at the bottom of the screen, letting you choose from Smile Detection, Wink Self-Timer, and Face Self-Timer. Use the cursor buttons or rear control dial to highlight one of these options, then press FUNC./SET to select it. With Smile Detection, the camera will take a picture whenever a person smiles; with the Wink Self-Timer, you need to press the shutter button halfway to be sure that a person's face is framed in a green rectangle on the LCD. Then, press the shutter button fully, and the LCD will say, Wink to Take Picture. Once the person whose face is in the green frame winks, the camera should take the picture within two seconds. Finally, with the Face Self-Timer, you focus on a group of people and press the shutter button. Then you run over and join the group; the camera will take the picture once it detects a new face (yours). If it doesn't detect a new face, it will take the picture anyway, after 15 seconds. If you find this feature of use, that's great; personally, I will stick to the regular old self-timer. When one of these settings is highlighted, you can press the up/down cursor buttons to select the number of shots to be taken when the shutter fires, up to 10.

■ **High Speed Burst HQ.** This is a super-fast continuous shooting mode (4.5 fps) that lets you grab as many as six full resolution shots in one sequence by holding down the shutter button. The G1 X is able to achieve this higher speed by locking the focus, exposure, and color balance at the settings for the first shot in the sequence, and not displaying the images on the LCD as they are captured. When you've reached the maximum number of six shots in a single set, a Busy indicator appears on the LCD, and the shots are then displayed on the screen.

The G1 X "stacks" all the images in the burst together, and during subsequent playback, only the first in the group is shown, along with a SET icon in the upper-left corner of the LCD. That's your cue to press the FUNC./SET button if you want to view all of them. Hiding a series of similar images in this way speeds picture review, but if you'd prefer to see all the images individually all the time, you can turn off the stacking feature by turning off Group Images in the Playback menu, as described in Chapter 4.

High Speed Burst HQ mode at 4.5 shots per second is faster than using the G1 X's conventional continuous shooting modes: Continuous (1.9 fps, with focus and exposure locked in when you press the shutter button halfway), Continuous Shooting AF (0.7 fps, with AF Frame locked at Center), and Continuous Shooting LV (0.7 fps). In Continuous Shooting LV (Live View), which is available when using Fireworks, AF lock, or Manual focus modes, focus is fixed for all shots and the LCD does not black out between shots.

■ **Handheld Night Scene.** This mode takes consecutive shots and combines them to produce a final image with the least amount of image noise and camera shake. You'll like this mode for shooting evening scenes without a tripod.

■ **Beach.** This setting provides properly exposed human subjects against a bright background of water, sand, and reflected sunlight. The metering mode is set to Evaluative.

- **Underwater.** This setting is intended specifically for use under the surface with the optional Canon Waterproof Case WP-DC-34. It sets the white balance to the Underwater setting to remove bluish color casts, and reduces the intensity of the flash.

- **Foliage.** Another saturation-rich setting for shooting trees and leaves, with emphasis on bright and vivid greens.

- **Snow.** Like Beach, this setting properly exposes people and other subjects, despite glaring ice and snow, while removing the blue tinge often caused by snow backgrounds.

- **Fireworks.** Offers vivid photos of fireworks with a multi-second exposure to capture an entire burst. You should set the camera firmly on a tripod and turn image stabilization off. The flash is forced off and cannot be turned on.

- **Stitch Assist 1 and 2.** These two settings (one for left-to-right shots and the other for right-to-left) are set up to help you take two or more overlapping images, as many as 26 in all, that are later merged to create a seamless panorama on your computer with the supplied PhotoStitch program.

Image Effects/Creative Filters Modes

The Image Effects position on the mode dial yields access to a series of 10 special effects. Press the FUNC./SET button to produce a listing of options. These include:

- **HDR.** With this setting, the camera uses its internal processing to take three pictures in rapid sequence in order to create a High Dynamic Range image. This processing results in a final image that includes a wider range of bright, well-exposed areas than could be recorded in a single shot. This feature can be especially useful if you are faced with a situation in which part of your subject is in bright sunlight and part in shadow. Using the different exposure levels from the three separate images, the camera essentially discards the excessively bright and excessively dark portions, and attempts to put together a pleasing final product. Because the camera needs to process the three images into one, it's best to use a tripod, though you may have reasonable success if you hold the camera very steady and the lighting is bright enough that a fast shutter speed will be used, to avoid blur from camera movement. It's also recommended that you disable image stabilization, which could interfere with the camera's ability to process the three images properly.

- **Color Effects.** When using the HDR setting, you can add various color effects. Press the Metering Mode button to activate a horizontal menu listing of effects: Off (no effect), Sepia, B/W, Super Vivid, or Poster Effect. Use the cursor buttons or rotate the rear control dial to select one of these, then press the Metering Mode button again to exit the selection menu.

- **Nostalgic.** This setting lets you ramp down the saturation of the colors in your images, giving the appearance of a faded, antique photograph. When you select this option, the camera puts a message on the LCD advising you to turn the front control dial to "age your pictures." If you then turn that dial to the right, the saturation of the colors will decrease. If you dial in all five of the available increments, the image will be black-and-white, and four increments will be almost completely drained of color. I find that three levels on the dial yields a noticeable, but not overwhelming, fading effect.

- **Fish-eye Effect.** This setting simulates the bulging, distorted view produced by an extreme wide-angle "fish-eye" lens. This is an interesting effect, and is worth playing around with to see if you find it can be of use, or of entertainment value in some situations. Here again, as with the Nostalgic effect, you can select the intensity of the alteration of the image. Use the front control dial to set the level of the fish-eye effect to Low, Medium, or High. You can see the effect of the setting on the LCD before you snap the shutter, to evaluate how high you want to set it. Note that, if you want to achieve a fish-eye effect without using a fish-eye lens, another way to do so is in post-processing software. For example, in Photoshop you can simulate a fish-eye effect for any image using the command Filter-Distort-Spherize. (See Figure 5.17.)

Figure 5.17
Fish-eye effect.

■ **Miniature Effect.** This option produces another interesting effect, along the lines of an optical illusion. The idea here is that you take a photo of a "real" subject, such as a full-sized house, but the camera blurs the image at the top and bottom, so that the final image looks like a photo of a miniaturized model of a house. When you're aiming at the subject, press the Metering Mode button to activate the white frame on the screen, then use the zoom lever and the rear control dial to enlarge or contract the frame and move it around, so you can choose how much of the middle of the image is kept sharp and un-blurred. While selecting the area, use the left/right cursor buttons to switch the orientation of the frame to vertical, and the up/down buttons to return to horizontal orientation of the effect.

This illusion works because photos of models are taken with the camera close to the subject, which makes the depth-of-field quite narrow, so it is difficult to have the entire model in focus. The blurring at the top and bottom of the image simulate this effect, so the eye is tricked into thinking it's actually looking at a model. Now, when and why would you want to use this effect? I haven't yet figured that out, unless it's just included as a neat effect to impress your friends. (See Figure 5.18.)

The effect can also be applied when shooting movies, to create interesting "miniature" shots with old-time speeded-up motion. See the sidebar, "Using Miniature Effect."

Figure 5.18
Miniature effect.

- **Toy camera.** This setting produces an effect found in cheap plastic cameras (like the infamous "Diana" model), complete with darker, blurred corners and modified colors. Use the front control dial to choose Standard, Warm, or Cool exaggerated color schemes.

- **Monochrome.** Use this setting to capture images in glorious monochrome, using the front control dial to select from black-and-white, sepia, or blue ("cyanotone") versions.

- **Super Vivid.** This setting increases the saturation of the colors in a scene, making them appear much richer and more intense than normal. Use it for dramatic effect, when appropriate.

- **Poster Effect.** This setting, like the previous one, is not intended for a specific type of scene; rather, it imposes a particular type of processing on the image. In this case, it provides a degree of "posterization," increasing contrast with bright color effects, to achieve a highly stylized effect reminiscent of pop-art on an entertainment poster. (See Figure 5.19.)

Figure 5.19
Poster effect.

- **Color Accent.** Lets you retain just one color in an image, converting the rest of the image to black-and-white. Once you have selected Color Accent, press the Metering Mode button, which will bring up a box at the bottom of the screen filled with a color. Then move the camera so the center frame is aimed at the one color you want to retain. Press the left cursor button, and the box at the bottom of the screen will fill with that color. (If you select no color, Green is used as the default.)

Use the up/down cursor buttons or turn the rear control dial to adjust the range of that color (from –5 to +5). A large negative number will retain *only* the selected color. As you progress into the positive numbers, more and more colors of similar hue will be retained. Press the Metering Mode button to return to shooting mode. Then press the shutter button, and only objects of your selected color range will retain any color in the final image (see Figure 5.20). This option is available when shooting movies, also.

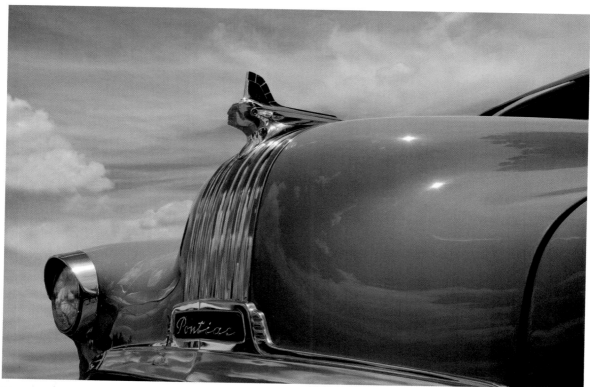

Figure 5.20 With the Color Accent option, you can tell the camera which single color to retain—in this case red; the rest of the image is transformed to black-and-white.

■ **Color Swap.** This operation is similar to Color Accent, except that, rather than retain the color you first select, you change objects of that color to the second color that you select. After pressing the Metering Mode key the original image and swapped image will be displayed one after another. The default replacement is to swap green with gray. To select another color combination, position the center frame over the object whose color you want to change, and press the left cursor button. The left box at the bottom of the screen will fill with that color. Then position the center frame over the color you want to change the first object to, and press the right cursor button. The right box at the bottom of the screen will fill with that color. Use the up/down cursor buttons or turn the rear control dial to adjust the range from −5 to +5, as above. Then take the picture, and any object of the first color will have been changed to the second color. This option is also available for movie shooting.

USING THE MINIATURE EFFECT

When you've selected Miniature Effect in the Creative Filters Function menu, you can further specify the position and orientation of the "sharp" area as well (for movies) as the playback speed. Press the Metering Mode button, and then use the following controls:

■ Rotate the rear control dial to move the sharp-area box from one side to the other (either vertically or horizontally, depending on orientation).

■ Press the left/right cursor buttons to switch from horizontal (wide) orientation of the sharp-area box to a vertical (tall) orientation. You can then use the left-right buttons (or rear control dial) to move the box's position. Press the up/down cursor buttons to return to horizontal orientation.

■ Rotate the front control dial to change movie playback speed, from 5X to 10X to 20X.

■ When finished making your adjustments, press the Metering Mode button to exit.

Adjusting Exposure with ISO Settings

Another important tool for achieving good exposure is the camera's capability for changing the ISO sensitivity setting. Sometimes photographers forget about this option, because the common practice is to set the ISO once for a particular shooting session (say, at ISO 100 or 200 for bright sunlight outdoors, or ISO 800 when shooting indoors) and then forget about ISO. ISOs higher than ISO 100 or 200 are seen as "bad" or "necessary evils." However, changing the ISO is a valid way of adjusting exposure settings, particularly with the Canon PowerShot G1 X, which produces good results at ISO settings that create grainy, unusable pictures with some other camera models.

Indeed, I find myself using ISO adjustment as a convenient alternate way of adding or subtracting EV when shooting in Manual mode, and as a quick way of choosing equivalent exposures when in automatic or semi-automatic modes. For example, suppose I've selected a Manual exposure with both f/stop and shutter speed suitable for my image using, say, ISO 200. I can change the exposure in full-stop increments by pressing the up button and selecting the ISO with the rear dial or directional keys. The difference in image quality/noise at the base setting of ISO 200 is negligible if I dial in ISO 100 to reduce exposure a little, or change to ISO 400 to increase exposure. I keep my preferred f/stop and shutter speed, but still adjust the exposure.

Or, perhaps, I am using Tv mode and the metered exposure at ISO 200 is 1/500th second at f/8. If I decide on the spur of the moment I'd rather use 1/500th second at f/5.6, I can switch to ISO 100. Of course, it's a good idea to monitor your ISO changes, so you don't end up at ISO 3200 accidentally. ISO settings can, of course, also be used to boost or reduce sensitivity in particular shooting situations.

The PowerShot G1 X has direct ISO settings from 100 to 12800:

- Press the up cursor button (ISO). When the ISO screen appears, use the left/right cursor buttons or the rear control dial to choose Auto, or fixed ISO settings from 100 to 12800 in 1/3 EV increments. The Metering Mode button will quickly set ISO Auto. (ISO Auto cannot be set when the mode dial is in the Manual exposure position.) Press the up button again to return to the shooting screen.

- Press the MENU button while the ISO screen is visible to choose the maximum ISO speed that will be used with the ISO Auto option. You can select ISO 400 to ISO 1600 in 1/3 EV increments. Press the MENU button again to exit.

When you choose the Auto ISO setting, the camera adjusts the sensitivity dynamically to suit the subject matter. Remember that if the Auto ISO ranges aren't suitable for you, individual ISO values can also be selected in any of the more advanced shooting modes (Av, Tv, P, and Manual).

Bracketing

Bracketing is a method for shooting several consecutive exposures using different settings, as a way of improving the odds that one will be exactly right. Before digital cameras took over the universe, it was common to bracket exposures, shooting, say, a series of three photos at 1/125th second, but varying the f/stop from f/8 to f/11 to f/16. In practice, smaller than whole-stop increments were used for greater precision. Plus, it was just as common to keep the same aperture and vary the shutter speed, although in the days before electronic shutters, film cameras often had only whole increment shutter speeds available.

Today, cameras like the PowerShot G1 X can bracket exposures much more precisely, taking three shots immediately at the press of the shutter release, and bracket focusing as well. While focus bracketing is sometimes used when there is a tricky situation involving manual focus, autoexposure bracketing (AEB) is used much more often. When this feature is activated, the camera takes three consecutive photos: one at the metered "correct" exposure, one with less exposure, and one with more exposure, using an increment of your choice up to plus 2/minus 2 stops. The procedure for setting up exposure bracketing is discussed in Chapter 4, in connection with the FUNC. menu.

Basically, you press the FUNC./SET key, scroll down to Bracketing, scroll over to the right to select Exposure Bracketing, and press the MENU button to get to the screen where you set the exposure interval, plus or minus 2 EV. One key point you need to bear in mind, which the camera does not warn you about: you need to have the flash turned off for bracketing to work.

Be sure to turn bracketing off when you're done with that feature. Bracketing is available only in P, Av, Tv, and M modes, though exposure bracketing is not available in M mode. Once bracketing is turned on, it remains in effect after the first set of three images is taken, and the setting will continue to be in effect even after the camera has been turned off and then back on, until you turn the electronic flash back on, or return to the FUNC. menu to cancel bracketing.

Bracketing and Merge to HDR

HDR (High Dynamic Range) photography is, at the moment, incredibly popular. There are entire books that do nothing but tell you how to shoot and process HDR images. If you aren't familiar with the technique, HDR involves shooting two or three or more images at different bracketed exposures, giving you an "underexposed" version with lots of detail in highlights that would otherwise be washed out; an "overexposed" rendition that preserves detail in the shadows; and several intermediate shots. These are combined to produce a single image that has an amazing amount of detail throughout the scene's entire tonal range.

The extreme, cartoonish implementations of HDR are somewhat of a fad, even though true HDR photography has been around since before digital techniques made it easier to accomplish. The current interest exists in the first place due to a (temporary, I hope) defect in current digital camera sensors. It's presently impossible to capture the full range of brightness that we perceive; digital cameras, including the PowerShot G1 X, can't even grab the full range of brightness that *film* can see, as I showed you in Figures 5.1 and 5.2 at the beginning of this chapter.

But as the megapixel race slows down, sensor designers have already begun designing capture electronics that have larger density (dynamic) ranges, and I fully expect to see cameras within a few years that can produce images similar to what we're getting now with HDR manipulation in image editors, and auto HDR features in cameras like the G1 X.

HDR works like this: Suppose you wanted to photograph a dimly lit room that had a bright window showing an outdoors scene. Proper exposure for the room might be on the order of 1/60th second at f/2.8 at ISO 200, while the outdoors scene probably would require f/11 at 1/400th second. That's almost a 7 EV step difference (approximately 7 f/stops) and well beyond the dynamic range of any digital camera, including the PowerShot G1 X. The camera's built-in auto HDR feature does a fairly good job of stretching the dynamic range of the camera, but more conventional HDR photography can do it better.

When you're using Merge to HDR Pro, a feature found in Adobe Photoshop (similar functions are available in other programs, including Photomatix [www.hdrsoft.com; free to try, $99 to buy]), you'd take several pictures. As I mentioned earlier, one would be exposed for the shadows, one for the highlights, and perhaps one for the midtones. Then, you'd use the Merge to HDR Pro command (or the equivalent in other software) to combine all of the images into one HDR image that integrates the well-exposed sections of each version. You can use the PowerShot G1 X's exposure bracketing feature to produce those images.

The images should be as identical as possible, except for exposure. So, it's a good idea to mount the camera on a tripod, use a remote release (or the self-timer), and take all the exposures in one burst. Just follow these steps:

1. **Set up your camera on a sturdy support.** Mount the PowerShot G1 X on a tripod and connect a remote release switch (such as the optional Canon RS60-E3), if available. If a remote is not available, set the self-timer to a delay of several seconds.

2. **Specify RAW.** Set the camera to shoot RAW images, as described in Chapter 4.

3. **Choose bracketing.** Set exposure bracketing to a two-stop increment, as described earlier in this chapter and in Chapter 4.

4. **Focus.** Manually focus or autofocus the camera.

5. **Use Av exposure mode.** You don't want the aperture to change between exposures, thus changing focus and depth-of-field. In Av mode the G1 X will adjust exposure using only the shutter speed.

6. **Take your shots.** Trigger the camera to expose your set of three images.

7. **Process the photos.** Copy your images to your computer and continue in Photoshop with the Merge to HDR Pro steps listed next.

The next steps show you how to combine the separate exposures into one merged High Dynamic Range image.

1. If you use an application to transfer the files to your computer, make sure it does not make any adjustments to brightness, contrast, or exposure. You want the real RAW information for Merge to HDR to work with. If you do everything correctly, you'll end up with three photos like the ones shown in Figure 5.21.

2. Load the images into Photoshop using your preferred RAW converter.

3. Save as .PSD files.

4. Activate Merge to HDR Pro by choosing File > Automate > Merge to HDR Pro.

5. Select the photos to be merged, as shown in Figure 5.22, where I have specified the three PSD files. You'll note a checkbox that can be used to automatically align the images if they were not taken with the camera mounted on a rock-steady support.

6. Once HDR merge has done its thing, you must save in the .PSD (Photoshop) file format, to retain the file's full color information, in case you want to work with the HDR image later. Otherwise, you can convert to a normal 24-bit file and save in any compatible format.

Figure 5.21 Make one exposure for the shadow areas, one for the middle tones, and one for the highlights, such as the sky.

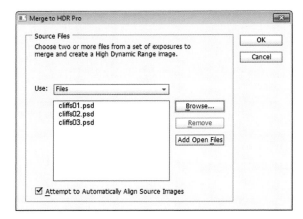

Figure 5.22
Use the Merge to HDR Pro command to combine the three images.

If you do everything correctly, you'll end up with a photo like the one shown in Figure 5.23, which has the properly exposed foreground and the well-exposed sky. Note that, ideally, nothing should move between shots. In the example pictures, the river is moving, but the exposures were made so close together that, after the merger, you can't really tell.

What if you don't have the opportunity, inclination, or skills to create several images at different exposures, as described? If you shoot in RAW format, you can still use Merge to HDR Pro, working with a *single* original image file. What you do is import the image into Photoshop several times, using Adobe Camera Raw to create multiple copies of the file at different exposure levels.

For example, you'd create one copy that's too dark, so the shadows lose detail, but the highlights are preserved. Create another copy with the shadows intact and allow the highlights to wash out. Then, you can use Merge to HDR to combine the two and end up with a finished image that has the extended dynamic range you're looking for.

Dealing with Noise

Image noise is that random grainy effect that some like to use as a visual effect, but which, most of the time, is objectionable because it robs your image of detail even as it adds that "interesting" texture. Noise is caused by two different conditions: high ISO settings and long exposures.

High ISO noise commonly appears when you raise your camera's sensitivity setting above ISO 1000. With the Canon G1 X camera, noise may become visible at ISO 1600, and is usually fairly noticeable at ISO 3200 and higher. This kind of noise appears as a result of the amplification needed to increase the sensitivity of the sensor. While higher ISOs do pull details out of dark areas, they also amplify non-signal information randomly, creating noise.

Figure 5.23
You'll end up with an extended dynamic range photo like this one.

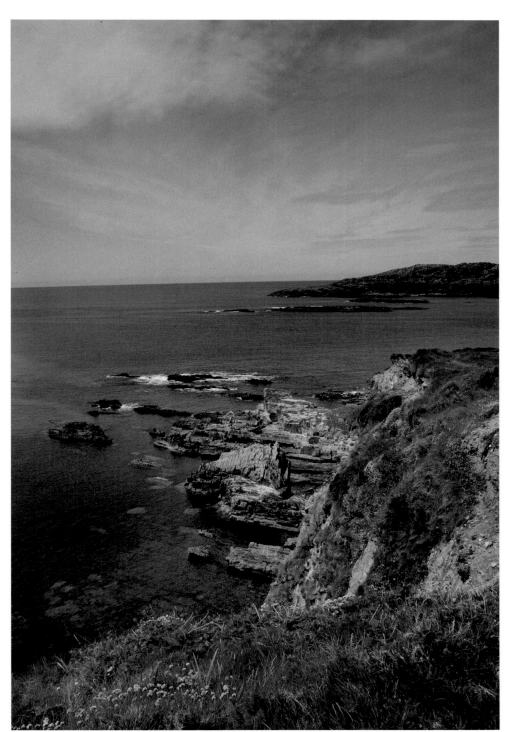

A similar noisy phenomenon occurs during long time exposures, which allow more photons to reach the sensor, increasing your ability to capture a picture under low light conditions. However, the longer exposures also increase the likelihood that some pixels will register random phantom photons, often because the longer an imager is "hot" the warmer it gets, and that heat can be mistaken for photons.

Fortunately, Canon's electronics geniuses have done a good job minimizing noise from all causes in the PowerShot G1 X. When the camera takes an exposure of longer than one second, you will notice a delay after the image is taken, while the camera uses its noise-reduction circuitry to minimize the visual noise in the image. It also processes high-ISO shots to reduce noise. However, there are no noise-related settings you can adjust yourself on the G1 X. You can apply noise reduction to some extent using Photoshop or similar software, and when converting RAW files to some other format, using your favorite RAW converter, or an industrial-strength product like Noise Ninja (www.picturecode.com) to wipe out noise after you've already taken the picture.

Fixing Exposures with Histograms

While you can often recover poorly exposed photos in your image editor, your best bet is to arrive at the correct exposure in the camera, minimizing the tweaks that you have to make in post-processing. However, you can't always judge exposure just by viewing the image on your PowerShot G1 X's LCD before or after the shot is made. Ambient light may make the LCD difficult to see, and the brightness level you've set can affect the appearance of the playback image.

Instead, you can use a histogram, which is a chart displayed on the PowerShot G1 X's LCD that shows the number of tones being captured at each brightness level. You can use the information to provide correction for the shot you are about to take, or for the next shot you take. The G1 X offers a histogram that shows overall brightness levels for an image, which can be displayed during shooting mode or playback mode.

A brightness histogram like that used in the PowerShot G1 X is a chart that includes a representation of up to 256 vertical lines on a horizontal axis that show the number of pixels in the image at each brightness level, from 0 (black) on the left side to 255 (white) on the right. (The 3-inch LCD of this PowerShot model doesn't have enough pixels to show each and every one of the 256 lines, but, instead, provides a representation of the shape of the curve formed.) The more pixels at a given level, the taller the bar at that position. If no bar appears at a particular position on the scale from left to right, there are no pixels at that particular brightness level.

A typical histogram produces a mountain-like shape, with most of the pixels bunched in the middle tones, with fewer pixels at the dark and light ends of the scale. Ideally, though, there will be at least some pixels at either extreme, so that your image has both

DISPLAYING HISTOGRAMS

To view histograms on your screen, press the DISP. button while an image is shown on the LCD, either before shooting or during playback. Keep pressing the button until the histogram is shown. The display will cycle between several levels of information, one of which will include the histogram. If you don't see the histogram while in shooting mode, go to Custom Display on the Shooting menu and change that setting so that histograms will be displayed. The histogram will display only in Program, Shutter priority, Aperture priority, Manual, and Quick Shot shooting modes. (It will display in Quick Shot mode even if you have turned it off on the Custom Display menu.) You also can display the histogram on the review image that displays right after you have taken a picture. Set that option by choosing Review Info from the Shooting menu, and then selecting Detailed. The histogram always displays on the detailed screen in playback mode. If you press the top cursor button while the histogram is displayed in playback mode, an RGB histogram appears, presenting the brightness graphs for the three component colors of the image. Press that button again to go back to the normal screen. In addition, on the detailed playback screen, any overexposed areas of the thumbnail image will blink to warn you that the highlights may be blown out.

a true black and a true white representing some details. Learn to spot histograms that represent over- and underexposure, and add or subtract exposure using an EV modification to compensate.

For example, Figure 5.24 shows the histogram for an image that is badly underexposed. You can guess from the shape of the histogram that many of the dark tones to the left of the graph have been clipped off. There's plenty of room on the right side for additional pixels to reside without having them become overexposed. Or, a histogram might look like Figure 5.25, which is overexposed. In either case, you can increase or decrease the exposure (either by changing the f/stop or shutter speed in Manual mode or by adding or subtracting an EV value in Program mode) to produce the corrected histogram shown in Figure 5.26, in which the tones "hug" the right side of the histogram to produce as many highlight details as possible. See "Making EV Changes," earlier in this chapter for information on dialing in exposure compensation.

The histogram can also be used to aid in fixing the contrast of an image, although gauging incorrect contrast is more difficult. For example, if the histogram shows all the tones bunched up in one place in the image, the photo will be low in contrast. If the tones are spread out more or less evenly, the image is probably high in contrast. In either case, your best bet may be to switch to RAW (if you're not already using that format) so you can adjust contrast in post-processing. However, you can also change to a user-defined setting using the My Colors feature (not available when shooting RAW), as covered in Chapter 4, with contrast set lower or higher as required.

Figure 5.24
This histogram shows an under-exposed image.

Figure 5.25
This histogram reveals that the image is overexposed.

Figure 5.26
A histogram for a properly exposed image should look like this.

6

Mastering the Mysteries of Autofocus

Getting the right exposure is one of the foundations of a great photograph, but a lot more goes into a compelling shot than good tonal values. A sharp image, proper white balance, good color, and other factors all can help elevate your image from good to exceptional. So, now that you've got a good understanding of exposure tucked away, you'll want to learn how to use the automatic and manual focusing controls available with the Canon PowerShot G1 X, and master some of the many ways you can fine-tune your images. We'll also discuss some creative ways to use exposure, including using very short or long exposures, and we'll look at techniques to improve your movie making with this camera.

Getting into Focus

Learning to use the Canon PowerShot G1 X's autofocus system is easy, but you do need to fully understand how the system works to get the most benefit from it. Once you're comfortable with autofocus, you'll know when it's appropriate to use the Manual focus option, too. The important thing to remember is that focus isn't absolute. For example, some things that appear to be in sharp focus at a given viewing size and distance might not be in focus at a larger size and/or closer distance. In addition, the goal of optimum focus isn't always to make things look sharp. Not all of an image will be or should be sharp. Controlling exactly what is sharp and what is not is part of your creative palette. Use of depth-of-field characteristics to throw part of an image out of focus while other parts are sharply focused, particularly when shooting close-up photos, is one of the most valuable tools available to a photographer. But selective focus works only when the desired areas of an image are in focus properly. For the digital camera photographer, correct focus can be one of the trickiest parts of the technical and creative process.

Your camera's autofocus sensors require a certain minimum amount of light to operate. If necessary, the AF assist beam built into the PowerShot G1 X and Canon's dedicated flash units provide additional light that helps assure enough illumination for autofocus.

Focus Modes and Options

As you've come to appreciate by now, the PowerShot G1 X offers many options for how it approaches photography. Focus is no exception. Of course, as with other aspects of this camera, you can set the shooting mode to Auto, and the camera will do just fine in its focusing in most situations. (Actually, the G1 X will still let you choose some autofocus options, such as Face Detect, even if the shooting mode is Auto.) But, if you want more creative control, the choices are there for you to make. The PowerShot's focus options actually provide you with more choices than any other aspect of the camera's operation.

Assuming you're not going to set the shooting mode to Auto, your first choice is whether to use autofocus or manual focus. (Manual focus is not available in some Scene modes, such as Fireworks.) Manual focus, of course, was the only choice available to photographers from the nineteenth-century days of Daguerreotypes until about the 1980s, when autofocus started becoming available. Manual focus presents you with great flexibility along with the challenge of keeping the image in focus under what may be challenging conditions, such as rapid motion of the subject, darkness of the scene, and the like. We'll talk more about manual focus later in this chapter. For now, we'll assume you're going to rely on the camera's AF capabilities.

The PowerShot G1 X has two basic AF modes: One-shot AF (also known as Single Autofocus) in which the camera locks in focus once and keeps it locked until the picture is taken, and Continuous AF, in which the camera continues to adjust focus to track subject movement. Oddly enough, what Canon calls One-shot AF with its digital SLR cameras is actually just Continuous AF (Off) with the G1 X; when you turn off Continuous AF, the camera switches to One-shot mode. There's a FUNC. menu setting for Standard Single Shot mode, which overrides the menu setting for Continuous AF. Beyond those two basic modes, there is a more specialized mode called Servo AF that is designed for one particular type of situation—tracking focus to follow moving subjects. Once you have decided on which AF mode to use, you also need to tell the camera how to set the AF Frame—the zone which is used to select the subject to focus on. In other words, after you tell the camera how to autofocus, you also have to tell it where to direct its focusing attention. I'll explain each of the three focus modes, and other aspects of focus, in more detail later in this section.

MANUAL FOCUS

With manual focus activated by pressing the left cursor key, your PowerShot G1 X lets you set the focus yourself by turning the rear control dial. There are some advantages and disadvantages to this approach. While your batteries will last slightly longer in manual focus mode, it will take you longer to focus the camera for each photo, a process that can be tricky. Modern digital cameras depend so much on autofocus that the viewfinders are no longer designed for optimum manual focus. The optical viewfinder on your PowerShot, for example, can't be used for manual focusing at all—you must rely on the view (magnified or otherwise) on the LCD. So, although manual focus is still an option for you to consider in certain circumstances, it's not as easy to use as it once was. I recommend that you try to use the camera's various AF options first, and switch to manual focus only if AF is not working for you. I'll explain more about manual focus later in this chapter.

How Autofocus Works

Although Canon began adding autofocus capabilities to its film cameras in the 1980s, prior to that focusing was always done manually. Honest. Imagine what it must have been like to focus manually under demanding, fast-moving conditions such as sports photography.

Focusing was problematic because our eyes and brains have poor memory for correct focus, which is why your eye doctor must shift back and forth between sets of lenses and ask "Does that look sharper—or was it sharper before?" in determining your correct prescription. Similarly, manual focusing involves jogging the focus ring back and forth as you go from almost in focus, to sharp focus, to almost focused again. The little clockwise and counterclockwise arcs decrease in size until you've zeroed in on the point of correct focus. What you're looking for is the image with the most contrast between the edges of elements in the image. (See Figure 6.1.)

The PowerShot G1 X's autofocus mechanism, like all such systems found in modern digital cameras, also evaluates these increases and decreases in sharpness, but it is able to remember the progression perfectly, so that autofocus can lock in much more quickly and, with an image that has sufficient contrast, more precisely. Unfortunately, while the PowerShot's focus system finds it easy to measure degrees of apparent focus at each of the focus points in the viewfinder, it doesn't really know with any certainty *which* object should be in sharpest focus. Is it the closest object? The subject in the center? Something lurking *behind* the closest subject? A person standing over at the side of the picture? Many of the techniques for using autofocus effectively involve telling the PowerShot G1 X exactly what it should be focusing on.

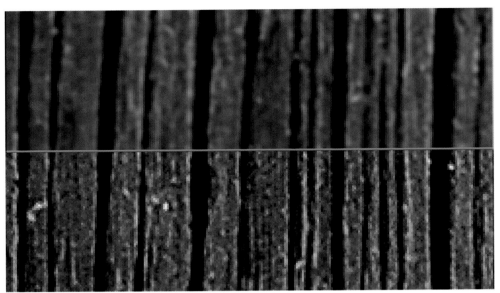

Figure 6.1
When an image is out of focus (top), the contrast between edges is low; in focus (bottom) and the contrast is at its highest point.

Adding Circles of Confusion

But there are other factors in play, as well. You know that increased depth-of-field brings more of your subject into focus. But more depth-of-field also makes autofocusing (or manual focusing) more difficult because the contrast is lower between objects at different distances. So, autofocus with the camera's lens set to its maximum 112mm effective focal length may be easier than at the minimum 28mm focal length (or zoom setting), because at the longer focal length the lens has less apparent depth-of-field.

To make things even more complicated, many subjects aren't polite enough to remain still. They move around in the frame, so that even if the PowerShot is sharply focused on your main subject, the subject may change position and require refocusing. An intervening subject may pop into the frame and pass between you and the subject you meant to photograph. You (or the PowerShot) have to decide whether to lock focus on this new subject, or remain focused on the original subject. Finally, there are some kinds of subjects that are difficult to bring into sharp focus because they lack enough contrast to allow the PowerShot's AF system (or our eyes) to lock in. Blank walls, a clear blue sky, or other subject matter may make focusing difficult.

If you find all these focus factors confusing, you're on the right track. Focus is, in fact, measured using something called a *circle of confusion*. An ideal image consists of zillions of tiny little points, which, like all points, theoretically have no height or width. There is perfect contrast between the point and its surroundings. You can think of each point as a pinpoint of light in a darkened room. When a given point is out of focus, its edges decrease in contrast and it changes from a perfect point to a tiny disc with blurry

Figure 6.2

When a pin-point of light (left) goes out of focus, its blurry edges form a circle of confusion (center and right).

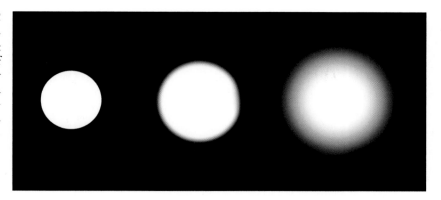

edges (remember, blur is the lack of contrast between boundaries in an image). (See Figure 6.2.)

If this blurry disc—the circle of confusion—is small enough, our eye still perceives it as a point. It's only when the disc grows large enough that we can see it as a blur rather than a sharp point that a given point is viewed as out of focus. You can see, then, that enlarging an image, either by displaying it larger on your computer monitor or by making a large print, also enlarges the size of each circle of confusion. Moving closer to the image does the same thing. So, parts of an image that may look perfectly sharp in a 5 × 7–inch print viewed at arm's length, might appear blurry when blown up to 11 × 14 and examined at the same distance. Take a few steps back, however, and the image may look sharp again.

To a lesser extent, the viewer also affects the apparent size of these circles of confusion. Some people see details better at a given distance and may perceive smaller circles of confusion than someone standing next to them. For the most part, however, such differences are small. Truly blurry images will look blurry to just about everyone under the same conditions.

Technically, there is just one plane within your picture area, parallel to the back of the camera (or sensor, in the case of a digital camera) that is in sharp focus. That's the plane in which the points of the image are rendered as precise points. At every other plane in front of or behind the focus plane, the points show up as discs that range from slightly blurry to extremely blurry. In practice, the discs in many of these planes will still be so small that we see them as points, and that's where we get depth-of-field. Depth-of-field is just the range of planes that include discs that we perceive as points rather than blurred splotches. The size of this range increases as the aperture is reduced in size and is allocated roughly one-third in front of the plane of sharpest focus, and two-thirds behind it. The range of sharp focus is always greater behind your subject than in front of it—although in many cases, depth-of-field will be very shallow, as shown in Figure 6.3.

Figure 6.3
Only the bird is in focus, but the area behind him appears blurry because the depth-of-field is limited.

Using Manual Focus

As I noted earlier, manual focus is not as attractive an option nowadays as it used to be when cameras were designed for that method of focusing and were equipped with readily visible focusing aids. But Canon's designers have done a good job of letting you exercise your initiative in the focusing realm, so you certainly should become familiar with the technique for those occasions when it makes sense to take control in this area. Here are the basic steps:

- **Select a shooting mode other than Auto, Fireworks, Kids & Pets, Sports Scene, Smile Shutter, or Stitch Assist modes.** If you set the mode to any of those options, the Focus Range/MF button won't let you choose manual focus.

- **Press the Focus Range/MF button (left cursor key).** Choose MF from the Macro/Normal/Manual Focus choices that appear. The large letters MF will appear on the screen, then fade to a small icon at the top right of the screen. An abbreviated focus scale appears on the right side of the LCD with 2 feet, 5 feet, 10 feet, and infinity marked (see Figure 6.4).

- **Aim at your subject and turn the rear control dial to focus.** The focusing block in the center of the screen will enlarge to help you assess whether the image is in focus. (That is, unless you turned off this feature, called MF-Point Zoom, through the Shooting menu.) Turn the dial until the subject appears to be in the sharpest possible focus. Be careful when turning the rear control dial. It's all too easy to hit a cursor key by mistake when rotating.

■ **Use the Safety MF feature to fine-tune the focus.** After you have made your focus adjustments with the rear control dial, you can press either the shutter button or the AF Frame/Trash button to "fine-tune" the focus. Actually, this just means that after going through all the trouble of using manual focus, you're going to punt and use autofocus after all, which may seem a bit strange. But, in some circumstances this could be a useful procedure, because you are getting the focus system started by showing it exactly where to focus, then letting it finish up the process. It also may help you get used to the manual focus procedure by practicing and comparing your results to those of the autofocus mechanism. This Safety MF feature is not available if you turn it off through the Shooting menu.

■ **If your subject is a particular, small area of the overall scene, set the camera to Single-shot AF (which, on the G1 X, is Continuous AF off), and set the AF Frame to FlexiZone.** Use the AF Frame entry in the Shooting menu to switch to FlexiZone, and then set the focus frame to its smallest size and move it over the area of the scene that needs to be in sharpest focus.

Figure 6.4
The scale shows the approximate distance focused.

Even veteran users sometimes don't realize that when you crank manual focus down to the minimum marked distance on the scale, you can continue to rotate the rear control dial to produce a *new* scale with 50cm down to 20cm markings. You don't need to activate Macro mode (which limits you to a defined range of focus distances) to activate this handy close-focusing capability. Just rotate the dial to focus from 50cm (about 19 inches) to 20cm (a little less than 8 inches).

Hyperfocal Distance—A Tool for Quick Candid Shots

There is one somewhat specialized area in which you might want to consider a particular advantage of using manual focus—to grab quick shots without using any of the autofocus options at all, and without having to manually focus the camera. In effect, this technique lets you convert your sophisticated autofocusing camera into something like a Kodak Brownie from days of old—a box camera that shoots with a fixed focus, but still manages to take quite presentable pictures.

The key here is to use manual focus, and preset it to what is called the camera's *hyperfocal distance*, which is defined as the focusing distance at which everything from half that distance to infinity will appear to be in sharp focus. Note that I say things will "appear" to be in sharp focus. As I discussed earlier in this chapter, there is only one mathematical plane in which images will actually be in perfectly sharp focus for a given lens, taking into account factors such as focal length and aperture. However, because of our old friends the circles of confusion, even though images may not be in perfect focus, if those circles are small enough, they will still appear to be in sharp enough focus to pass our visual inspection.

If you aspire to what some call "street photography"—snapping candid shots of people and other subjects on city streets (or in other public locations) when you see something that catches your eye, you may want to try this technique. With the camera's focus preset, you don't have to fiddle with any controls or settings; you can just fire away at anything that catches your interest within the zone of sharp focus. There are many varied approaches taken by different photographers in this area, and you will need to experiment to find a system that works for you. Following is one possible way to set up the PowerShot G1 X for quick, candid shots using the hyperfocal distance:

- **Set up the camera's other shooting options.** I suggest setting the shooting mode to Aperture priority (Av) and using as small an aperture as you can manage, given the prevailing lighting conditions. Try to use at least f/4.5 to widen the depth-of-field. I suggest using Evaluative exposure metering, auto white balance, and RAW + L image size and quality to leave your options open for post-processing. Set the flash to forced off. Set continuous shooting on, so you can snap lots of shots when the right moment comes. You may want to turn off the camera's operational sounds to avoid attracting attention. With the PowerShot G1 X, consider using the swivel screen at an angle so you don't have to face in the direction you're shooting.

- **Set the camera to manual focus at the hyperfocal distance.** This step requires that you do some homework before you go out on your candid-shooting expedition. You can go to www.dofmaster.com to find tools to calculate the camera's hyperfocal distance. You have to base the calculation on the actual focal length of the camera's lens. In our case, although the 35mm equivalent focal length of the PowerShot G1 X's lens at its wide-angle setting is 28mm, its actual focal length (marked on the lens) is 15.1mm. Using that value, and f/5.6 as our aperture, the answer is that the hyperfocal distance for the PowerShot's lens is about 6.5 feet. This means that, if you set the camera's manual focus to 6.5 feet and leave it there, everything you shoot, from a distance of about 3.25 feet (half of 6.5 feet) to infinity will appear sharp, as long as you're using the full wide-angle setting for your lens. Of course, the PowerShot camera does not have a focusing scale that shows exactly where 6.5 feet is. If you want to be as exact as possible, get a measuring tape and set the camera up exactly 6.5 feet from a subject, then adjust the manual focus control until focus is sharp, and note exactly where the focusing bar reaches on the camera's scale.

- **Save all of these settings to C2.** Once all of the above settings are just the way you want them, choose Save Settings from the Shooting menu and save all of them to C2 on the mode dial. (I suggest C2 just because it's the last setting on the dial, and might be easier to turn to in a hurry than C1.)

- **When you see a likely subject, turn to C2 and fire away.** Try these settings for a while and check out the results. If they don't measure up, change various settings until you have created the perfect instrument for super street photography.

Your Autofocus Mode Options

Choosing the right autofocus mode and the way in which focus points are selected is your key to success. Using the wrong mode for a particular type of photography can lead to a series of pictures that are all sharply focused—on the wrong subject. When I first started shooting sports with an autofocus camera (back in the film camera days), I covered one baseball game alternating between shots of base runners and outfielders with pictures of a promising young pitcher, all from a position next to the third base dugout. The base runner and outfielder photos were great, because their backgrounds didn't distract the autofocus mechanism. But all my photos of the pitcher had the focus tightly zeroed in on the fans in the stands behind him. Because I was shooting with film instead of a digital camera, I didn't know about my gaffe until the film was developed. A simple change, such as locking in focus or focus zone manually, or even manually focusing, would have done the trick.

To save battery power, your PowerShot ordinarily doesn't start to focus the lens until you partially depress the shutter release. But, autofocus isn't some mindless beast out there snapping your pictures in and out of focus with no feedback from you after you press that button. There are several settings you can modify that return a fair amount of control to you. Your first decision should be whether you set the PowerShot G1 X to Continuous or Continuous Off (what the rest of the world calls One Shot AF). Or, you can use the FUNC. menu to set Standard Single Shot focus, which leaves the Continuous menu setting on. Follow these steps:

1. Press the MENU button and navigate to the Shooting menu.

2. Scroll to the entry called Continuous AF. (See Figure 6.5.)

3. Set Continuous AF to On or Off.

4. Press the MENU button again to exit.

Figure 6.5
Press the left/right cursor keys until the AF choice you want is selected.

The following sections detail what each of the available autofocus modes do.

Single Autofocus/Continuous AF Off

If you've elected to leave Continuous AF turned off, you'll be using the mode also called *Single Autofocus* by most of the universe. In this mode, focus is set when you press the shutter button halfway and remains locked at that focus setting until the button is fully depressed, taking the picture, or until you release the shutter button without taking a shot. For non-action photography, this option is usually your best choice, as it minimizes out-of-focus pictures, at the expense of spontaneity, because the camera will not take a picture at all while it is seeking focus. You're locked out of shooting until the autofocus mechanism is happy with the current focus setting. Continuous AF Off/ One-shot AF/Single Autofocus is sometimes referred to as *focus priority* for that reason. Because of the small delay while the camera zeroes in on correct focus, you might experience slightly more shutter lag. This mode uses less battery power than Continuous AF.

When sharp focus is achieved, the focus frame will turn green and you'll hear a little beep (assuming you have normal shooting and setup options enabled). If you've set AF Point Zoom to On, a magnified central image is shown instead. By keeping the shutter button depressed halfway, you'll find you can reframe the image by moving the camera to aim at another angle while retaining the focus (and exposure) that's been set.

Continuous AF

Continuous AF is a mode you might want to use when photographing sports, young kids at play, and other fast-moving subjects. In this mode, the autofocus system continues to operate all the time, even when the shutter button is not depressed halfway. In other words, the camera always attempts to focus the image. When you use this mode, the camera will be ready to fine-tune its focus quickly once you decide on a final subject at which to aim the camera, because the focusing apparatus is doing its best to be ready for the current focusing conditions. Of course, this option drains battery power quite quickly, so turn it off unless you have a definite need for it (or have an endless supply of batteries). In addition, this option can have the drawback of the camera's switching its focus to any subject that enters the focus frame, thereby drawing the focus away from a subject you were interested in. That's where the next AF mode comes into play.

Servo AF

Servo AF is another option that can be turned on from the Shooting menu (see Figure 6.6) and can be used alone, or with Continuous AF activated. This option tells the camera to lock autofocus on the subject in the focus frame when you press the shutter release halfway, and then continue to keep that subject in focus, as long as it remains within the focus frame.

Figure 6.6
Select Servo AF from the Shooting menu when you want to keep the focus on a particular moving subject.

The focus frame in the center turns blue when you lock on to a subject in this way, and the camera will continue to lock its focus on the subject within that blue frame, as long as you are able to keep the subject in the focus frame. This option is designed for situations such as tracking a particular athlete at a sporting event, a particular performer at a concert, or a particular child racing around on a playground. This focus mode addresses the situation we just discussed in connection with Continuous AF mode, in which a new subject moves into the frame and steals the focus away from the subject you are most interested in, by ensuring that the subject you want to focus on stays in focus (as long as you keep it within the blue frame). Again, as with Continuous AF (which can be used at the same time as Servo AF), this option puts a strain on your battery supply, so preserve it for occasions when it is of definite use.

I know these three focus options can be confusing, so Table 6.1 is a summary of when to use each of them.

Setting the AF Frame

You're not done yet with choosing the settings for autofocus on these PowerShot models. The settings already discussed—Continuous AF Off/Single-Shot AF, Continuous AF, Servo AF, and Manual focus, all tell the camera *how* to focus. But, with the AF

Table 6.1 Autofocus Modes		
Mode	**What It Does**	**When to Use**
Continuous AF Off (Single autofocus)	Locks focus only when shutter release is pressed halfway, and does not refocus if subject moves. Camera will shoot picture only when focus is achieved.	When shooting subjects that are not in motion, when you want to minimize the number of out-of-focus shots.
Continuous AF	Tries to focus at all times, even before shutter release is pressed halfway. Camera will shoot picture even if focus is not achieved.	On moving subjects, when you want the camera to focus and refocus for a possible shot.
Servo AF	Locks focus on subject within focus frame when shutter release is pressed halfway, and refocuses if the subject moves but remains within the focus frame. Camera will shoot picture even if focus is not achieved.	Use when you want to lock focus on a particular subject that may be moving, and want the camera to ignore other moving objects that come into the frame *after* you've pressed the shutter release button halfway. Use with or without Continuous AF, so the camera will/will not also focus *before* pressing the shutter halfway.

modes, the camera needs to be told not only how to focus, but *where* to focus. That is the subject of our next discussion—telling the camera where to focus, by setting the options for the AF Frame. (This function is not available in Movie or Auto modes.)

The PowerShot G1 X offers a fairly impressive array of autofocus frame options, which help you dictate exactly where in the scene the sharpest focus should be. To select the AF Frame mode, follow these steps:

1a. Press the MENU button, navigate to the Shooting menu, select the top entry (AF Frame), and press the left/right cursor keys to select from among the choices available with your current shooting mode. (With some modes, the choice will be either On or Off.) Press MENU again to exit.

Or:

1b. Press the AF Frame/Trash button on the back right of the camera, followed by the * button located to the right of the AF Frame button.

2. As you press the * button, the AF Frame mode cycles among the modes available using your current shooting mode setting. When you've selected the mode you want to use, press the AF Frame button again to confirm it. You can move the frame with the cursor keys or the rear control dial.

With the G1 X, Canon has streamlined and consolidated the AF Frame choices somewhat. With this PowerShot model, the only three choices on the Shooting menu in most shooting modes are Face AiAF, FlexiZone, and Tracking AF.

- **Face AiAF.** The camera will display frames for up to nine detected faces. You can press the AF Frame button to enter Face Select mode, in which the camera places a frame over what it believes to the be main subject, and up to two additional faces. (Similar to Figure 6.7.)

  - **Change to a different face.** You can move this frame to another face by pressing the AF Frame button. The Face Select: On message appears on the LCD, with the currently selected face marked with a dual-bordered box. Press the AF Frame button to switch to another detected face. The camera will track the selected face within the frame and continue to focus on it. Take the picture. Exposure mode will be set to Evaluative metering, and white balance to AWB automatically.

  - **In Auto shooting mode.** Only Face AiAF is available (the AF Frame option vanishes from the Shooting menu).

  - **In other shooting modes.** If FlexiZone is selected, the frame is moved to Center if the LCD display is turned off. (That makes sense, because you would have a hard time moving the focus frame around the screen if you couldn't see the screen!)

Figure 6.7
In Face AiAF mode, the PowerShot will detect up to nine faces, placing a white block around the main subject's face, and gray blocks around additional faces.

- **FlexiZone.** The AF Frame starts out as a white rectangle in the center of the screen. When you press the shutter release halfway, the frame turns green, signifying that focus is locked. Make sure you've set AF-Point Zoom to Off.

  - **Reframe after locking focus.** Keep the shutter button pressed down as you reframe.

  - **Change the size of the focus frame.** Press the AF Frame button (northwest of the cursor pad). The frame turns orange. Press the MENU button to change from a larger frame to a smaller frame, and vice versa.

  - **Move the focus frame.** Press the AF Frame button. After the frame turns orange, you can move either size focus frame around the screen with the four cursor keys or the rear control dial. You can move the focus frame rapidly with the rear control dial, or in finer steps with the four cursor buttons.

  - **Confirm choices.** When finished sizing/moving the focus frame, press the AF Frame button again.

- **Tracking AF.** In this mode, you can choose the subject to be tracked by the auto-focus system. When you choose this option, the focus area on the screen becomes a small white box with four little lines sticking out in each direction. (See Figure 6.8.) Place this box over your subject (such as a fidgety child or pet), and press the AF Frame/Trash button, to the upper left above the rear control dial. The camera will then attempt to keep your chosen subject in its focus frame, even as it (or the camera) moves. (See Figure 6.9.) When you're ready to take the picture, press the shutter button halfway to calculate focus and exposure; the focus box will turn blue, and the camera will continue to adjust focus and exposure on your subject until you press the shutter button all the way to take the picture.

Figure 6.8 In Tracking AF mode, first select the subject to be followed.

Figure 6.9 Your subject will be tracked until you take the photo, or cancel tracking by pressing the AF Frame button.

So, what should a photographer do when faced with all of these focusing options? Following are some general guidelines based on my own preferences. You very well may develop a different set of guidelines that are more suitable for your own situations.

- If you're taking casual snapshots or are in a hurry and don't have time to make detailed settings, set the shooting mode to Auto and the chances are very good that the pictures will be in focus.

- If your subject is an orderly group of people standing still, set the focus mode to Single-shot AF (Continuous AF off) and set the AF Frame to Face AiAF.

- If your subject is a general group of people, animals, or other objects in constant motion, set the camera to Continuous AF and set the AF Frame to Face AiAF.

- If your subject is a particular person or other object among a general group of people, animals, or objects in constant motion, set the camera to Continuous AF and to Servo AF; set the AF Frame to Tracking AF. Then aim the AF Frame at your particular subject using Tracking AF, and press the shutter button halfway, and keep the blue focus frame locked on your subject until you take the picture.

- If your subject is a particular, small area of the overall scene, set the camera to Single-shot AF (Continuous AF off), and set the AF Frame to FlexiZone. Then set the focus frame to its smallest size and move it over the area of the scene that needs to be in sharpest focus.

Focus Bracketing

In Focus-BKT mode, three images are captured each time you press the shutter release. The first image is shot at the distance you select using manual focus, and the other two slightly closer and slightly farther. The G1 X doesn't allow you to use continuous shooting when focus bracketing, because the camera by default shoots all three bracketed shots consecutively and continually. Just follow these steps:

1. **Activate Focus Bracketing.** In the Function menu, scroll down to the bracketing icon and choose Focus-BKT.

2. **Press the MENU button to select the increment.** A scale will appear along the bottom of the screen. Use the rear control dial or left/right cursor buttons to choose from three increasingly wider preset increments. (You can't control the amount each increment represents, because the actual distances will change depending on your initial focus distance setting.)

   Or you can set or change the increment by pressing the right cursor button, choosing MF (manual focus), and pressing the MENU button.

3. **Take your picture.** Press the shutter release and the three exposures bracketed for focus will be taken immediately (any self-timer settings are ignored).

Macro Shooting

Shooting with the macro focusing option, which means shooting extreme close-ups, is an entire branch of photography in itself. The most serious practitioners of macro photography use highly specialized equipment, including special lenses, extension tubes, bellows, racks, tripods, lights, and on and on. But, with the PowerShot G1 X, you actually have an amazingly capable instrument for general macro photography, which can be of considerable use to you even if you don't join the ranks of the true macro-philes.

Although macro shooting is not something you're likely to do every day unless you're a coin collector, student of insects, or aficionado of other very small things, the chances are you will have some occasion to use the capabilities of the PowerShot G1 X closely (see Figure 6.10). Without the use of any add-on lenses or other extra equipment, this

Figure 6.10
These crayons were photographed from just eight inches away.

camera can focus down to 20 centimeters from the end of the lens—that is a little less than 8 inches. And the camera can achieve this close focusing while still using its various autofocus modes, though, of course, several of them (Face AiAF, Servo AF, etc.) would not be useful while shooting at that range, or anywhere close to it. Note that the 20-centimeter distance is available only when the PowerShot's lens is zoomed back to its wide-angle setting; when it's zoomed in to its full telephoto focal length of 112mm, the closest it can focus in Macro mode is 30 centimeters (about 12 inches).

Before I detail the steps for successful use of the macro focusing mode, here are some ideas for how you might make use of it:

- Document the contents of coin and stamp collections, or collections of any small items.

- Take close-up shots of flowers and plants while they're in full bloom. Explore them in different lighting conditions and from various angles to uncover different aspects of their beauty.

- Get close enough to insects, reptiles, and other living creatures to capture their activities and appearances in documentary-like detail.

- Unleash your creative side by putting together elaborate (or simple) tabletop still-life tableaus in the spirit of Salvador Dali, or that are just fun to look at.

- Take sharply focused close-ups from various angles to illustrate items you are selling on eBay or other online auction sites.

- If you need a quick copy of a receipt, instruction sheet, check, or other document and don't have access to a copy machine, pull out your trusty PowerShot G1 X and make a perfectly serviceable photographic copy. You can view the image on your camera's display (magnified to show details if need be), display it on a computer screen, send it by e-mail, or print it out.

Chances are there's something in that list that you may want to do at some point. So let's go through the steps that will accomplish a solid macro photograph. Of course, if you're in a hurry you won't have time to carry out all of these steps, but here's the full list for when you do have time:

1. Secure the camera firmly on a solid tripod. Turn Image Stabilization off.

2. Arrange for lighting that will not be blocked by the camera itself, which is likely to cast a shadow because of its extreme proximity to the subject.

3. Select a shooting mode that fits the situation at hand. Consider using Aperture priority and setting the aperture as small as possible with the lighting available, to achieve the greatest depth-of-field you can so as to keep the subject in sharp focus.

4. Turn Continuous AF off, so the camera focuses only once. In the alternative, use manual focus, with Safety MF turned on. Turn AF-Point Zoom off, unless you want a magnified central image.

5. Set the AF Frame mode to FlexiZone and set the AF Frame to its smallest size.

6. Press the Focus Mode/Macro button (left cursor key) to engage Macro mode.

7. Press the AF Frame button, then press the MENU button to make the frame as small as possible. Use the cursor keys to move the AF Frame to cover the part of the subject that needs to be in sharpest focus.

8. Activate the self-timer or use the remote Switch RS60-E3 so the shutter will be tripped without your pressing the shutter button and possibly shaking the camera.

9. Compose the shot, check the focus, press the shutter button, and stand clear while the self-timer counts down, to make sure that you don't cast any shadows over the subject and that you don't touch the camera while it's making the exposure.

Focus Stacking

If you are doing macro (close-up) photography of flowers, or other small objects at short distances, the depth-of-field often will be extremely narrow. In some cases, it will be so narrow that it will be impossible to keep the entire subject in focus in one photograph. Although having part of the image out of focus can be a pleasing effect for a portrait of a person, it is likely to be a hindrance when you are trying to make an accurate photographic record of a flower, or small piece of precision equipment. One solution to this problem is focus stacking, a procedure that can be considered like HDR translated for the world of focus—taking multiple shots with different settings, and, using software as explained below, combining the best parts from each image in order to make a whole that is better than the sum of the parts. Focus stacking requires a non-moving object, so some subjects, such as flowers, are best photographed in a breezeless environment, such as indoors.

For example, see Figures 6.11 through 6.13, in which I took photographs of three colorful crayons. As you can see from these images, the depth-of-field was extremely narrow, and only a small part of the subject was in focus for each shot.

Now look at Figure 6.14, in which the entire subject is in reasonably sharp focus. This image is a composite, made up of the three shots above, as well as 10 others, each one manually focused on the same scene, but at very gradually increasing distances from the camera's lens. All 13 images were then combined in Adobe Photoshop using the focus stacking procedure.

Figures 6.11, 6.12, and 6.13 These three shots were all focused on different distances within the same scene. No single shot could bring the entire subject into sharp focus.

Figure 6.14
Three partially out-of-focus shots have been merged, along with ten others, through a focus stacking procedure in Adobe Photoshop, to produce a single image with the entire subject in focus.

Here are the steps you can take to combine shots for the purpose of achieving sharp focus in this sort of situation:

1. **Set the camera firmly on a solid tripod.** A tripod or other equally firm support is absolutely essential for this procedure.

2. **Set the G1 X for remote control (optional).** You'll get the best results, with the least amount of camera movement between shots, if you use the optional RS-60E3 wired remote control. If you don't have this accessory available, press the shutter release button gently each time.

3. **Set the camera to manual focus mode.** Use the procedure described in the previous section to activate manual focus.

4. **Set the exposure, ISO, and white balance manually.** Use test shots if necessary to determine the best values. This step in the Shooting menu will help prevent

visible variations from arising among the multiple shots that you'll be taking. You don't want the G1 X to change the ISO setting or white balance between shots.

5. **Set the quality of the images to NEF (RAW) +JPEG FINE.** Use the Shooting menu to make this adjustment. Having both formats will give you flexibility when combining the images.

6. **Turn off Image Stabilization.** Navigate to the Shooting menu and turn off IS. You don't need it when the camera is securely mounted on a tripod, and disabling stabilization will keep the camera from making any sort of image adjustment between exposures.

7. **Focus manually on the very closest point of the subject to the lens.** Change the focus.

8. **Trip the shutter.** Use the remote or a gentle press of the shutter.

9. **Carefully refocus.** Gently rotate the rear control dial to focus on a point slightly farther away from the lens and trip the shutter again.

10. **Repeat.** Continue taking photographs in this way until you have covered the entire subject with in-focus shots.

The next step is to process the images you've taken in Photoshop. Transfer the images to your computer, and then follow these steps:

1. In Photoshop, select File > Scripts > Load Files into Stack. In the dialog box that then appears, navigate on your computer to find the files for the photographs you have taken, and highlight them all.

2. At the bottom of the next dialog box that appears, check the box that says, "Attempt to Automatically Align Source Images," then click OK. The images will load; it may take several minutes for the program to load the images and attempt to arrange them into layers that are aligned based on their content.

3. Once the program has finished processing the images, go to the Layers panel and select all of the layers. You can do this by clicking on the top layer and then Shift-clicking on the bottom one.

4. While the layers are all selected, in Photoshop go to Edit > Auto-Blend Layers. In the dialog box that appears, select the two options, Stack Images and Seamless Tones and Colors, then click OK. The program will process the images, possibly for a considerable length of time.

5. If the procedure worked well, the result will be a single image made up of numerous layers that have been processed to produce a sharply focused rendering of your subject. If it did not work well, you may have to take additional images the next time, focusing very carefully on small slices of the subject as you move progressively farther away from the lens.

Although this procedure can work very well in Photoshop, you also may want to try it with programs that were developed more specifically for focus stacking and related procedures, such as Helicon Focus (www.heliconsoft.com), PhotoAcute (www.photoacute.com), or CombineZM (www.hadleyweb.pwp.blueyonder.co.uk).

7

Movie Making with Your Canon PowerShot G1 X

Canon has considerably beefed up the movie-making capabilities of the PowerShot G1 X, compared to the fairly rudimentary video features of its predecessors, including "little brother" PowerShot G12. The G1 X can record 1920 × 1080–pixel (Full HD) movies at 24 frames per second, 1280 × 720–pixel (Standard HD) movies at 30 fps, and 640 × 480–pixel (VGA-format) movies at 30 fps.

In addition, it can capture iFrame movies, an Apple-developed simplified movie format with an HDTV-like 16:9 aspect ratio of 960 × 540 pixels at 30 fps. Movies using the G1 X's Miniature Effect processing can be captured at 6, 3, and 1.5 fps, which produces a speeded-up playback that works well with "miniaturized" clips. Finally, the camera can capture Movie Digest clips to accompany still pictures, providing video vignettes of a day's activity.

The camera can output its high-quality HD footage to an HDTV with great fidelity through an HDMI connection. Of course, as you might expect, the G1 X is not a serious rival to a dedicated camcorder or to some of the high-end Canon still cameras, such as the EOS 5D Mark III, which are endowed with advanced video capabilities. But, depending on the size of your memory card and recording format chosen, the PowerShot G1 X can record up to about half an hour of HD video in one continuous shot, and can record up to an hour of uninterrupted standard-quality video. If you're out and about and develop a sudden need to make a video record of an event, from a school sports event to a breaking news story, your G1 X will get the footage down on your SD card with very acceptable quality.

Making Movies

I'll show you how to optimize your settings before you start shooting video, but here are some considerations to be aware of as you get started. Many of these points will be covered in more detail later in this chapter:

- **Use the right card.** You'll want to use an SD, SDHC, or SDXC card with Class 6 or higher speed; if you use a slower card, like a Class 4 or especially Class 2, the recording may stop after a minute or two. Chose a memory card with at least 4GB capacity; 8GB or 16GB are even better. If you're going to be recording a lot of HD video, that could be a good reason to take advantage of the ability to use SDXC cards of 64GB capacity. Just make sure your memory card reader is SDXC compatible and your computer can read the files from that type of card. I've standardized on fast Class 6 or Class 10 16GB SDHC cards when I'm shooting movies; one of these cards will hold at least three hours of video. However, the camera cannot shoot a continuous movie scene for more than 29 minutes. You can start shooting the next clip right away, though, missing only about 30 seconds of the action. Of course that assumes there's enough space on your memory card and adequate battery power.

- **Minimize zooming.** While it's great to be able to use the zoom (1X to 4X in optical zoom mode; up to 16X in digital zoom mode) for filling the frame with a distant subject, think twice before zooming. Unless you are using an external mic, the sound of the zoom motor will be picked up and it will be audible when you play a movie. Any more than the occasional minor zoom will be very distracting to friends who watch your videos. And digital zoom will definitely degrade image quality. Don't use the digital zoom if quality is more important than recording a specific subject, such as a famous movie star from a distance.

- **Use a fully charged battery.** A fresh battery will allow about one hour of filming at normal (non-Winter) temperatures. Individual HD clips can be no longer than 29 minutes, although VGA mode video can run up to an hour.

- **Keep it cool.** Video quality can suffer terribly when the imaging sensor gets hot so keep the camera in a cool place. When shooting on hot days especially, the sensor can get hot more quickly than usual; when there's a risk of overheating, the camera will stop recording and it will shut down about five seconds later. Give it time to cool down before using it again.

- **Press the Movie button.** Located on the camera's right corner with a red dot, you don't have to hold it down. Press it again when you're done to stop recording.

Here are the basic points you need to know before you start shooting video:

- **Set the mode dial to Movie mode—or not.** You can begin shooting movies immediately when the G1 X is set to any exposure mode, but you'll have no control over the exposure. Just press the red Movie button at the top-right edge of the back of the camera. Exposure is automatic, and ignores your setting of the exposure compensation dial that rings the mode dial. If you want to adjust exposure when movie shooting, rotate the mode dial to the Movie icon. That will give you control over exposure compensation (but, not with the dial: you need to press the exposure lock button, marked with an asterisk, and then dial in your compensation with the rear control dial).

- **Choose a shooting mode.** When the mode dial is set to SCN or Filter Effects modes, you can activate any of a selection of Scene modes, which will be applied when you press the Movie button to activate video capture. The available modes include Portrait, Landscape, Beach, Underwater, Foliage, Snow, Fireworks, Nostalgic, Fish-eye Effect, Miniature Effect, Monochromatic, Super Vivid, Poster Effect, Color Accent, Color Swap, and iFrame Movie.

  In other words, if you select HDR, Toy Camera, Kids & Pets, Sports, Smart Shutter, High Speed Burst HQ, Handheld Night Scene, or Stitch Assist as a mode, it will not be activated when you press the red Movie button.

- **Choose a Movie mode.** When the Movie icon is selected on the mode dial, Use the FUNC. menu, discussed in Chapter 4, to choose the video shooting mode, either Standard or iFrame (which produces iFrame clips for editing with iFrame-compatible software).

- **Choose your resolution.** The last selection at the bottom of the FUNC. menu lets you choose the resolution for your movie. There are just three possibilities: Full HD quality at 1920 × 1080 pixels/24 fps (Full HD), 1280 × 720 pixels/30 fps (Standard HD), and standard VGA quality at 640 × 480 pixels. An indicator at the right shows how many minutes of video you can record on your current memory card, using the resolution that is highlighted. All video is recorded in PCM stereo sound in the Motion JPEG format, resulting in file extensions of .MOV. This is the format used by Apple's QuickTime software, and is an excellent format for viewing and editing on either PC or Macintosh computers.

- **Make other settings if desired.** The settings mentioned above are the only ones you really need to make to get ready to record your video. The camera will take care of most other settings, using autofocus with the AF Frame set to Face AiAF and adjusting the exposure as you record using Evaluative metering. But, if you want, you can use manual focus, and you can adjust white balance, image stabilization, digital zoom, and a few other items, using the Shooting menu. On the FUNC. menu, in addition to the basic settings discussed above, you can set white balance, My Colors, and the neutral-density filter.

- **Use the right card.** As I mentioned, you'll want to use an SD Class 6 memory card or better to store your clips; slower cards may not work properly. Choose a memory card with at least 4GB capacity. 8GB or 16GB are even better. If you're going to be recording a lot of HD video, that could be a good reason to take advantage of the G1 X's ability to use SDXC cards of 64GB capacity. Just make sure your computer can read the files from the card.

- **Use a fully charged battery.** Canon says that a fresh battery will allow about one hour of filming at normal (non-Winter) temperatures.

- **Press the Movie button.** You don't have to hold it down. Press it again when you're done.

THE MINIATURE EFFECT REDUX

As I noted in Chapter 5, when you've selected Miniature Effect in the Creative Filters Function menu, you can further specify the position and orientation of the "sharp" area as well the playback speed for movies. Press the Metering Mode button, and then use the following controls:

- Rotate the rear control dial to move the sharp-area box from one side to the other (either vertically, or horizontally, depending on orientation).

- Press the left/right cursor buttons to switch from horizontal (wide) orientation of the sharp-area box to a vertical (tall) orientation. You can then use the left-right buttons (or rear control dial) to move the box's position. Press the up/down cursor buttons to return to horizontal orientation.

- Rotate the front rear control dial to change movie playback speed, from 5X to 10X to 20X.

- When finished making your adjustments, press the Metering Mode button to exit.

GETTING INFO

The information display shown on the LCD screen when shooting movies is quite sparse; the screen will show time elapsed and the REC indicator to show that you are shooting a movie. The only other option is to display grid lines or the electronic level, or both, if you have selected those features through the Shooting menu under Custom Display.

Editing Movies in the Camera

The PowerShot G1 X provides a very basic capability for editing movies in the camera. This is not a technique I would recommend for general use in editing your videos, and you won't be doing a lot of post-production work with this simple tool, but there may be a situation in which you have no computer available and you need to trim the beginning or end of a video by a few seconds so you can show it on a TV set, perhaps at a conference. Here's how to do it:

1. **Get the video on the screen.** Press the Playback button and press the Jump key (marked with an asterisk), then move with the down cursor button to the fourth icon, for stills/movies. Press either the left or right cursor button to select movies. Press the FUNC./SET button to confirm that you want to view only movies, and then turn the rear control dial to find the movie you're looking for.

2. **Press the FUNC./SET key twice.** Once to select the movie you want, and again to call up the playback and editing controls (see Figure 7.1).

Figure 7.1
View the movie during playback.

Exit *Play* *Slow Motion* *Skip Backward* *Previous Frame* *Next Frame* *Skip Forward* *Edit*

Movie Editing Bar *Frame Indicator* *Elapsed Time* *Total Length*

3. **Select the Scissors icon.** Scroll with the rear control dial or with the left/right cursor buttons highlight the icon of a pair of scissors. Press FUNC./SET to select it. The screen shown in Figure 7.2 will appear.

4. **Select beginning or end to trim.** At the top left of the screen, scroll with the down cursor button to either the icon showing the scissors before a frame of film (trim beginning) or the scissors after a frame of film (trim end).

5. **Scroll to select the portion to trim.** Using the right cursor button (if trimming beginning) or left cursor button (if trimming end), or the rear control dial for faster selection, move the orange marker along the bar at the bottom of the screen that represents the length of the film.

6. **Select and use the trimming tool.** Use the down cursor button to move down the column of icons at the top left of the screen to the next-to-last icon, labeled "Save." Select it, and the camera will prompt you with three choices: New File, Overwrite, and Cancel. Your safest option is to choose New File, unless you're 100% sure that it's safe to overwrite the existing movie with the new, shorter version.

7. **Repeat to trim the other end.** If you also want to remove some of your clip from the other end of the video, repeat steps 1–6.

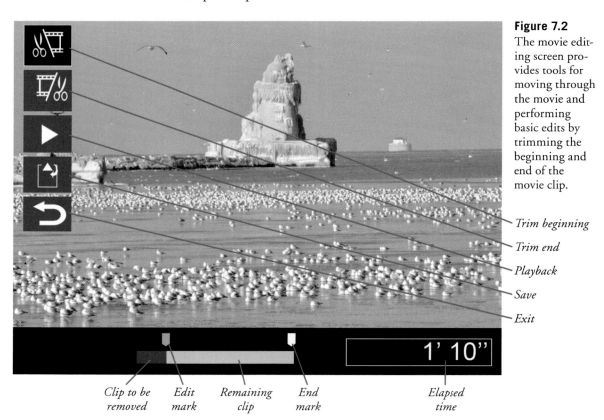

Figure 7.2
The movie editing screen provides tools for moving through the movie and performing basic edits by trimming the beginning and end of the movie clip.

Trim beginning

Trim end

Playback

Save

Exit

1' 10"

Clip to be removed   *Edit mark*   *Remaining clip*   *End mark*   *Elapsed time*

Tips for Shooting Better Video

Once upon a time, the ability to shoot video with a digital still camera was one of those "Gee whiz" gimmicks camera makers seemed to include just to have a reason to get you to buy a new camera. That hasn't been true for a couple of years now, as the video quality of many digital still cameras has gotten quite good. The Canon G1 X is a stellar example. It's capable of HD-quality video and is actually able to outperform typical modestly priced digital video camcorders.

Producing good-quality video is more complicated than just buying good equipment. There are techniques that make for gripping storytelling and a visual language the average person is very used to, but also pretty unaware of. We're used to watching the best productions that television, video, and motion pictures can offer. Whether it's fair or not, our efforts are compared to what we're used to seeing produced by experts. While this book can't make you a professional videographer in half a chapter, there is some advice I can give you that will help you improve your results with the camera.

There are a number of different things to consider when planning a video shoot, and when possible, a shooting script and storyboard can help you produce a higher quality video.

Keep Things Stable and on the Level

Camera shake's enough of a problem with still photography, but it becomes even more of a nuisance when you're shooting video. While the Canon G1 X's image-stabilization feature can help minimize this, it can't work miracles. Placing your camera on a tripod will work much better than trying to handhold it while shooting. One bit of really good news is that compared to pro dSLRs the Canon G1 X can work very effectively on a lighter tripod.

Shooting Script

A shooting script is nothing more than a coordinated plan that covers both audio and video and provides order and structure for your video. A detailed script will cover what types of shots you're going after, what dialogue you're going to use, audio effects, transitions, and graphics.

Storyboards

A storyboard is a series of panels providing visuals of what each scene should look like. While the storyboards produced by Hollywood are generally of very high quality, there's nothing that says drawing skills are important for this step. Stick figures work just fine if that's the best you can do. The storyboard just helps you visualize locations,

Figure 7.3 A storyboard is a series of simple sketches or photos to help visualize a segment of video.

placement of actors/actresses, props and furniture, and also helps everyone involved get an idea of what you're trying to show. It also helps show how you want to frame or compose a shot. You can even shoot a series of still photos and transform them into a "storyboard" if you want, as in Figure 7.3.

Storytelling in Video

Today's audience is used to fast-paced, short-scene storytelling. In order to produce interesting video for such viewers, it's important to view video storytelling as a kind of shorthand code for the more leisurely efforts print media offers. Audio and video should always be advancing the story. While it's okay to let the camera linger from time to time, it should only be for a compelling reason and only briefly.

It only takes a second or two for an establishing shot to impart the necessary information. For example, many of the scenes for a video documenting a model being photographed in a rock 'n' roll music setting might be close-ups and talking heads, but an establishing shot showing the studio where the video was captured helps set the scene.

Provide variety too. Change camera angles and perspectives often and never leave a static scene on the screen for a long period of time. (You can record a static scene for a reasonably long period and then edit in other shots that cut away and back to the longer scene with close-ups that show each person talking.)

When editing, keep transitions basic! I can't stress this one enough. Watch a television program or movie. The action "jumps" from one scene or person to the next. Fancy transitions that involve exotic "wipes," dissolves, or cross fades take too long for the average viewer and make your video ponderous.

Composition

In movie shooting, several factors restrict your composition, and impose requirements you just don't always have in still photography (although other rules of good composition do apply). Here are some of the key differences to keep in mind when composing movie frames:

- **Horizontal compositions only.** Some subjects, such as basketball players and tall buildings, just lend themselves to vertical compositions. But movies are shown in horizontal format only. So if you're interviewing a local basketball star, you can end up with a worst-case situation like the one shown in Figure 7.4. If you want to show how tall your subject is, it's often impractical to move back far enough to show him full-length. You really can't capture a vertical composition. Tricks like getting down on the floor and shooting up at your subject can exaggerate the perspective, but aren't a perfect solution.

- **Wasted space at the sides.** Moving in to frame the basketball player as outlined by the yellow box in Figure 7.4 means that you're still forced to leave a lot of empty space on either side. (Of course, you can fill that space with other people and/or interesting stuff, but that defeats your intent of concentrating on your main subject.) So when faced with some types of subjects in a horizontal frame, you can be creative, or move in *really* tight. For example, if I was willing to give up the "height" aspect of my composition, I could have framed the shot as shown by the green box in the figure, and wasted less of the image area at either side.

Figure 7.4
Movie shooting requires you to fit all your subjects into a horizontally oriented frame.

■ **Seamless (or seamed) transitions.** Unless you're telling a picture story with a photo essay, still pictures often stand alone. But with movies, each of your compositions must relate to the shot that preceded it, and the one that follows. It can be jarring to jump from a long shot to a tight close-up unless the director—you—is very creative. Another common error is the "jump cut" in which successive shots vary only slightly in camera angle, making it appear that the main subject has "jumped" from one place to another. (Although everyone from French New Wave director Jean-Luc Goddard to Guy Ritchie—Madonna's ex—have used jump cuts effectively in their films.) The rule of thumb is to vary the camera angle by at least 30 degrees between shots to make it appear to be seamless. Unless you prefer that your images flaunt convention and appear to be "seamy."

■ **The time dimension.** Unlike still photography, with motion pictures there's a lot more emphasis on using a series of images to build on each other to tell a story. Static shots where the camera is mounted on a tripod and everything is shot from the same distance are a recipe for dull videos. Watch a television program sometime and notice how often camera shots change distances and directions. Viewers are used to this variety and have come to expect it. Professional video productions are often done with multiple cameras shooting from different angles and positions. But many professional productions are shot with just one camera and careful planning, and you can do just fine with your Canon G1 X.

Here's a look at the different types of commonly used compositional tools:

■ **Establishing shot.** Much like it sounds, this type of composition establishes the scene and tells the viewer where the action is taking place. Let's say you're shooting a video of your offspring's move to college; the establishing shot could be a wide shot of the campus with a sign welcoming you to the school in the foreground. Another example would be for a child's birthday party; the establishing shot could be the front of the house decorated with birthday signs and streamers or a shot of the dining room table decked out with party favors and a candle-covered birthday cake. Or, in Figure 7.5, I wanted to show the studio where the video was shot.

■ **Medium shot.** This shot is composed from about waist to head room (some space above the subject's head). It's useful for providing variety from a series of close-ups and also makes for a useful first look at a speaker. (See Figure 7.6.)

■ **Close-up.** The close-up, usually described as "from shirt pocket to head room," provides a good composition for someone talking directly to the camera. Although it's common to have your talking head centered in the shot, that's not a requirement. In Figure 7.7 the subject was offset to the right. This would allow other images, especially graphics or titles, to be superimposed in the frame in a "real" (professional) production. But the compositional technique can be used with Canon G1 X videos, too, even if special effects are not going to be added.

Figure 7.5 An establishing shot from a distance sets the stage for closer views.

Figure 7.6 A medium shot is used to bring the viewer into a scene without shocking them. It can be used to introduce a character and provide context via their surroundings.

Figure 7.7 A close-up generally shows the full face with a little head room at the top and down to the shoulders at the bottom of the frame.

Figure 7.8 An extreme close-up is a very tight shot that cuts off everything above the top of the head and below the chin (or even closer!). Be careful using this shot since many of us look better from a distance!

Figure 7.9 A "two-shot" features two people in the frame. This version can be framed at various distances such as medium or close up.

Figure 7.10 An "over-the-shoulder" shot is a popular shot for interview programs. This point of view helps make the viewers feel like they're the one asking the questions.

■ **Extreme close-up.** When I went through broadcast training back in the '70s, this shot was described as the "big talking face" shot and we were actively discouraged from employing it. Styles and tastes change over the years and now the big talking face is much more commonly used (maybe people are better looking these days?) and so this view may be appropriate. Just remember, the Canon G1 X is capable of shooting in high-definition video and you may be playing the video on a high-def TV; be careful that you use this composition on a face that can stand up to high definition. (See Figure 7.8.)

■ **"Two shot."** A two shot shows a pair of subjects in one frame. They can be side by side or one in the foreground and one in the background. (See Figure 7.9.) This does not have to be a head to ground composition. Subjects can be standing or seated. A "three shot" is the same principle except that three people are in the frame.

■ **Over the shoulder shot.** Long a composition of interview programs, the "over the shoulder shot" uses the rear of one person's head and shoulder to serve as a frame for the other person. This puts the viewer's perspective as that of the person facing away from the camera. (See Figure 7.10.)

Lighting for Video

Much like in still photography, how you handle light pretty much can make or break your videography. Lighting for video can be more complicated than lighting for still photography, since both subject and camera movement is often part of the process.

Lighting for video presents several concerns. First off, you want enough illumination to create a useable video. Beyond that, you want to use light to help tell your story or increase drama. Let's take a better look at both.

Illumination

You can significantly improve the quality of your video by increasing the light falling in the scene. This is true indoors or out, by the way. While it may seem like sunlight is more than enough, it depends on how much contrast you're dealing with. If your subject is in shadow (which can help them from squinting) or wearing a ball cap, a video light can help make them look a lot better.

Lighting choices for amateur videographers are a lot better these days than they were a decade or two ago. An inexpensive incandescent video light, which will easily fit in a camera bag, can be found for $15 or $20. You can even get a good-quality LED video light for less than $100. Work lights sold at many home improvement stores can also serve as video lights since you can set the camera's white balance to correct for any color casts. You'll need to mount these lights on a tripod or other support, or, perhaps, to a bracket that fastens to the tripod socket on the bottom of the camera.

Much of the challenge depends upon whether you're just trying to add some fill light on your subject versus trying to boost the light on an entire scene. A small video light will do just fine for the former. Neither will handle the latter. Fortunately, the versatility of the Canon G1 X comes in quite handy here. Since the camera shoots video in Auto ISO mode, it can compensate for lower lighting levels and still produce a decent image. For best results though, better lighting is necessary.

Creative Lighting

While ramping up the light intensity will produce better technical quality in your video, it won't necessarily improve the artistic quality of it. Whether we're outdoors or indoors, we're used to seeing light come from above. Videographers need to consider how they position their lights to provide even illumination while up high enough to angle shadows down low and out of sight of the camera.

When considering lighting for video, there are several factors. One is the quality of the light. It can either be hard (direct) light or soft (diffused). Hard light is good for showing detail, but can also be very harsh and unforgiving. "Softening" the light, but diffusing it somehow, can reduce the intensity of the light but make for a kinder, gentler light as well.

While mixing light sources isn't always a good idea, one approach is to combine window light with supplemental lighting. Position your subject with the window to one side and bring in either a supplemental light or a reflector to the other side for reasonably even lighting.

Lighting Styles

Some lighting styles are more heavily used than others. Some forms are used for special effects, while others are designed to be invisible. At its most basic, lighting just illuminates the scene, but when used properly it can also create drama. Let's look at some types of lighting styles:

- **Three-point lighting.** This is a basic lighting setup for one person. A main light illuminates the strong side of a person's face, while a fill light lights up the other side. A third light is then positioned above and behind the subject to light the back of the head and shoulders. (See Figure 7.11.)

- **Flat lighting.** Use this type of lighting to provide illumination and nothing more. It calls for a variety of lights and diffusers set to raise the light level in a space enough for good video reproduction, but not to create a particular mood or emphasize a particular scene or individual. With flat lighting, you're trying to create even lighting levels throughout the video space and minimize any shadows. Generally, the lights are placed up high and angled downward (or possibly pointed straight up to bounce off of a white ceiling). (See Figure 7.12.)

Figure 7.11 With three-point lighting, two lights are placed in front and to the side of the subject (45-degree angles are ideal) and positioned about a foot higher than the subject's head. Another light is directed on the background in order to separate the subject and the background.

Figure 7.12 Flat lighting is another approach for creating even illumination. Here the lights can be bounced off of a white ceiling and walls to fill in shadows as much as possible. It is a flexible lighting approach since the subject can change positions without needing a change in light direction.

- **"Ghoul lighting."** This is the style of lighting used for old horror movies. The idea is to position the light down low, pointed upward. It's such an unnatural style of lighting that it makes its targets seem weird and ghoulish.

- **Outdoor lighting.** While shooting outdoors may seem easier because the sun provides more light, it also presents its own problems. As a general rule of thumb, keep the sun behind you when you're shooting video outdoors, except when shooting faces (anything from a medium shot and closer) since the viewer won't want to see a squinting subject. When shooting another human this way, put the sun behind her and use a video light to balance light levels between the foreground and background. If the sun is simply too bright, position the subject in the shade and use the video light for your main illumination. Using reflectors (white board panels or aluminum foil-covered cardboard panels are cheap options) can also help balance light effectively.

Audio

When it comes to making a successful video, audio quality is one of those things that separates the professionals from the amateurs. We're used to watching top-quality productions on television and in the movies, yet the average person has no idea how much effort goes in to producing what seems to be "natural" sound. Much of the sound you hear in such productions is actually recorded on carefully controlled sound stages and "sweetened" with a variety of sound effects and other recordings of "natural" sound.

Tips for Better Audio

Since recording high-quality audio is such a challenge, it's a good idea to do everything possible to maximize recording quality. Here are some ideas for improving the quality of the audio your camera records:

- **Get the camera and its microphone close to the subject.** The farther the microphone is from the audio source, the less effective it will be in picking up that sound. While having to position the camera and microphone closer to the subject affects your lens choices and lens perspective options, it will make the most of your audio source. Of course, if you're using a very wide-angle lens, getting too close to your subject can have unflattering results, so don't take this advice too far.

- **Turn off any sound makers you can.** Little things like fans and air handling units aren't obvious to the human ear, but will be picked up by the microphone. Turn off any machinery or devices that you can plus make sure cell phones are set to silent mode. Also, do what you can to minimize sounds such as wind, radio, television, or people talking in the background.

- **Make sure to record some "natural" sound.** If you're shooting video at an event of some kind, make sure you get some background sound that you can add to your audio as desired in post-production.

- **Consider recording audio separately.** Lip-syncing is probably beyond most of the people you're going to be shooting, but there's nothing that says you can't record narration separately and add it later. It's relatively easy if you learn how to use simple software video-editing programs like iMovie (for the Macintosh) or Windows Movie Maker (for Windows PCs). Any time the speaker is off-camera, you can work with separately recorded narration rather than recording the speaker on-camera. This can produce much cleaner sound.

WIND NOISE REDUCTION

The camera's built-in mics include a low-cut filter to reduce wind noise. However, it can also affect other sounds. You can disable the low-cut filter for the G1 X's internal microphone by choosing Off for Wind Filter in the Shooting menu.

Lens Craft

I'll cover the use of lenses with the Canon G1 X in more detail in Chapter 10, but a discussion of lens selection when shooting movies may be useful at this point. In the video world, not all focal lengths are created equal. The two most important considerations are depth-of-field, or the beneficial lack thereof, and zooming. I'll address each of these separately.

Depth-of-Field and Video

Have you wondered why professional videographers have gone nuts over still cameras that can also shoot video? The producers of *Saturday Night Live* could afford to have Alex Buono, their director of photography, use the niftiest, most expensive high-resolution video cameras to shoot the opening sequences of the program. Instead, Buono opted for a pair of digital SLR cameras. One thing that makes digital still cameras so attractive for video is that they have relatively large sensors, which provides improved low-light performance and results in the oddly attractive reduced depth-of-field, compared with most professional video cameras.

Figure 7.13 provides a comparison of the relative size of sensors. The typical size of a professional video camera sensor is shown at right, just below a graphic representing the size of the earlier PowerShot G12 camera's sensor. At upper left is the sensor size of the typical APS-C digital SLR, such as the Canon EOS Rebel T3i. It's relatively huge. Just south of that is the sensor used in the G1 X. (The yellow lines represent the portion of the sensor actually used for HD video, with the top and bottom cropped out.)

You can see that the G1 X's sensor is much larger than the pro video version, and massive when compared to the sensor found in the earlier G12. Of course, the APS-C sensor shown at upper left, and a full-frame FX sensor (not shown) are even larger. But, compared with the sensors used in many pro video cameras and the even smaller sensors found in the typical camcorder, the Canon G1 X's image-grabber is much larger.

As you'll learn in Chapter 9, a larger sensor calls for the use of longer focal lengths to produce the same field of view, so, in effect, a larger sensor has reduced depth-of-field. And *that's* what makes cameras like the Canon G1 X attractive from a creative standpoint. Less depth-of-field means greater control over the range of what's in focus. Your G1 X, with its larger sensor, compared to many other compact cameras, and the PowerShot G12 in particular, has a distinct advantage over consumer camcorders in this regard, and even does a slightly better job than professional video cameras.

Figure 7.13
Sensor size
comparison.

Zooming and Video

When shooting still photos, a zoom is a zoom is a zoom. The key considerations for a zoom lens used only for still photography are the maximum aperture available at each focal length ("How *fast* is this lens?"), the zoom range ("How far can I zoom in or out?"), and its sharpness at any given f/stop ("Do I lose sharpness when I shoot wide open?").

When shooting video, the priorities may change, and there are two additional parameters to consider. The first two I listed, lens speed and zoom range, have roughly the same importance in both still and video photography. Zoom range gains a bit of importance in videography, because you can always/usually move closer to shoot a still photograph, but when you're zooming during a shot most of us don't have that option (or the funds to buy/rent a dolly to smoothly move the camera during capture). But, oddly enough, overall sharpness may have slightly less importance under certain conditions when shooting video. That's because the image changes in some way many times per second (24 or 30 times per second with the Canon G1 X), so any given frame doesn't hang around long enough for our eyes to pick out every single detail. You want a sharp image, of course, but your standards don't need to be quite as high when shooting video.

Here are the remaining considerations, and the two new ones:

- **Zoom lens maximum aperture.** The speed of the lens matters in several ways. A zoom with a relatively large maximum aperture lets you shoot in lower light levels, and a big f/stop allows you to minimize depth-of-field for selective focus. Keep in mind that the maximum aperture may change during zooming, down to f/5.8 at the maximum telephoto position.

- **Zoom range.** Use of zoom during actual capture should not be an everyday thing, unless you're shooting a kung-fu movie. However, there are effective uses for a zoom shot, particularly if it's a "long" one from extreme wide angle to extreme close-up (or vice versa). Most of the time, you'll use the zoom range to adjust the perspective of the camera *between* shots, and a longer zoom range can mean less trotting back and forth to adjust the field of view. Zoom range also comes into play when you're working with selective focus (longer focal lengths have less depth-of-field), or want to expand or compress the apparent distance between foreground and background subjects. A longer range gives you more flexibility.

- **Power zoom.** The Canon G1 X's zoom is not specifically optimized for video shooting, and can produce jerky images, even with vibration reduction turned on.

- **Linearity.** Unless a lens is optimized for video shooting a particular lens may not necessarily be linear. Zooming in or out at a constant speed doesn't always produce a smooth zoom. There may be "jumps" as the elements of the lens shift around during the zoom. Keep that in mind if you plan to zoom during a shot.

Part III

Advanced Tools

This part consists of four chapters that will help you dig even deeper into the use of the more advanced tools available with your Canon PowerShot G1 X, such as your camera's zoom lens, and the things you can do with the creative application of light, both natural and electronic. As with previous parts, you can start with any of the chapters that pique your interest the most, following these guidelines:

- **If you want to explore some special techniques, read:** *Chapter 8: Advanced Shooting* with Your Canon PowerShot G1 X. This chapter introduces some interesting photo tricks, including uses for long and short exposures, infrared photography, and a few things you can do with the latest tablet computers.

- **If you know that using your G1 X's lens effectively involves more than just pressing the zoom lever, you'll want to go to:** *Chapter 9: Getting the Most from Your Zoom.* Discover what telephoto and wide-angle perspectives can do for your photos, and how to avoid the most common pitfalls of each end of the zoom scale. Learn about macro shooting, and discover some interesting add-ons that make your zoom even more versatile.

- **If you'd like to use light more effectively to create a mood or effect, read:** *Chapter 10: Making Light Work for You.* Available light and electronic flash are powerful tools, but you need to understand how they work to harness their capabilities. This chapter shows you how to choose between continuous illumination and flash, and the best way to progress beyond the limitations of your PowerShot G1 X's built-in flash.

- **If you want to jump ahead and begin working with your images on your computer, you'll want to look at:** *Chapter 11: Downloading and Editing Your Images.* It's not a how-to chapter for image editing. Instead, it explains your options for transferring images and then processing them with easy-to-use, but powerful, software options, from Canon's Digital Photo Pro to Photoshop.

Advanced Shooting with Your Canon PowerShot G1 X

Getting the right exposure is one of the foundations of a great photograph, but a lot more goes into a compelling shot than good tonal values. So, now that you've got a good understanding of exposure tucked away, you'll want to learn some creative ways to use exposure, including using very short or long exposures, and work with the infrared portion of the electromagnetic spectrum.

More Exposure Options

In Chapter 5, you learned techniques for getting the *right* exposure, but I haven't explained all your exposure options just yet. You'll want to know about the *kind* of exposure settings that are available to you with the Canon PowerShot G1 X. There are options that let you control when the exposure is made, or even how to make an exposure that's out of the ordinary in terms of length. The sections that follow explain your camera's special exposure features, and even discuss a few it does not have, to put the others in context.

A Tiny Slice of Time

Exposures that seem impossibly brief can reveal a world we didn't know existed. In the 1930s, Dr. Harold Edgerton, a professor of electrical engineering at MIT, pioneered high-speed photography using a repeating electronic flash unit he patented called the *stroboscope.* As the inventor of the electronic flash, he popularized its use to freeze objects in motion, and you've probably seen his photographs of bullets piercing balloons and drops of milk forming a coronet-shaped splash.

Electronic flash freezes action by virtue of its extremely short duration—as brief as 1/50,000th second or less. Although the PowerShot G1 X's built-in pop-up flash unit can give you these ultra-quick glimpses of moving subjects, an external flash, such as one of the Canon Speedlites, offers even more versatility. You can read more about using electronic flash to stop action in Chapter 10.

Of course, the PowerShot is fully capable of immobilizing all but the fastest movement using only its shutter speeds, which range all the way up to a speedy 1/4,000th second. Indeed, you'll rarely have need for such a brief shutter speed in ordinary shooting. If you wanted to use an aperture of f/2.8 at ISO 100 outdoors in bright sunlight, for some reason, a shutter speed of 1/4,000th second would more than do the job. You'd need a faster shutter speed only if you moved the ISO setting to a higher sensitivity (but why would you do that?). Under less than full sunlight, 1/4,000th second is more than fast enough for any conditions you're likely to encounter.

Most sports action can be frozen at 1/2,000th second or slower, and for many sports a slower shutter speed is actually preferable—for example, to allow the wheels of a racing automobile or motorcycle, or the propeller on a classic aircraft to blur realistically. But if you want to do some exotic action-freezing photography without resorting to electronic flash, the PowerShot's top shutter speed is at your disposal. Here are some things to think about when exploring this type of high-speed photography:

- **You'll need a lot of light.** High shutter speeds cut very fine slices of time and sharply reduce the amount of illumination that reaches your sensor. To use 1/4,000th second at an aperture of f/6.3, you'd need an ISO setting of 800—even in full daylight. To use an f/stop smaller than f/6.3 or an ISO setting lower than 1600, you'd need *more* light than full daylight provides. (That's why electronic flash units work so well for high-speed photography when used as the sole illumination; the short duration of the flash—1/1,000th second or less—provides both the effect of a brief shutter speed and the high levels of illumination needed.) Of course, the G1 X has a built-in neutral-density filter to cut down the amount of light reaching the sensor.

- **Forget about reciprocity failure.** If you're an old-time film shooter, you might recall that very brief shutter speeds (as well as very high light levels and very *long* exposures) produced an effect called *reciprocity failure,* in which given exposures ended up providing less than the calculated value because of the way film responded to very short, very intense, or very long exposures of light. Solid-state sensors don't suffer from this defect, so you don't need to make an adjustment when using high shutter speeds (or brief flash bursts).

■ **No elongation effect.** This is another old bugaboo that has largely been solved through modern technology, but I wanted to bring it to your attention anyway. In olden times, cameras used shutters that traveled horizontally. To achieve faster shutter speeds, focal plane shutters (located just in front of the focal plane) open only a smaller-than-frame-sized slit so that, even though the shutter is already traveling at its highest rate of speed, the film/sensor is exposed for a briefer period of time as the slit moves across the surface. At very short shutter speeds, and with subjects moving horizontally at very fast velocities, it was possible for the subject to partially "keep up" with the shutter if it were traveling in the same direction as the slit, producing an elongated effect. Conversely, subjects moving in the opposite direction of shutter motion could be compressed. Today, shutters like those in the PowerShot move vertically and at a higher maximum rate of speed. So, unless you're photographing a model rocket blasting into space, and holding the camera horizontally to boot (or shooting a racing car in vertical orientation), it's almost impossible to produce unwanted elongation/compression.

Working with Short Exposures

You can have a lot of fun exploring the kinds of pictures you can take using very brief exposure times, whether you decide to take advantage of the action-stopping capabilities of your built-in or external electronic flash or work with the Canon PowerShot G1 X's faster shutter speeds. Here are a few ideas to get you started:

■ **Take revealing images.** Fast shutter speeds can help you reveal the real subject behind the façade, by freezing constant motion to capture an enlightening moment in time. Legendary fashion/portrait photographer Philippe Halsman used leaping photos of famous people, such as the Duke and Duchess of Windsor, Richard Nixon, and Salvador Dali to illuminate their real selves. Halsman said, "*When you ask a person to jump, his attention is mostly directed toward the act of jumping and the mask falls so that the real person appears.*" Try some high-speed portraits of people you know in motion to see how they appear when concentrating on something other than the portrait. (See Figure 8.1.)

■ **Create unreal images.** High-speed photography can also produce photographs that show your subjects in ways that are quite unreal. A helicopter in mid-air with its rotors frozen or a motocross cyclist leaping over a ramp, but with all motion stopped so that the rider and machine look as if they were frozen in mid-air, make for an unusual picture.

Figure 8.1
The act of jumping shows how your subjects appear when concentrating on something other than the portrait.

- **Capture unseen perspectives.** Some things are *never* seen in real life, except when viewed in a stop-action photograph. Edgerton's balloon bursts were only a starting point. Freeze a hummingbird in flight for a view of wings that never seem to stop. Or, capture the splashes as liquid falls into a bowl, as shown in Figure 8.2. No electronic flash was required for this image (and wouldn't have illuminated the water in the bowl as evenly). Instead, a clutch of high-intensity lamps and an ISO setting of 1600 allowed the camera to capture this image at 1/2,000th second.

- **Vanquish camera shake and gain new angles.** Here's an idea that's so obvious it isn't always explored to its fullest extent. A high enough shutter speed is even better at correcting for camera movement than the G1 X's built-in image stabilization feature. It can free you from the tyranny of a tripod in light levels too low for even IS to counter camera shake, making it easier to capture new angles, or to shoot quickly while moving around, especially with longer lenses. I tend to use a monopod or tripod for almost everything when I'm not using vibration reduction, and I end up missing some shots because of a reluctance to adjust my camera support to get a higher, lower, or different angle. If you have enough light and can use an f/ stop wide enough to permit a high shutter speed, you'll find a new freedom to choose your shots.

Figure 8.2 A large amount of artificial illumination and an ISO 1600 sensitivity setting allowed capturing this shot, taken at 1/2,000th second without use of an electronic flash.

Long Exposures

Longer exposures are a doorway into another world, showing us how even familiar scenes can look much different when photographed over periods measured in seconds. At night, long exposures produce streaks of light from moving, illuminated subjects like automobiles or amusement park rides. Extra-long exposures of seemingly pitch-dark subjects can reveal interesting views using light levels barely bright enough to see by. At any time of day, including daytime (in which case you'll often need the help of the neutral-density filter to make the long exposure practical), long exposures can cause moving objects to vanish entirely, because they don't remain stationary long enough to register in a photograph.

Three Ways to Take Long Exposures

There are actually three common types of lengthy exposures: *timed exposures, bulb exposures,* and *time exposures.* The PowerShot G1 X offers only the first one of these, but it's helpful to understand what other options exist, to put this camera's capability into context. Because of the length of the exposure, all of the following techniques should be used with a tripod to hold the camera steady.

■ **Timed exposures.** These are long exposures from 1 second to 15 seconds, measured by the camera itself. To take a picture in this range with the PowerShot G1 X, simply use Manual or Tv mode and use the control dial to set the shutter speed to the length of time you want, choosing from preset speeds of 1.0, 1.3, 1.6, 2.0,

2.5, 3.2, 4.0, 5.0, 6.0, 8.0, 10.0, 13.0, 15.0, 30.0, or 60.0 seconds. The advantage of timed exposures is that the camera does all the calculating for you. There's no need for a stopwatch. If you review your image on the LCD and decide to try again with the exposure doubled or halved, you can dial in the correct exposure with precision. The disadvantage of timed exposures is that you can't take a photo with this camera for longer than 60 seconds.

- **Bulb exposures.** This type of exposure, not available with the G1 X, is so-called because in the olden days the photographer squeezed and held an air bulb attached to a tube that provided the force necessary to keep the shutter open for the desired period of time.

- **Time exposures.** This is a setting found on some cameras to produce longer exposures. Although the G1 X lacks this capability, with cameras that implement this option, the shutter opens when you press the shutter release button, and remains open until you press the button again.

Working with Long Exposures

Because the PowerShot G1 X produces such good images at longer exposures, and there are so many creative things you can do with long-exposure techniques, you'll want to do some experimenting. Get yourself a tripod or another firm support and get started. Here are some things to try:

- **Make people invisible.** One very cool thing about long exposures is that objects that move rapidly enough won't register at all in a photograph, while the subjects that remain stationary are portrayed in the normal way. That makes it possible to produce people-free landscape photos and architectural photos at night or, even, in full daylight if you use the neutral-density filter (set from the FUNC. menu) to allow an exposure of at least a few seconds. If you find the technique isn't working, you may need to wait for an overcast day to allow for a long enough exposure, if daylight people-vanishing is your goal. They'll have to be walking *very* briskly and across the field of view (rather than directly toward the camera) for this to work. At night, it's much easier to achieve this effect with the 60-second exposures that are possible with the G1 X, as you can see in Figures 8.3 and 8.4.

- **Create streaks.** If you aren't shooting for total invisibility, long exposures with the camera on a tripod can produce some interesting streaky effects, as shown in Figure 8.5. You don't need to limit yourself to indoor photography, however. Depending on the light conditions, using the neutral-density filter may darken the scene sufficiently to allow you to take photographs outdoors with a shutter speed slow enough to paint streaks on your image.

Figure 8.3 This alleyway is thronged with people, as you can see in this two-second exposure using only the available illumination.

Figure 8.4 With the camera still on a tripod, a longer 60-second exposure rendered the passersby almost invisible.

Figure 8.5 The dancers produced a swirl of color as they moved during the 1/4 second exposure.

- **Produce light trails.** At night, car headlights and taillights and other moving sources of illumination can generate interesting light trails. Your camera doesn't even need to be mounted on a tripod; handholding the PowerShot for longer exposures adds movement and patterns to your trails, as in Figure 8.6. If you're shooting fireworks, a longer exposure may allow you to combine several bursts into one picture.

- **Blur waterfalls, etc.** You'll find that waterfalls and other sources of moving liquid produce a special type of long-exposure blur, because the water merges into a fantasy-like veil that looks different at different exposure times, and with different waterfalls. Cascades with turbulent flow produce a rougher look at a given longer exposure than falls that flow smoothly. (See Figure 8.7.)

- **Show total darkness in new ways.** Even on the darkest, moonless nights, there is enough starlight or glow from distant illumination sources to see by, and, if you use a long exposure, there is enough light to take a picture, too, as in Figure 8.8.

Figure 8.6 Holiday lights produce interesting light trails when you zoom through a long exposure.

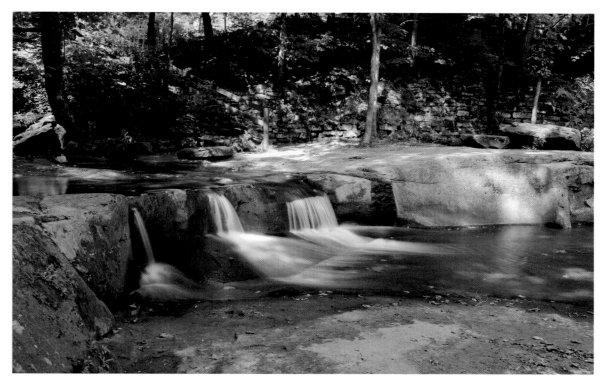

Figure 8.7 Long exposures of waterfalls have become almost a cliché, but one that can still be used effectively.

Figure 8.8 Although this time exposure appears to be taken at twilight, it actually was snapped at 10 p.m.

Delayed Exposures

Sometimes it's desirable to have a delay of some sort before a picture is actually taken. Perhaps you'd like to get in the picture yourself, and would appreciate it if the camera waited 10 seconds after you press the shutter release to actually take the picture. Maybe you want to give a tripod-mounted camera time to settle down and damp any residual vibration after the release is pressed to improve sharpness for an exposure with a relatively slow shutter speed. It's possible you want to explore the world of time-lapse photography. The next sections present your delayed exposure options.

Self-Timer

The PowerShot G1 X has a built-in self-timer with a range of delay options from 0 to 30 seconds. (I'm not sure why you'd want a zero second delay, but it's there.) Your camera also has a self-timer/multiple shot setting that allows taking 1 to 10 shots after the delay. You call the self-timer into action from the FUNC./SET menu. The operation of the self-timer is easy to follow from the camera's prompts, but if you need a refresher, see Chapter 4.

Forget to bring along your tripod, but still want to take a close-up picture with a precise focus setting? Set your digital camera to the Self-timer function, then put the camera on any reasonably steady support, such as a fence post or a rock. When you're ready to take the picture, press the shutter release. The camera might totter back and forth for a second or two, but it will settle back to its original position before the self-timer activates the shutter.

Beyond Visible Light with Infrared

Congratulations—you have won the Infrared Lottery! What I mean by that is, by your wise choice of purchasing a PowerShot G1 X, you have acquired one of the modern digital cameras that is capable of using infrared light to take some very interesting and unusual-looking photographs. Not every digital camera can take infrared photographs in this way. Many cameras nowadays have an infrared-blocking filter built into them, so they can't take advantage of the exotic-looking properties of infrared images.

You can test any digital camera for infrared picture–taking ability by aiming an infrared remote control at the camera's lens and clicking any button on the remote a few times, or holding it down. If the camera is sensitive to infrared light, you will see a bright light being emitted from the remote, though it's invisible to the naked eye. The PowerShot G1 X model passes this test quite nicely. This camera is not designed for infrared picture taking, and may not be as good at it as some other cameras that are built (or converted) for that purpose, but I consider this model to do a pretty decent job in this esoteric area.

So, what do you do with your newfound power to take infrared photographs? If you want, you can delve quite deeply into the topic and become immersed in lots of arcane information about how infrared works. An Internet search on "infrared digital photography" will get you going on that endeavor.

The purpose of this book, though, is to give you enough practical information to get you started without bogging you down. So, to give you a sample of what the PowerShot G1 X can do in this area, I'll give you a set of steps you can take to enter the world of infrared photography. These steps represent just one approach, but they will work. Here is my suggested scenario:

- **Get an adapter and an infrared filter.** In order to take interesting-looking infrared photographs, you need not only to have a camera like the PowerShot G1 X, which can "see" infrared light, you also need to have a way to block the normal, humanly visible light. If you don't take that step, the visible light will overwhelm the infrared light and the resulting photograph will look rather ordinary. In the past, some people used exposed, developed photographic film as a makeshift infrared filter. You would be better off, though, with a commercially available photographic filter such as the Hoya R72, available from good photo supply firms. Then you need to find a way to secure it in front of the lens. You could try cobbling together a holder from a cardboard tube or the like, or you could get a more permanent device such as the FA-DC58C filter adapter sold by Canon (about $29), which accepts 58mm filters. Or you could start out by just holding it firmly in front of the lens.

- **Set the camera on a tripod.** This is required because the infrared filter is quite dark, and you will need a long exposure, possibly of more than one second, to get a usable image.

- **Use custom white balance.** If you need a refresher on the procedure, see Chapter 4's discussion of the Function menu. But there is a twist here: instead of aiming the camera at a white (or gray) surface to get the white balance set, for infrared, I suggest you aim at green foliage, if possible (trees, grass, bushes), because those make some of the best subjects for infrared photos, which render green objects in white in dramatic contrast to their normal appearance.

- **Use Aperture priority (Av) mode.** Because the camera is on a tripod, you don't have to worry about having a long exposure. Try f/4.5 for a start. The camera will probably select a long exposure, of one second or more.

- **Find a suitable subject.** As I noted above, you might want to start with green trees and plants outdoors. Include sky and clouds as well, if possible, for contrast, dramatic images. Once you've gotten started, though, experiment with a variety of subjects.

- **Use the self-timer.** This isn't a strong requirement, but I like to use the self-timer when possible, to avoid camera shake for long exposures.

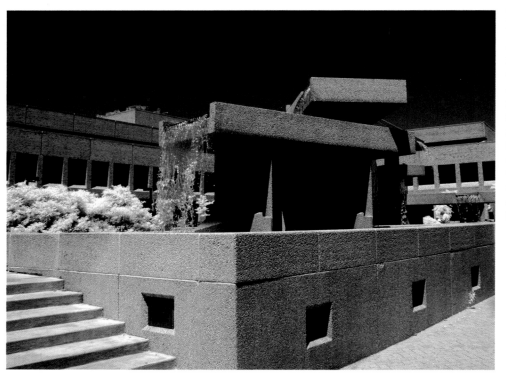

Figure 8.9
This infrared shot was taken in Aperture priority mode with a Hoya R72 filter, exposed at f/3.5 for 4 seconds at ISO 800. Custom white balance was set based on the color of the green bushes at left.

See Figure 8.9 for an example of a photograph shot using the above technique.

Wi-Fi

These days, GPS and Wi-Fi capabilities work together with your G1 X in interesting new ways. Wireless capabilities allow you to upload photos directly from your G1 X to your computer at home or in your studio, or, through a hotspot at your hotel or coffee shop back to your home computer or to a photo sharing service like Facebook or Flickr. A special Wi-Fi-enabled memory card that you slip in the SD slot of your camera performs the magic. GPS capabilities—built right into some of those Wi-Fi cards—allow you to mark your photographs with location information, so you don't have to guess where a picture was taken.

Both capabilities are very cool. Wi-Fi uploads can provide instant backup of important shots and sharing. Geotagging is most important as a way to associate the geographical location where the photographer was when a picture was taken, with the actual photograph itself. It can be done with the location-mapping capabilities of the Wi-Fi card.

Figure 8.10
The Eye-Fi card
is an SD card
with built-in
Wi-Fi features.

A relatively affordable solution is offered by Eye-Fi (www.eye.fi). The Eye-Fi card (see Figure 8.10) is an SDHC memory card with a wireless transmitter built in. You insert it in your camera just as with any ordinary card, and then specify which networks to use. You can add as many as 32 different networks. The next time your camera is on within range of a specified network, your photos and videos can be uploaded to your computer and/or to your favorite sharing site. During setup, you can customize where you want your images uploaded. The Eye-Fi card will only send them to the computer and to the sharing site you choose. Upload to any of 25 popular sharing websites, including Flickr, Facebook, MobileMe, Costco, Adorama, Smugmug, YouTube, Shutterfly, or Walmart. Online sharing is included as a lifetime, unlimited service with all X2 cards.

When uploading to online sites, you can specify not just where your images are sent, but how they are organized, by specifying preset album names, tags, descriptions, and even privacy preferences on certain sharing sites. Some Eye-Fi cards also include a geo-tagging service, which helps you view uploaded photos on a map, and sort them by location. Eye-Fi's geotagging uses Wi-Fi Positioning System (WPS) technology. Using built-in Wi-Fi, the Eye-Fi card senses surrounding Wi-Fi networks as you take pictures. When photos are uploaded, the Eye-Fi service then adds the geotags to your photos. You don't need to have the password or a subscription for the Wi-Fi networks the card accesses; it can grab the location information directly without the need to "log in." You don't need to set up or control the Eye-Fi card from your camera. Software on your computer manages all the parameters. (See Figure 8.11.)

Your G1 X has an Eye-Fi Settings entry in the Setup menu that allows you to enable or disable this capability. This menu option has two subitems. The first lets you choose Enable to help ensure that the Eye-Fi card's transmitter is functioning. The other item, Connection Info, provides information about what Wi-Fi access point, if any, the card

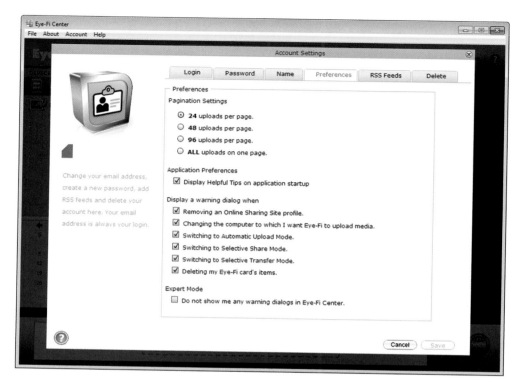

Figure 8.11
Functions of the
Eye-Fi card can
be controlled
from your
computer.

is connected to. If you are having trouble getting your Eye-Fi card to transmit images, use these menu settings to help correct the problem. Also, if you are using an Eye-Fi card for image storage but have no network available at a given time, you can choose Disable on this menu so the camera does not waste its power in trying to help the Eye-Fi card connection when no connection is available. You'll also want to turn off Eye-Fi when traveling on an airplane (just as you disable your cell phone, tablet, or laptop's wireless capabilities when required to do so). In addition, use of Wi-Fi cards may be restricted or banned outside the United States, because the telecommunications laws differ in other countries.

If you frequently travel outside the range of your home (or business) Wi-Fi network, an optional service called Hotspot Access is available, allowing you to connect to any AT&T Wi-Fi hotspot in the U.S. In addition, you can use your own Wi-Fi accounts from commercial network providers, your city, even organizations you belong to such as your university.

The card has another interesting feature called Endless Memory. When pictures have been safely uploaded to an external site, the card can bet set to automatically erase the oldest images to free up space for new pictures. You choose the threshold where the card starts zapping your old pictures to make room.

Eye-Fi currently offers several models starting at about $50. All of them can be used to transmit your photos from the camera to a computer on your home network (or any other network you set up somewhere, say, at a family reunion). Software allows you to upload your images from your camera through your computer network directly to websites and digital printing services already mentioned. The most sophisticated option is Eye-Fi Pro X2, an 8GB SDHC card that adds geographic location labels to your photo (so you'll know where you took it), and frees you from your own computer network by allowing uploads from more than 10,000 Wi-Fi hotspots around the U.S. Very cool, and the ultimate in picture backup.

Tablets, Smart Phones, and the PowerShot G1 X

Although tablets and smart phones are still in their infancies, in the future, your iPhone, iPad/tablet computer, iPod Touch/MP3 player, smart phone, or Google Android portable device will be one of the most important accessories you can have for your G1 X (or other) digital camera. We're only now seeing the beginnings of the trend. The relevant platforms are these:

- **Old-style smart phones.** I include in this category all smart phones that are *not* iPhones or phones based on Google's Android operating system. You can buy lots of interesting apps for these phones, although not many applications specifically for photography. This type of phone should be on its way out, too, with iPhone and Android smart phones dominating, simply because it's easier to write applications for the iPhone's iOS and Android than to create them for multiple "old" smart phone platforms.

- **Android smart phones.** There are already more Android-based smart phones on the market than for all other types, including iOS. Although Apple had a head start, the number of Android applications is rapidly catching up.

- **iPhones.** It might sound strange to say that the skyrocketing sales of iPhones has been held in check, but it's true. The real or imagined short-comings of AT&T's data network—which only got worse as more users grabbed iPhones—have kept many from switching to the iOS platform. The difficulties may even have contributed to the rapid growth of Android-based phones, which have been offered by Verizon and other suppliers seen as having "better" communications networks. Even so, iOS leads in number of applications, especially for photography apps. When my first app was developed, it appeared for the iOS platform first. With Verizon entering the iOS picture, it's possible that iPhone sales *will* genuinely skyrocket. Or, Android may have picked up enough steam to blunt any dramatic increase in iPhone sales.

- **iPod Touch.** Basically, the latest iPod Touch is an iPhone that can't make phone calls. (Although there are some hacks around that limitation.) Virtually all of the apps that run on the iPhone under iOS also run on the iPod Touch. You need a Wi-Fi connection to access features that use network capabilities, but, these days, Wi-Fi hot spots aren't that difficult to find. Tethering and Mi-Fi (which allow another device to serve as a hot spot for non-connected gadgets like the Touch), and *automobiles* that include built-in Wi-Fi (!) make connectivity almost universal. In my travels through Europe in the last year, I found free Wi-Fi connections in the smallest towns. (Indeed, the only time I was asked to pay for it was when staying in an upscale hotel.) So, for many who are tied to a non-iPhone cell phone, the iPod Touch is a viable alternative.

- **Tablet computers.** I've been welded to my iPad (shown alongside my iPhone in Figure 8.12) since I bought it the first day they became available. I use them to access e-mail, useful apps, and as a portable portfolio. Today, there are alternative tablet computers running Android. I recently picked up an Amazon Kindle Fire, which also does e-mail and a limited number of apps, and which has a Gallery feature (see Figure 8.13) that transforms it into a compact portfolio almost as useful for that purpose as an iPad. (However, only 6 of the Kindle Fire's 8GB of storage are available to the user, so you'll have to limit the size of your portfolio.

I use the Kindle Fire and both an iPhone and iPad. (If I'm traveling overseas where my iPhone can't be used, I usually take along the iPod Touch instead.) The iPhone/iPod slips in a pocket and can be used anywhere. I don't even have to think about taking it with me, because I always have one or the other. I have to remember to tote along the iPad or Kindle Fire, and, I do, to an extent you'd probably find surprising. (After the movie finally starts, I fold them into their cases and use them as a tray for my popcorn bucket.) Tablet computers can do everything a pocket-sized device can do, and are easier to read/view/type on. When I am out shooting, I prefer to have all my apps in a smaller device that I can slip in the camera bag, but if there's room, the iPad goes along instead. Because my iPad (unlike the Kindle Fire) has 3G connectivity, I don't need a Wi-Fi connection to use it almost anywhere. I do have a Wi-Fi hot spot built into my iPhone that I can use to connect the Kindle Fire to the net if I need to.

Figure 8.12
The iPad, iPod, and other devices open a whole world of useful apps to the photographer.

Figure 8.13
The Kindle Fire is a smaller, more affordable alternative to the iPad.

What Else Can You Do with Them?

Many of these devices can serve as a backup for your PowerShot G1 X's memory cards. I've got Apple's camera connection kit, and can offload my pictures to my iPad's 64GB of memory, then upload them to Flickr or Facebook, or send to anyone through e-mail. My iPad also makes a perfect portable portfolio, too. I have hundreds of photos stored on mine, arranged into albums (see Figure 8.12, earlier) ready for instant display, either individually, or in slide shows. I have the same photo library on my iPhone and iPod Touch, and more than a few pictures available for showing on my Kindle Fire.

But the real potential for using these devices comes from specialized apps written specifically to serve photographic needs. Here are some of the kinds of apps you can expect in the future. (I'm working on more than a few of them myself.)

- **Camera guides.** Even the rotten manual that came with your camera is too large to carry around in your camera bag all day. I'm converting many of my own camera-specific guides to app form, while adding interactive elements, including hyperlinks and videos. You can already put a PDF version of your camera manual on your portable device and read it, if you like. In the future, you should be able to read any of the more useful third-party guides anywhere, anytime.

- **Exposure estimator.** Choose a situation and the estimated exposure will be provided. Useful as a reality check and in difficult situations, such as fireworks, where the camera's meters may falter.

- **Shutter speed advisor.** The correct shutter speed for a scene varies depending on whether you want to freeze action, or add a little blur to express motion. Other variables include whether the subject is crossing the frame, moving diagonally, or headed toward you. The photographer also needs to consider the focal length of the lens, and presence/absence of image stabilization features, tripod, monopod, etc. This app will allow you to tap in all the factors and receive advice about what shutter speed to use.

- **Hyperfocal length calculator.** In any given situation, set the focus point at the distance specified for your lens's current focal length setting, and everything from half that distance to infinity will be in focus. But the right setting differs at various focal lengths. This app tells you, and is a great tool for grab shots.

- **Accessory selector.** Confused about what flash, remote control, battery grip, lens hood, filter, or other accessory to use with your camera or lens? This selector lists the key gadgets, which ones fit which cameras, and explains how to use them.

- **Before and after.** Images showing before/after versions of dozens of situations with and without corrective/in-camera special effects applied.

- **Fill light.** Pesky shadows on faces from overhead lighting indoors? This turns your iPod/iPhone or (best of all) iPad into a bright, diffuse fill light panel. Choose from white fill light, or *colors* for special effects. Makes good illumination for viewing your camera's buttons and dials in dark locations, too.

- **Gray card.** Turn your i-device into an 18 percent gray card for metering and color balance.

- **Super links.** If you don't find your answer in the Toolkit, you can link to websites, including mine, with more information.

- **How It's Made.** A collection of inspiring photos, with details on how they were taken in camera—or manipulated in Photoshop (if that's your thing).

- **Quickie guides.** Small apps that lead you, step-by-step, through everything you need to photograph lots of different types of scenes. Typical subjects would be sports, landscape photography, macro work, portraits, concerts/performances, flowers, wildlife, and nature.

As you can see, the potential for apps is virtually unlimited. You can expect your smart phone, tablet computer, or other device to be a mainstay in your camera bag within a very short time.

9

Getting the Most from Your Zoom

The 28–112mm f/2.8 zoom lens mounted on your Canon PowerShot G1 X is the "eye" of your camera. It captures the light that's focused on the sensor to produce the image. Through its zooming capability, the lens changes the magnification of the image, and, indirectly, the perspective of your photograph. The maximum aperture (or f/stop) of your lens also affects your ability to shoot under varying light conditions. The size of the lens opening you choose helps determine the range of sharpness (depth-of-field) and the absolute *amount* of sharpness.

Those aspects are very important to your picture taking. With a camera like the G1 X, the lens is fixed and cannot be interchanged (although you can adjust its characteristics with add-on attachments). So, the quality and features of the lens itself are the most crucial factors you should consider in choosing a camera. Fortunately, the lens mounted on the G1 X is a very good one, and to a large extent, one of the key reasons why these cameras are so popular.

This chapter explains some of the things you should keep in mind when using your zoom, how to select the best focal lengths for the kinds of photography you want to do, and things you can do to increase the versatility of your camera's built-in optics.

Using Step Zoom

Although the G1 X zooms smoothly from 28mm to 112mm using the zoom lever concentric with the shutter release, your camera doesn't provide much feedback about what zoom setting you're using. The zoom status bar at the top of the screen lengthens and shrinks as you zoom in and out, and a readout tells you what the focus range is at the current zoom setting (in meters, of course, so when it says 1.3 meters to infinity at 112mm you may not intuitively know what your limits are).

Fortunately, the G1 X has a feature called Step Zoom (not available in Movie mode) that allows you to flip between preset focal lengths of 28mm, 35mm, 50mm, 85mm, or 112mm equivalents. That's especially handy for photo veterans who know instinctively that, say, 28mm is considered wide; 50mm is thought of as "normal"; 85mm is excellent for head-and-shoulders portraits; and 100mm or 112mm is useful for sports. To work with Step Zoom, follow these steps:

1. Assign Zoom to the front control dial, using the Set Dial Functions entry in the Shooting menu, as described in Chapter 4.

2. Turn the dial clockwise to zoom in to any of the five increments.

3. Turn the dial counterclockwise to zoom back out.

4. The front control dial won't zoom in any digital zoom range, but rotating it counterclockwise will exit digital zoom and set the lens to 112mm. The G1 X stores the last used zoom position, even when powered down, and will start up using that setting.

How Lenses Affect Your Pictures

The first thing to get out of the way is the notion of absolute and equivalent focal lengths. Your 28–112mm zoom lens is actually a 15.1–60.4mm zoom in absolute terms, because those are the true focal lengths available from the optics built into the camera. The effective focal lengths in use, however, are customarily given in the form of the *equivalent* focal length compared to a 35mm film camera or "full-frame" digital camera. Because the sensor on the G1 X measures just 14 × 18.7mm, rather than the 24 × 36mm of a full-frame camera, the smaller sensor in your PowerShot requires shorter focal lengths to produce the same field of view.

That is, at 15.1mm, your lens has the same field of view as a 28mm lens on a full-frame camera; at 60.4mm, it has the same field of view as a 112mm telephoto on a full-frame camera. Because various cameras in this class have sensors of varying sizes, it makes sense to always convert their "real" focal lengths to the full-frame equivalent. So, in specifications for digital cameras, and throughout this book, I'll always refer to the *equivalent* focal lengths, and ignore the "real" focal lengths, because the latter have little meaning to the average photographer.

- **Change magnification.** Zooming in and out changes the magnification of your image in the viewfinder, on the LCD, and in the final image captured by your sensor. With the G1 X, this magnification factor is 1X to 4X. In Figure 9.1 you can see that the image at the 112mm maximum zoom position (bottom) is four times larger than the image produced at the 28mm setting (top).

Figure 9.1
At its 28mm setting, the PowerShot's zoom lens provides a true wide-angle view (top); at 112mm, the zoom offers a telephoto perspective.

- **Change perspective.** As you move closer or farther away from your subject, your perspective changes. At closer distances, with the lens zoomed out wider, objects in the foreground become exaggerated in size and more prominent compared to shots taken from a greater distance, and the lens zoomed in to telephoto settings. This change in perspective is intertwined with the magnification of your zoom. To keep an image the same size in the frame, you can zoom in or out, changing the magnification, or you can move closer or farther away, changing the perspective.

- **Control exposure.** The aperture built into your lens controls the exposure, as well as what exposures you can use. For example, with the G1 X, the maximum aperture is f/2.8 (at the wide-angle setting) and the smallest f/stop available is f/16. So, you can use only exposure combinations that call for f/2.8 to f/16. For example, on a bright day with an ISO setting of ISO 100, you could shoot at 1/200th second at f/16 to 1/4000th second at f/3.5.

Of course, these figures assume the G1 X's lens is at the wide-angle setting. At longer zoom positions, the maximum aperture decreases. At 28mm, it's f/2.8; at 50mm, it's f/4.5; at 85mm, it's f/5.6; at the maximum zoom setting of 112mm, it's f/5.8. The minimum effective aperture remains at f/16 in all cases.

■ **Affects depth-of-field.** The range of sharpness of your image, also called depth-of-field (DOF), is affected by the size of the f/stop. Your camera has the least amount of DOF at f/2.8, and the most at f/16. Fortunately (and unfortunately), the smaller sensor and smaller sensor size means that the 15.1–60.4 *true* focal lengths of your lens provide relatively large amounts of depth-of-field at any of these f/stops at normal shooting distances. Whether you're using f/2.8 or f/16 you'll probably have more than enough DOF, except when shooting macro pictures, when even the DOF provided at f/16 may not be enough. The *unfortunate* part comes from having so much DOF in most instances that selective focus techniques may be more difficult or impossible.

■ **Affects sharpness.** The f/stop built into your lens affects the absolute sharpness, too, not just the range of sharpness. As with most camera lenses the largest f/stop does not produce the best image quality; f/2.8 is good, but not as good as f/4 or f/5.6. At f/8 and smaller, lenses start to lose a little sharpness because of a phenomenon called *diffraction*. (The light entering the lens is scattered slightly by the edges of the aperture's diaphragm.) Diffraction grows worse as lens focal lengths become shorter, which is one of the reasons why the G1 X's lens stops at f/16 and doesn't continue on to smaller stops, such as f/22 or f/32, found in many lenses for other types of cameras, including digital SLRs. (Sensor design can affect diffraction, too, and optical physics is another limitation on the minimum f/stop available with cameras like the G1 X.)

So, what can you do with the zoom built into your Canon PowerShot G1 X? Here's what you need to know:

■ **Bring you closer.** A longer focal length brings distant subjects closer to you, offers better control over depth-of-field, and avoids the perspective distortion that wide-angle lenses provide. They compress the apparent distance between objects in your frame.

■ **Wider perspective.** Sometimes you need the widest view that your lens offers. Often, your back is up against a wall and you *can't* take a step backward to take in more subject matter. Perhaps you're standing on the rim of the Grand Canyon, and you want to take in as much of the breathtaking view as you can. You might find yourself just behind the baseline at a high school basketball game and want an interesting shot with a little perspective distortion tossed in the mix. In all these cases, you'll need to use the widest focal length that your lens offers, which in the G1 X provides the same field of view as a 28mm lens on a full-frame camera.

- **Bring your camera (a little) closer.** The macro setting of your lens allows you to autofocus from 7.9 inches to 27.6 inches at the wide-angle zoom position, and 33.6 inches to 5.2 feet at the telephoto position. This is not considered a very impressive macro range. Your macro subject area is roughly 8 × 10 inches in size. However, the G1 X's macro capabilities provides a little flexibility when you want to vary your subject distance (say, to avoid spooking a skittish creature).

- **More speed.** Your lens's f/2.8 maximum aperture at 28mm (f/5.8 at 112mm) means you can shoot many scenes in available light, using reasonable ISO speeds of ISO 1600 or below. ISO 12800 can be used only at the risk of increased visual noise in your images. You have to evaluate whether the image you want to capture is worth the noise penalty of higher IS settings.

- **Special features.** The optical image stabilization built into your lens makes your lens "faster" by allowing you to shoot at a slower shutter speed. For example, if 1/30th second at f/2.8 won't cut it, and raising the ISO isn't an option (say, you're already at ISO 1600), you can often grab your shot at an even slower shutter speed, assuming that it's camera shake and not subject movement you're trying to freeze. Your PowerShot can often get good images at 1/15th second or even 1/8th second, if you've turned on the Image Stabilization feature in the Shooting menu.

Using the Wide-Angle Zoom Settings

The zoom settings from 28mm to about 45mm are considered wide angle with your PowerShot G1 X. To use these focal lengths effectively, you need to understand how they affect your photography. Here's a quick summary of the things you need to know.

- **More depth-of-field.** Practically speaking, even with the copious amounts of depth-of-field that your camera's true 15.1–60.4mm focal length range offers, wide-angle settings still offer more depth-of-field at a particular subject distance and aperture. (But see the sidebar below for an important note.) You'll find that helpful when you want to maximize sharpness of a large zone, but not very useful when you'd rather isolate your subject using selective focus (telephoto focal lengths are better for that).

- **Stepping back.** Wide-angle focal lengths have the effect of making it seem that you are standing farther from your subject than you really are. They're helpful when you don't want to back up, or can't because there are impediments in your way.

- **Wider field of view.** While making your subject seem farther away, as implied above, a wide-angle setting also provides a larger field of view, including more of the subject in your photos.

■ **More foreground.** As background objects retreat, more of the foreground is brought into view by a wide-angle setting. That gives you extra emphasis on the area that's closest to the camera. Photograph your home with a medium zoom setting, and the front yard probably looks fairly conventional in your photo (that's why these medium focal lengths are called "normal"). Switch to a wider setting and you'll discover that your lawn now makes up much more of the photo. So, wide-angle focal lengths are great when you want to emphasize that lake in the foreground, but problematic when your intended subject is located farther in the distance.

■ **Perspective distortion.** When you tilt the camera so the plane of the sensor is no longer perpendicular to the vertical plane of your subject, some parts of the subject are now closer to the sensor than they were before, while other parts are farther away. So, buildings, flagpoles, or NBA players appear to be falling backward, as you can see in Figure 9.2. While this kind of apparent distortion (it's not caused by a defect in the lens) can happen with any focal length, it's most apparent when a wide-angle lens setting is used.

Figure 9.2
When you tilt the camera upward, tall buildings appear to be falling backward.

■ **Super-sized subjects.** The tendency of a wide-angle lens to emphasize objects in the foreground, while de-emphasizing objects in the background can lead to a kind of size distortion that may be more objectionable for some types of subjects than others. Shoot a bed of flowers up close with a wide-angle setting, and you might like the distorted effect of the larger blossoms nearer the lens. Take a photo of a family member with the same lens from the same distance, and you're likely to get some complaints about that gigantic nose in the foreground. Figure 9.3 shows a dry creek bed using a medium focal length at top. At bottom, a wide-angle setting emphasizes the rocks in the foreground, making them appear huge, and making the background trees (and even the horizon) seem farther away.

Figure 9.3
At top, a normal view of a dry creek bed. At bottom, the wide-angle perspective from a slightly lower angle makes the small rocks in the foreground appear to be huge.

- **Steady cam.** You'll find that you can handhold a wide-angle focal length at slower shutter speeds, without need for image stabilization, than you can with a telephoto lens setting. The reduced magnification of the wide-zoom setting doesn't emphasize camera shake like a telephoto setting does.

- **Interesting angles.** Many of the factors already listed combine to produce more interesting angles when shooting with wide-angle focal lengths. Raising or lowering a telephoto lens a few feet probably will have little effect on the appearance of the distant subjects you're shooting. The same change in elevation can produce a dramatic effect for the much-closer subjects typically captured with a wide-zoom setting.

DOF IN DEPTH

The depth-of-field (DOF) advantage of wide-angle focal lengths is diminished when you enlarge your picture; believe it or not, a wide-angle image enlarged and cropped to provide the same subject size as a telephoto shot would have the *same* depth-of-field. Try it: take a wide-angle photo of a friend from a fair distance, and then zoom in to duplicate the picture in a telephoto image. Then, enlarge the wide shot so your friend is the same size in both. The wide photo will have the same DOF (and will have much less detail, too).

Potential Wide-Angle Problems

Wide-angle focal lengths have a few quirks that you'll want to keep in mind when shooting. Here's a checklist of common problems:

- **Symptom: converging lines.** Unless you want to use wildly diverging lines as a creative effect, it's a good idea to keep horizontal and vertical lines in landscapes, architecture, and other subjects carefully aligned with the sides, top, and bottom of the frame. That will help you avoid undesired perspective distortion. Sometimes it helps to shoot from a slightly elevated position so you don't have to tilt the camera up or down.

- **Symptom: color fringes around objects.** Lenses are often plagued with fringes of color around backlit objects, produced by *chromatic aberration*, which comes in two forms: *longitudinal/axial*, in which all the colors of light don't focus in the same plane; and *lateral/transverse*, in which the colors are shifted to one side. Lens designers must use special techniques to reduce these effects.

- **Symptom: lines that bow outward.** Some wide-angle focal lengths cause straight lines to bow outward, with the strongest effect at the edges. You can minimize barrel distortion simply by framing your photo with some extra space all around, so the edges where the defect is most obvious can be cropped out of the picture.

- **Symptom: light and dark areas when using a polarizing filter.** If you know that polarizers work best when the camera is pointed 90 degrees away from the sun and have the least effect when the camera is oriented 180 degrees from the sun, you know only half the story. With focal lengths in the 28mm vicinity, the angle of view (75 degrees diagonally, or 44 degrees horizontally) is extensive enough to cause problems. Think about it: when a 28mm lens is pointed at the proper 90-degree angle from the sun, objects at the edges of the frame will be oriented at 112 to 68 degrees, with only the center at exactly 90 degrees. Either edge will have much less of a polarized effect. The solution is to avoid using a polarizing filter with focal lengths having an equivalent focal length of less than about 35mm. Zoom out, if necessary, and avoid extreme wide-angle shots.

Using Telephoto Settings

Telephoto focal lengths also can have a dramatic effect on your photography. Here are the most important things you need to know. In the next section, I'll concentrate on telephoto considerations that can be problematic—and how to avoid those problems.

- **Selective focus.** Long focal lengths have reduced depth-of-field within the frame, allowing you to use selective focus to isolate your subject. You can open the lens up as wide as possible to create shallow depth-of-field, or close it down a bit to allow more to be in focus. The flip side of the coin is that when you *want* to make a range of objects sharp, you'll need to use a smaller f/stop to get the depth-of-field you need. Like fire, the depth-of-field of a telephoto lens can be friend or foe. Figure 9.4 shows a photo of a statue with an ugly background, so I photographed it using the 112mm setting and the widest f/stop available to de-emphasize the background.

- **Getting closer.** Telephoto focal lengths bring you closer to wildlife, sports action, and candid subjects. No one wants to get a reputation as a surreptitious or "sneaky" photographer (except for paparazzi), but when applied to candids in an open and honest way, a long lens setting can help you capture memorable moments while retaining enough distance to stay out of the way of events as they transpire.

- **Reduced foreground/increased compression.** Telephoto focal lengths have the opposite effect of wide angles: they reduce the importance of things in the foreground by squeezing everything together. This compression even makes distant objects appear to be closer to subjects in the foreground and middle ranges. You can use this effect as a creative tool.

■ **Accentuates camera shakiness.** Telephotos magnify any camera shake. It's no wonder that image stabilization is popular in longer focal lengths.

■ **Interesting angles require creativity.** Telephoto focal lengths require more imagination in selecting interesting angles, because the "angle" you do get on your subjects is so narrow. Moving from side to side or a bit higher or lower can make a dramatic difference in a wide-angle shot, but raising or lowering a telephoto lens a few feet probably will have little effect on the appearance of the distant subjects you're shooting.

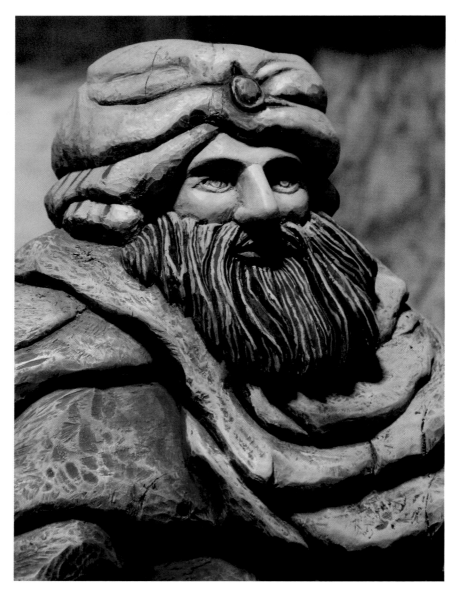

Figure 9.4
A wide f/stop and telephoto focal length helped isolate this statue from its background.

Avoiding Telephoto Lens Problems

Many of the "problems" that telephoto focal lengths pose are really just challenges and not that difficult to overcome. Here is a list of the seven most common picture maladies and suggested solutions.

■ **Symptom: flat faces in portraits.** Head-and-shoulders portraits of humans tend to be more flattering when a focal length in the 50mm to 85mm range is used. Longer focal lengths compress the distance between features like noses and ears, making the face look wider and flat. A wide-angle might make noses look huge and ears tiny when you fill the frame with a face. So stick with 50mm to 85mm focal length ranges, going longer only when you're forced to shoot from a greater distance, and wider only when shooting three-quarters/full-length portraits, or group shots.

■ **Symptom: blur due to camera shake.** Use a higher shutter speed (boosting ISO if necessary), and image stabilization, or mount your camera on a tripod, monopod, or brace it with some other support. Of those three solutions, only the first will reduce blur caused by *subject* motion; IS (image stabilization) or a tripod won't help you freeze a race car in mid-lap.

■ **Symptom: color fringes.** Chromatic aberration is the most pernicious optical problem found in telephoto focal lengths in cameras like the G1 X. There are others, including spherical aberration, astigmatism, coma, curvature of field, and similarly scary-sounding phenomena. Your only solution may be to correct the fringing in your favorite RAW conversion tool or image editor. Photoshop's Lens Correction filter offers sliders that minimize both red/cyan and blue/yellow fringing.

■ **Symptom: lines that curve inward.** Pincushion distortion is sometimes found at many telephoto focal lengths. You might find after a bit of testing that it is worse at certain focal lengths with your particular zoom lens. Like chromatic aberration, it can be partially corrected using tools like Photoshop's Lens Correction filter.

■ **Symptom: low contrast from haze or fog.** When you're photographing distant objects, a long focal length shoots through a lot more atmosphere, which generally is muddied up with extra haze and fog. That dirt or moisture in the atmosphere can reduce contrast and mute colors. Some feel that a skylight or UV filter can help, but this practice is mostly a holdover from the film days. Digital sensors are not sensitive enough to UV light for a UV filter to have much effect.

■ **Symptom: low contrast from flare.** To reduce flare from bright light sources at the periphery of the picture area, or completely outside it, avoid pointing your camera directly at the sun. Because telephoto focal length settings often create images that are lower in contrast in the first place, you'll want to be especially careful, and perhaps shade the front of the lens with your hand.

■ **Symptom: dark flash photos.** A long lens setting might make a subject that's 50 feet away look as if it's right next to you, but your camera's flash isn't fooled. You'll need extra power for distant flash shots, and probably more power than your built-in flash provides. The shoe-mount Canon 580EX II Speedlite, for example, can automatically zoom its coverage down to that of a medium telephoto lens, providing a theoretical full-power shooting aperture of about f/8 at 50 feet and ISO 400. (Try *that* with the built-in flash!) Of course, this flash is expensive and larger than your entire camera. One of the other Canon external flash units might be all you need, however. I'll explain more about flash in Chapter 10.

Image Stabilization

Image stabilization provides you with camera steadiness that's the equivalent of at least two or three shutter speed increments. This extra margin can be invaluable when you're shooting under dim lighting conditions or handholding with the camera set for its longest optical focal length of 112mm. Perhaps that shot of a foraging deer calls for a shutter speed of 1/250th second at f/5.6, and you fear that the image will be blurry. Relax, with image stabilization turned on, you can shoot at 1/250th second and get virtually the same results as if you had used 1/500th or even 1/100th second, as long as the deer doesn't decide to bound off.

Or, maybe you're shooting a high-school play without a tripod or monopod, and you'd really, really like to use 1/15th second at f/4. Assuming the actors aren't flitting around the stage at high speed, your PowerShot and its IS feature can let you grab the shot at the wide-angle position. However, keep these facts in mind:

■ **IS doesn't stop action.** Unfortunately, no image stabilization is a panacea to replace the action-stopping capabilities of a higher shutter speed. Image stabilization applies only to camera shake. You still need a fast shutter speed to freeze action. IS works great in low light, when you're using long focal lengths, and for macro photography. It's not always the best choice for action photography, unless there's enough light to allow a sufficiently high shutter speed. If so, IS can make your shot even sharper.

■ **IS slows you down.** The process of adjusting the lens elements takes time, just as autofocus does, so you might find that IS adds to the lag between when you press the shutter and when the picture is actually taken. That's another reason why image stabilization might not be a good choice for sports.

■ **Use when appropriate.** In some situations, IS can produce worse results if used while you're panning the camera from side to side during exposure. The camera can confuse the motion with camera shake and overcompensate. You might want to switch off IS when panning or when your camera is mounted on a tripod.

■ **Do you need IS at all?** Remember that an inexpensive monopod might be able to provide the same additional steadiness as IS. If you're out in the field shooting wild animals or flowers and think a tripod isn't practical, try a monopod first.

Working with Filters

If you purchase the FA-DC58C filter adapter, you can use an enormous range of 58mm filter add-ons, including close-up attachments that will help you overcome the macro focusing limitations of the G1 X. Other types of filters add a lot more versatility. Just among Cokin-style filters alone, there are hundreds of different filter models offered for special effects, color correction, neutral density, diffusion, and other applications. As you investigate the Cokin system, you'll see that its flexibility accounts for much of its popularity.

There are more than 200 different Cokin filters, but other manufacturers also produce filters and holders in the standard Cokin sizes. You can place two different square filters in the pair of slots on the holder. They're held in place by friction, so you can move them up and down to partially or fully cover the lens when you want to vary your effect. A third, circular filter, can be dropped into a special slot that's closest to the camera lens. These include star filters, polarizers, and other filters, and they can be rotated within the slot to produce a particular effect (say, to vary the amount of polarization).

Polarizers

Polarizing filters, first mentioned earlier in this chapter, are a type of filter that can provide richer and more vibrant colors while reducing some of the reflective glare that affects many photos taken in bright daylight. Polarizing filters operate in much the same way as polarized sunglasses. The polarizer itself consists of two rings; one is attached to the lens, while the outer ring rotates the polarizing glass. This lets you selectively filter out different light waves. You can rotate the ring until the effect you want is visible. The amount of glare reduction depends heavily on the angle from which you take the photograph, and the amounts of scattered light in the reflections (which is determined by the composition of the subject). Polarizers work best when the sun is low in the sky and at a 90-degree angle from the camera and subject (that is, off to your left or right shoulder). Blue sky and water, which can contain high amounts of scattered light, can be made darker and more vibrant as glare is reduced. You can also reduce or eliminate reflections from windows and other nonmetallic surfaces. Figure 9.5 shows an example of how an image can be improved with a polarizing filter.

Figure 9.5

If the sky is too light (top), a polarizing filter can darken it and enrich the other colors in your image.

Neutral-Density Filters

Although your G1 X has a built-in ND filter, found in the FUNC. menu, sometimes you can use a little more filtration. In such cases, you'll want to use an add-on filter. Neutral-density filters are one of those high-concept tools with a function that's easy to grasp: they add nothing to the image except density (by preventing some of the light from reaching the sensor), and they are neutral (so the colors remain the same). A straight gray ND (neutral-density) filter increases the amount of exposure required, so that you'll need to use a larger aperture, slower shutter speed, or higher ISO setting to achieve correct exposure with the filter in place. You can even use all three in appropriate proportions, if you like. The net effect is the same as if there were less light illuminating the subject, so extra exposure is required.

The exact amount of neutral density supplied can be found in the filter's name, which usually includes either the *filter factor* or *optical density* of the particular filter. For example, you might see neutral-density filters labeled ND2, ND4, and ND8, which would signify that these filters would require 1 stop (2X), 2 stops (4X), and 3 stops (8X), of additional exposure, respectively. If you think about the relationship between f/stops—a one-stop difference requires twice as much exposure, a two-stop difference calls for four times as much exposure—the nomenclature makes sense. Your camera's built-in filter is an 8X ND filter, and will reduce exposure by three stops; add-on filters offer different amounts of filtration.

Given the eternal quest for faster and more sensitive sensors, what good are neutral-density filters? You'll find them useful anytime you want to use a slower shutter speed or a larger f/stop in a situation in which your camera's lowest ISO setting won't allow the use of one or the other. A slow shutter speed (for creative blurring purposes) *and* wide f/stop (also for creative selective focus applications) may be almost impossible to achieve. Proper use of ND filters can give you both options. As I mentioned, you can *split* the effects among all the exposure factors: an ND8 filter (like the one built into the G1 X) has three-stops of light-blocking power that will let you use a shutter speed that is half as fast, an f/stop that is twice as large, and an ISO setting that is twice as sensitive, all in the same photograph if that's what you want.

- **Slower shutter speeds.** Your G1 X has a minimum ISO setting of ISO 100. Your lens has a minimum f/stop of f/16. So, outdoors in bright daylight you may find it impossible to use a shutter speed longer than 1/100th second. If your mountain stream is not in bright sunlight, it's still unlikely you'll be able to use a shutter speed any longer than about 1/30th to 1/15th second. That's a shame when you have a beautiful waterfall or crashing ocean waves in your viewfinder and want to add a little creative motion blur. An ND8 filter can give you the 1/2 second to several-second exposures you'll need for truly ethereal water effects.

- **Larger f/stops.** Frequently there is too much light to use the large f/stop you want to apply to reduce depth-of-field. The wide-open f/stop you prefer for selective focus applications might demand shutter speeds of 1/4,000th second or higher. With a 2X or 4X ND filter, you can use the widest f/stop available at 1/4,000th second.

- **Countering overwhelming electronic flash.** I have several older manual studio flash units that are simply too powerful for *both* my available range of f/stops and ISO settings, even when switched from full power to half power. (Newer units generally offer 1/4, 1/8, 1/16, and 1/32 power options and may be continuously variable over that or an even larger range.) An ND filter allows me to shoot flash pictures with these strobes at my camera's lowest ISO setting and apertures larger than f/8.

■ **Vanishing act.** Create your own ghost town despite a fully populated image by using a longer shutter speed. With an ND8 filter and shutter speeds of 15 to 30 seconds, moving vehicular and pedestrian traffic doesn't remain in one place long enough to register in your image. With enough neutral density, you can even make people and things vanish in full daylight.

■ **Sky and foreground balance.** A special kind of neutral density, the split ND, or graduated ND filter, is a special tool for landscape photographers. In the average scene, the sky is significantly brighter than the foreground and well beyond the ability of most digital camera sensors to capture detail in both. An ND filter that is dark at the top and clear at the bottom can even out the exposure, restoring the puffy white clouds and clear blue sky to your images. There are other types of split and graduated filters available, as you'll learn from the next section.

Split-density and graduated filters are available in both traditional round screw-in filter types as well as in square versions that can be slipped into a Cokin or similar filter holder. The most useful variety is the graduated neutral-density filter, which is a "must have" filter that belongs in any serious photographer's kit.

A graduated ND filter (or its kin, the non-graduated split-density filter) has gray coloration in its "top" half, and clear glass in its "bottom" region. In practice, though, the filter can be rotated in use so that the neutral density is placed in the bottom or left/right orientations. The filter holds back light in the neutral-density region, while allowing all the light to pass through the clear portion. The most common usage is to darken the sky in landscape photos shot in horizontal format (which would otherwise be overexposed) and allow the foreground area of the scene to be exposed normally. Because the filter can be rotated, you can use it for this purpose when shooting vertical landscape photos, as well, or, simply to darken the left, right, or bottom of an image when taking pictures in any orientation.

Infrared Filters

One of the most exciting emerging applications for digital cameras is infrared photography, which I mentioned in Chapter 8 as an "advanced" technique. IR shooting provides a new and eerie perspective on many familiar subjects. The majority of cameras are fully capable of taking photographs using only infrared illumination when equipped with a *cut-off* filter that blocks visible light and allows only IR light to continue on to the sensor. An IR filter will let you produce images with dramatic dark skies, vivid puffy white clouds, and ghostly foliage on trees. IR can be used on subjects other than landscapes, too, to image humans with strange, pale complexions, and architecture quite unlike anything you may have seen before. However, because your camera itself includes a filter designed to *pass* visible light and *block* most (but not all) infrared illumination, you'll have to shoot using very slow shutter speeds, because so little light is left for the exposure once the majority of both visible and infrared light have been removed.

Even though an IR filter seems virtually black to the human eye, and will obscure your image on the LCD, the G1 X is perfect for infrared photography, because you can view, unhindered, through the camera's optical viewfinder.

To use an IR filter, you'll almost always want to mount the camera on a tripod. First, set your white balance manually—but point the lens at a subject that reflects a lot of IR, such as grass or foliage. Then, set up the camera, frame your image, focus, and set exposure with the camera set on Manual (start with ISO 200 and about 1/4 second at f/8). You might want to use the self-timer to avoid residual camera shake that can result from pressing the shutter release button.

Review your image on the camera's LCD. If you've set the white balance correctly, the image will appear in a black-and-white or sandstone-and-gray color scheme. (See Figure 9.6.) Otherwise, the image may be tinted slightly red. You can remove color casts later in your image editor (see my book *David Busch's Digital Infrared Pro Secrets* for detailed

Figure 9.6
Infrared photography provides other-worldly effects.

instructions on post-processing IR photos). The most important thing to look for during the shooting session is proper exposure. If the image appears too dark or light, change the exposure appropriately. It might be a good idea to bracket your shots (making several exposures of more and less than your first guesstimate) in any case.

Special Effects Filters

You can make your own special effects filters. With a little work, you can sometimes duplicate the effects of filters that would be quite costly to buy, or create brand-new filters that have never been seen before outside your imagination. It's easy to manufacture new filters out of ordinary, otherwise-useless filters like skylight or UV filters. You can use a Cokin-style filter holder and make square filters.

Here are some ideas for some do-it-yourself special effects filters:

- **Glamour filter.** Take an old UV filter (it doesn't even matter if it is scratched), and carefully smear the outer edges with petroleum jelly. Such a filter is a great tool for romantic portraits of females who want to be seen with flawless skin. The smaller the center spot, the larger the area of diffusion.

- **More glamour.** A piece of stocking material or other material with texture can be used to provide even more diffusion over the entire image—or cut a hole in the middle to allow the central portion of the image to remain sharp. Many years ago, Hollywood cinematographers photographed aging stars through a chicken feather to provide the needed softening effect. (One wag pointed out that a certain actress was so wrinkled that it would be advisable to use an entire chicken, instead.)

- **Starry night.** A piece of window screen material can produce a star-point effect. The advantage of going the do-it-yourself route is that your screen "filter" can be fitted even to lenses that don't normally accept filters. Just use a large enough piece.

- **Split filters.** Get yourself a sample book of Lee or Roscoe lighting filter swatches and use pieces to construct a split neutral-density filter (use gray swatches) or split color filters. While lighting filters may not have the optical quality you need for super sharp photos, you may find them good enough for experimentation.

- **Go wild.** Anything that you can fit in front of your lens, from a kaleidoscope with the colored-speckle end removed, to diffraction gratings can be used to produce a special effects filter. You can try out various possibilities just by holding them in front of the camera lens; then convert the ones that work best into permanent make-shift filters.

10

Making Light Work for You

Successful photographers and artists have an intimate understanding of the importance of light in shaping an image. Rembrandt was a master of using light to create moods and reveal the character of his subjects. Late artist Thomas Kinkade's official tagline was "Painter of Light." Dean Collins, co-founder of Finelight Studios, revolutionized how a whole generation of photographers learned and used lighting. It's impossible to underestimate how the use of light adds to—and how misuse can detract from—your photographs.

All forms of visual art use light to shape the finished product. Sculptors don't have control over the light used to illuminate their finished work, so they must create shapes using planes and curved surfaces so that the form envisioned by the artist comes to life from a variety of viewing and lighting angles. Painters, in contrast, have absolute control over both shape and light in their work, as well as the viewing angle, so they can use both the contours of their two-dimensional subjects and the qualities of the "light" they use to illuminate those subjects to evoke the image they want to produce.

Photography is a third form of art. The photographer may have little or no control over the subject (other than posing human subjects) but can often adjust both viewing angle *and* the nature of the light source to create a particular compelling image. The direction and intensity of the light sources create the shapes and textures that we see. The distribution and proportions determine the contrast and tonal values: whether the image is stark or high key, or muted and low in contrast. The colors of the light (because even "white" light has a color balance that the sensor can detect), and how much of those colors the subject reflects or absorbs, paint the hues visible in the image.

As a PowerShot G1 X photographer, you must learn to be a painter and sculptor of light if you want to move from *taking* a picture to *making* a photograph. This chapter provides an introduction to using the two main types of illumination: *continuous* lighting (such as daylight, incandescent, or fluorescent sources) and the brief, but brilliant snippets of light we call *electronic flash*.

Continuous Illumination versus Electronic Flash

Continuous lighting is exactly what you might think: uninterrupted illumination that is available all the time during a shooting session. Daylight, moonlight, and the artificial lighting encountered both indoors and outdoors count as continuous light sources (although all of them can be "interrupted" by passing clouds, solar eclipses, a blown fuse, or simply by switching off a lamp). Indoor continuous illumination includes both the lights that are there already (such as incandescent lamps or overhead fluorescent lights indoors) and fixtures you supply yourself, including photoflood lamps or reflectors used to bounce existing light onto your subject.

The surge of light we call electronic flash is produced by a burst of photons generated by an electrical charge that is accumulated in a component called a *capacitor* and then directed through a glass tube containing xenon gas, which absorbs the energy and emits the brief flash. Electronic flash is notable because it can be much more intense than continuous lighting, lasts only a fraction of a moment, and can be much more portable than supplementary incandescent sources. It's a light source you can carry with you and use anywhere.

Indeed, your PowerShot G1 X has an electronic flash unit built in, as shown in Figure 10.1. But you can also use an external flash, either mounted on the camera's accessory shoe or used off-camera and linked with a cable to the accessory shoe with an adapter, or triggered by a slave light (which sets off a flash when it senses the firing of another unit). Studio flash units are electronic flash, too, and aren't limited to "professional"

Figure 10.1
One form of light that's always available is the built-in flash on your PowerShot G1 X.

shooters, as there are economical "monolight" (one-piece flash/power supply) units available in the $200 price range. A serious PowerShot G1 X photographer (or someone who uses a G1 X as a backup to a digital SLR) might want to buy a couple to store in a closet and use to set up a home studio, or use as supplementary lighting when traveling away from home.

There are advantages and disadvantages to each type of illumination. Here's a quick checklist of pros and cons:

- **Lighting preview—Pro: continuous lighting.** With continuous lighting, you always know exactly what kind of lighting effect you're going to get and, if multiple lights are used, how they will interact with each other. With electronic flash, the general effect you're going to see may be a mystery until you've built some experience, and you may need to review a shot on the LCD, make some adjustments, and then reshoot to get the look you want. (In this sense, a digital camera's review capabilities replace the Polaroid test shots pro photographers relied on in decades past.)

- **Lighting preview—Con: electronic flash.** While some external flash units have a modeling light function (consisting of a series of low-powered bursts that flash for a period of time), your PowerShot G1 X lacks such a capability in its internal flash, and, in any case, this feature is no substitute for continuous illumination, or an always-on modeling lamp like that found in studio flash. As the number of flash units increases, lighting previews, especially if you want to see the proportions of illumination provided by each flash, grow more complex.

- **Exposure calculation—Pro: continuous lighting.** Your PowerShot G1 X has no problem calculating exposure for continuous lighting, because the illumination remains constant and can be measured through a sensor that interprets the light reaching the viewfinder. The amount of light available just before the exposure will, in almost all cases, be the same amount of light present when the shutter is released. The PowerShot G1 X's Spot metering mode can be used to measure and compare the proportions of light in the highlights and shadows, so you can make an adjustment (such as using more or less fill light) if necessary. You can even use a handheld light meter to measure the light yourself and set the exposure in Manual mode.

- **Exposure calculation—Con: electronic flash.** Electronic flash illumination doesn't exist until the flash fires, and so can't be measured by the PowerShot G1 X's exposure sensor during the exposure. Instead, the light must be measured by interpreting the intensity of a pre-flash triggered an instant before the main flash, as it is reflected back to the camera and through the lens. If you have a do-it-yourself bent, there are handheld flash meters, too, including models that measure both flash and continuous light.

■ **Evenness of illumination—Pro/con: continuous lighting.** Of continuous light sources, daylight, in particular, provides illumination that tends to fill an image completely, lighting up the foreground, background, and your subject almost equally. Shadows do come into play, of course, so you might need to use reflectors or fill-in light sources to even out the illumination further, but barring objects that block large sections of your image from daylight, the light is spread fairly evenly. Indoors, however, continuous lighting is commonly less evenly distributed. The average living room, for example, has hot spots and dark corners. But on the plus side, you can *see* this uneven illumination and compensate with additional lamps.

■ **Evenness of illumination—Con: electronic flash.** Electronic flash units (like continuous light sources such as lamps that don't have the advantage of being located 93 million miles from the subject) suffer from the effects of their proximity. The *inverse square law*, first applied to both gravity and light by Sir Isaac Newton, dictates that as a light source's distance increases from the subject, the amount of light reaching the subject falls off proportionately to the square of the distance. In plain English, that means that a flash or lamp that's eight feet away from a subject provides only one-quarter as much illumination as a source that's four feet away (rather than half as much). (See Figure 10.2.) This translates into relatively shallow "depth-of-light."

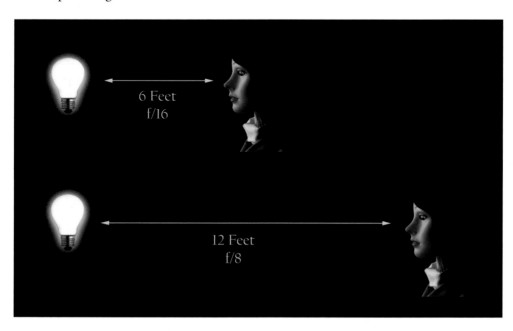

Figure 10.2
A light source that is twice as far away provides only one-quarter as much illumination.

- **Action stopping—Con: continuous lighting.** Action stopping with continuous light sources is completely dependent on the shutter speed you've dialed in on the camera. And the speeds available are dependent on the amount of light available and your ISO sensitivity setting. Outdoors in daylight, there will probably be enough sunlight to let you shoot at 1/2,000th second and f/6.3 with a non-grainy sensitivity setting of ISO 400. That's a fairly useful combination of settings if you're not using a super-telephoto with a small maximum aperture. But inside, the reduced illumination quickly has you pushing your PowerShot G1 X to its limits. For example, if you're shooting indoor sports, there probably won't be enough available light to allow you to use a 1/2,000th second shutter speed (although I routinely shoot indoor basketball at ISO 1600 and 1/500th second at f/4). In many indoor sports situations, you may find yourself limited to 1/500th second or slower.

- **Action stopping—Pro: electronic flash.** When it comes to the ability to freeze moving objects in their tracks, the advantage goes to electronic flash. The brief duration of electronic flash serves as a very high "shutter speed" when the flash is the main or only source of illumination for the photo. Your PowerShot G1 X's shutter speed may be set for 1/200th second during a flash exposure, but if the flash illumination predominates, the *effective* exposure time will be the 1/1,000th to 1/50,000th second or less duration of the flash, because the flash unit reduces the amount of light released by cutting short the duration of the flash. Figure 10.3 shows an eye-catching "hammer breaks bulb" photo by talented Cleveland photographer Kris Bosworth, who reports that syncing the flash with the event was the trickiest part of the whole experiment. The only fly in the ointment is that, if the ambient light is strong enough, it may produce a secondary, "ghost" exposure, as I'll explain later in this chapter.

- **Cost—Pro: continuous lighting.** Incandescent or fluorescent lamps are generally much less expensive than electronic flash units, which can easily cost several hundred dollars. I've used everything from desktop high-intensity lamps to reflector floodlights for continuous illumination at very little cost. There are lamps made especially for photographic purposes, too, priced up to $50 or so. Maintenance is economical, as well; many incandescent or fluorescent lamps use bulbs that cost only a few dollars.

- **Cost—Con: electronic flash.** Electronic flash units aren't particularly cheap. The lowest-cost dedicated flash designed specifically for the Canon digital cameras is about $110. (I'll tell you about specific flash units later in this chapter.) Such units are limited in features, however. Plan to spend some money to get the features that a sophisticated electronic flash offers.

- **Flexibility—Con: continuous lighting.** Because incandescent and fluorescent lamps are not as bright as electronic flash, the slower shutter speeds required (see Action stopping, above) mean that you may have to use a tripod more often, especially when shooting portraits. The incandescent variety of continuous lighting gets hot, especially in the studio, and the side effects range from discomfort (for your human models) to disintegration (if you happen to be shooting perishable foods like ice cream). The heat also makes it more difficult to add filtration to incandescent sources.

- **Flexibility—Pro: electronic flash.** Electronic flash's action-freezing power allows you to work without a tripod in the studio (and elsewhere), adding flexibility and speed when choosing angles and positions. Flash units can be easily filtered, and, because the filtration is placed over the light source rather than the lens, you don't need to use high-quality filter material. Roscoe or Lee lighting gels, which may be too flimsy to use in front of the lens, can be mounted or taped in front of your flash with ease.

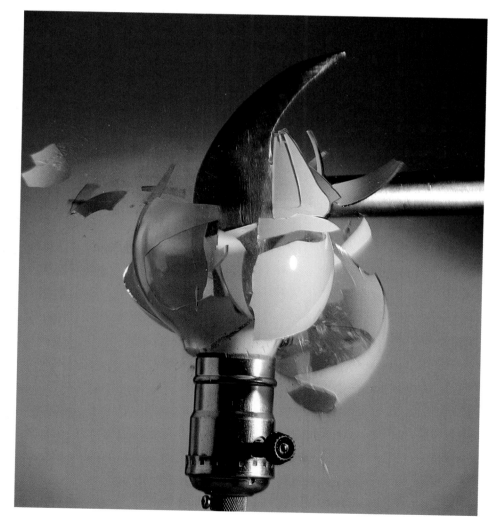

Figure 10.3
A switch that was closed by the impact of the hammer on the bulb triggered the electronic flash that froze this action.

Continuous Lighting Basics

While continuous lighting and its effects are generally much easier to visualize and use than electronic flash, there are some factors you need to take into account, particularly the color temperature of the light. (Color temperature concerns aren't exclusive to continuous light sources, of course, but the variations tend to be more extreme and less predictable than those of electronic flash.)

Color temperature, in practical terms, is how "bluish" or how "reddish" the light appears to be to the digital camera's sensor. Indoor illumination is quite warm, comparatively, and appears reddish to the sensor. Daylight, in contrast, seems much bluer to the sensor. Our eyes (our brains, actually) are quite adaptable to these variations, so white objects don't appear to have an orange tinge when viewed indoors, nor do they seem excessively blue outdoors in full daylight. Yet, these color temperature variations are real and the sensor is not fooled. To capture the most accurate colors, we need to take the color temperature into account in setting the color balance (or *white balance*) of the PowerShot G1 X—either automatically using the camera's smarts or manually, using our own knowledge and experience.

Color temperature can be confusing, because of a seeming contradiction in how color temperatures are named: warmer (more reddish) color temperatures (measured in degrees Kelvin) are the *lower* numbers, whereas cooler (bluer) color temperatures are *higher* numbers. It might not make sense to say that 3,400K is warmer than 6,000K, but that's the way it is. If it helps, think of a glowing red ember contrasted with a white-hot welder's torch, rather than fire and ice.

The confusion comes from physics. Scientists calculate color temperature from the light emitted by a theoretical object called a black body radiator, which absorbs all the radiant energy that strikes it, and reflects none at all. Such a black body not only *absorbs* light perfectly, but it *emits* it perfectly when heated (and since nothing in the universe is perfect, that makes it theoretical).

At a particular physical temperature, this imaginary object always emits light of the same wavelength or color. That makes it possible to define color temperature in terms of actual temperature in degrees on the Kelvin scale that scientists use. Incandescent light, for example, typically has a color temperature of 3,200K to 3,400K. Daylight might range from 4,500K to 6,000K. Each type of illumination we use for photography has its own color temperature range—with some cautions. The next sections will summarize everything you need to know about the qualities of these light sources.

Daylight

Daylight is produced by the sun, and so is moonlight (which is just reflected sunlight). Daylight is present, of course, during daytime hours, even when you can't see the sun. When sunlight is direct, it can be bright and harsh. If daylight is diffused by clouds, softened by bouncing off objects such as walls or your photo reflectors, or filtered by shade, it can be much dimmer and less contrasty.

Daylight's color temperature can vary quite widely. It is highest (most blue) at noon when the sun is directly overhead because the light is traveling through a minimum amount of the filtering layer we call the atmosphere. The color temperature at high noon may be 6,000K. At other times of day, the sun is lower in the sky and the particles in the air provide a filtering effect that warms the illumination to about 5,500K for most of the day. Starting an hour before dusk and for an hour after sunrise, the warm appearance of the sunlight is even visible to our eyes when the color temperature may dip to 5,000–4,500K, as shown in Figure 10.4.

Because you'll be taking so many photos in daylight, you'll want to learn how to use or compensate for the brightness and contrast of sunlight, as well as how to deal with its color temperature. I'll provide some hints later in this chapter.

Figure 10.4 At dawn and dusk, the color temperature of daylight may dip as low as 4,500K.

Incandescent/Tungsten Light

The term incandescent or tungsten illumination is usually applied to the direct descendants of Thomas Edison's original electric lamp. Such lights consist of a glass bulb that contains a vacuum, or is filled with a halogen gas, and contains a tungsten filament that is heated by an electrical current, producing photons and heat. Tungsten-halogen lamps are a variation on the basic light bulb, using a more rugged (and longer-lasting) filament that can be heated to a higher temperature, housed in a thicker glass or quartz envelope, and filled with iodine or bromine ("halogen") gases. The higher temperature allows tungsten-halogen (or quartz-halogen/quartz-iodine, depending on their construction) lamps to burn "hotter" and whiter. Although popular for automobile headlamps today, they've also been popular for photographic illumination.

Although incandescent illumination isn't a perfect light source, it's close enough that the color temperature of such lamps can be precisely calculated and used for photography without concerns about color variation (at least, until the very end of the lamp's life).

The other qualities of this type of lighting, such as contrast, are dependent on the distance of the lamp from the subject, type of reflectors used, and other factors that I'll explain later in this chapter.

Fluorescent Light/Other Light Sources

Fluorescent light has some advantages in terms of illumination, but some disadvantages from a photographic standpoint. This type of lamp generates light through an electro-chemical reaction that emits most of its energy as visible light, rather than heat, which is why the bulbs don't get as hot. The type of light produced varies depending on the phosphor coatings and type of gas in the tube. So, the illumination fluorescent bulbs produce can vary widely in its characteristics.

That's not great news for photographers. Different types of lamps have different "color temperatures" that can't be precisely measured in degrees Kelvin, because the light isn't produced by heating. Worse, fluorescent lamps have a discontinuous spectrum of light that can have some colors missing entirely. A particular type of tube can lack certain shades of red or other colors (see Figure 10.5), which is why fluorescent lamps and other alternative technologies such as sodium-vapor illumination can produce ghastly looking human skin tones. Their spectra can lack the reddish tones we associate with healthy skin and emphasize the blues and greens popular in horror movies.

Figure 10.5
The fluorescent lighting in this gym added a distinct green-ish cast to the image.

Adjusting White Balance

I showed you how to adjust white balance in Chapter 4, using the PowerShot G1 X's built-in presets and custom white balance capabilities.

In most cases, however, the PowerShot G1 X will do a good job of calculating white balance for you, so Auto can be used as your choice for the white balance setting most of the time. Use the preset values or set a custom white balance that matches the current shooting conditions when you need to. The only really problematic light sources are likely to be fluorescents. Some lighting vendors, such as GE and Sylvania, may actually provide a figure known as the *color rendering index* (or CRI), which is a measure of how accurately a particular light source represents standard colors, using a scale of 0 (some sodium-vapor lamps) to 100 (daylight and most incandescent lamps). Daylight fluorescents and deluxe cool white fluorescents might have a CRI of about 79 to 95, which is perfectly acceptable for most photographic applications. Warm white fluorescents might have a CRI of 55. White deluxe mercury vapor lights are less suitable, with a CRI of 45, while low-pressure sodium lamps can vary from CRI 0–18. As mentioned earlier in the book, the G1 X has two fluorescent light settings and a Shooting menu option for correcting illumination from mercury-vapor lamps.

Remember that if you shoot RAW, you can specify the white balance of your image when you import it into Photoshop, Photoshop Elements, or another image editor using your preferred RAW converter. While color-balancing filters that fit on the front of the lens exist, they are primarily useful for film cameras, because film's color balance can't be tweaked as extensively as that of a digital camera's sensor.

Electronic Flash Basics

Until you delve into the situation deeply enough, it might appear that serious photographers have a love/hate relationship with electronic flash. You'll often hear that flash photography is less natural looking, and that the built-in flash in most cameras should never be used as the primary source of illumination because it provides a harsh, garish look. Indeed, most "pro" cameras like the Canon EOS-1D X and EOS-5D Mark III don't have a built-in flash at all. Available ("continuous") lighting is praised, and built-in flash photography seems to be roundly denounced.

In truth, however, the bias is against *bad* flash photography. Indeed, flash has become the studio light source of choice for pro photographers, because it's more intense (and its intensity can be varied to order by the photographer), freezes action, frees you from using a tripod (unless you want to use one to lock down a composition), and has a snappy, consistent light quality that matches daylight. And even pros will concede that the built-in flash of the Canon PowerShot G1 X has some important uses as an adjunct to existing light, particularly to fill in dark shadows.

But electronic flash isn't as inherently easy to use as continuous lighting. As I noted earlier, electronic flash units are more expensive, don't show you exactly what the lighting effect will be (unless you use a second source called a *modeling light* for a preview), and the exposure of electronic flash units is more difficult to calculate accurately.

How Electronic Flash Works

The built-in flash is somewhat limited in range (Canon rates it effective out to 23 feet); you'll see why external flash units are often a good idea later in this chapter.

An electronic flash (whether built in or connected to the PowerShot G1 X through its hot shoe) is triggered at the instant of exposure, during a period when the sensor is fully exposed by the shutter. The PowerShot G1 X has a combination mechanical and electronic shutter. The shutter completely opens, at which point the flash can be triggered. This is called *1st-curtain sync*, although in the case of the G1 X there is no "curtain" (the term refers to the pair of curtains that travel across the sensor frame with so-called *focal plane* shutters). The flash fires; then, after a delay that can vary from 60 seconds to 1/2,000th second with the PowerShot G1 X, the shutter closes. If the flash is triggered just before the shutter starts to close, then *2nd-curtain sync* is used. In both cases, though, a shutter speed of 1/2000th second is the maximum that can be used to take a photo using the internal flash. External flash units are limited to a 1/250th second top shutter speed, except with units that support *high-speed sync* mode, which I'll explain later in this chapter. If you try to set the PowerShot G1 X's shutter to a faster speed in Tv or M mode while using flash, the camera will automatically adjust the shutter speed down to that model's maximum shutter speed when using flash.

Ghost Images

The difference between triggering the flash when the shutter just opens, or just when it begins to close might not seem like much. But whether you use 1st-curtain sync (the default setting) or 2nd-curtain sync (an optional setting) can make a significant difference to your photograph *if the ambient light in your scene also contributes to the image.*

At faster shutter speeds, particularly 1/500th second or faster, there isn't much time for the ambient light to register, unless it is very bright. It's likely that the electronic flash will provide almost all the illumination, so the choice of 1st-curtain sync or 2nd-curtain sync isn't very important. However, at slower shutter speeds, or with very bright ambient light levels, there is a significant difference, particularly if your subject is moving, or the camera isn't steady.

In any of those situations, the ambient light will register as a second image accompanying the flash exposure, and if there is movement (of camera or subject), that additional image will not be in the same place as the flash exposure. It will show as a ghost image and, if the movement is significant enough, as a blurred ghost image trailing in front of or behind your subject in the direction of the movement.

As I noted, when you're using 1st-curtain sync, the flash's main burst goes off the instant the shutter opens fully (a pre-flash is used to measure exposure in auto flash modes fires *before* the shutter opens). This burst produces an image of the subject on the sensor. Then, the shutter remains open for an additional period (in the range of 60 seconds to 1/2,000th second, as I said). If your subject is moving, say, toward the right side of the frame, the ghost image produced by the ambient light will produce a blur on the right side of the original subject image, making it look as if your sharp (flash-produced) image is chasing the ghost. For those of us who grew up with lightning-fast superheroes who always left a ghost trail *behind them*, that looks unnatural (see Figure 10.6).

So, Canon uses 2nd-curtain sync to remedy the situation. In that mode, the shutter opens, as before. The shutter remains open for its designated duration, and the ghost image forms. If your subject moves from the left side of the frame to the right side, the

Figure 10.6 1st-curtain sync produces an image that trails in front of the flash exposure (top), while 2nd-curtain sync creates a more "natural looking" trail behind the flash image.

ghost will move from left to right, too. *Then*, about 1.5 milliseconds before the second shutter curtain closes, the flash is triggered, producing a nice, sharp flash image *ahead* of the ghost image. Voilà! We have monsieur *Speed Racer* outdriving his own trailing image.

Avoiding Sync Speed Problems

In the past, before cameras and flash units became as sophisticated as they are today, photographers sometimes ran into problems when the camera's shutter speed was too fast to synchronize properly with the flash. Nowadays, I generally end up with sync speed problems only when shooting using third-party flash units, rather than my PowerShot G1 X's built-in flash or a Canon dedicated Speedlite. That's because if you're using either type of "smart" flash, the camera knows that a strobe is attached, and remedies any unintentional goof in shutter speed settings. That luxury is not available when using non-dedicated, "dumb" flash units.

In addition, the PowerShot G1 X can sync with the external flash at any speed up to 1/250th second, and when using a Canon dedicated external flash it can sync at speeds up to 1/4,000th second. If you happen to set the PowerShot G1 X's shutter to a faster speed in Tv or M mode, the camera will automatically adjust the shutter speed down to the fastest allowable speed on the G1 X. In Av, P, or any of the more automatic shooting modes, where the PowerShot G1 X selects the shutter speed, it will never choose a shutter speed that's too high when using flash.

Determining Exposure

Calculating the proper exposure for an electronic flash photograph is a bit more complicated than determining the settings by continuous light. The right exposure isn't simply a function of how far away your subject is (which the PowerShot G1 X can figure out based on the autofocus distance that's locked in just prior to taking the picture). Various objects reflect more or less light at the same distance so, obviously, the camera needs to measure the amount of light reflected back and through the lens. Yet, as the flash itself isn't available for measuring until it's triggered, the PowerShot G1 X has nothing to measure.

The solution is to fire the flash twice. The initial shot is a pre-flash that can be analyzed, then followed by a main flash that's given exactly the calculated intensity needed to provide a correct exposure. As a result, the primary flash may be longer for distant objects and shorter for closer subjects, depending on the required intensity for exposure. This through-the-lens evaluative flash exposure system operates whenever the built-in internal flash is used, or if you have attached a Canon dedicated flash unit to the PowerShot G1 X.

Guide Numbers

Guide numbers, usually abbreviated GN, are a way of specifying the power of an electronic flash in a way that can be used to determine the right f/stop to use at a particular shooting distance and ISO setting. In fact, before automatic flash units became prevalent, the GN was actually used to do just that. Today, guide numbers are most useful for comparing the power of various flash units, and Canon doesn't even provide GN figures for the G1 X's built-in flash. They are available for external flash units, described later in this chapter, and you can use the guide numbers to directly compare how powerful these add-on flashes are.

Using the Built-In Flash

The Canon PowerShot G1 X's built-in flash is a handy accessory because it is available as required, without the need to carry an external flash around with you constantly. This section explains how to use the built-in flash in the various shooting modes. This explanation is not as quick and easy as you might expect, because this camera, as you've already seen, is quite sophisticated in its general shooting capabilities, and it's also no slouch in the area of flash control options. There are numerous features and functions that I need to describe before I get into the nitty-gritty of which settings to use when. I also need to make a few general points about the nature of your camera's built-in flash.

The Always-Ready Flash

Although this is an obvious point, it's worth emphasizing. The built-in flash of the PowerShot G1 X is always available for use once you pop it up by pressing the flash button on the top-left edge of the camera. One bit of good news in this area: as I'll discuss a bit later in this section, with the PowerShot G1 X, unlike some other cameras in this class, you can *always* force the flash to its Off setting, even when shooting in the Auto mode and even if the flash is elevated. Otherwise, if you need to use it to fill in dark shadows as fill flash when shooting in sunlight, pop up the flash, and it's ready to go. (See Figure 10.7.)

Figure 10.7
The G1 X's built-in flash is instantly ready for fill-flash duties to brighten shadows in daylight shots.

Range and Angle of View

The PowerShot G1 X's built-in flash unit has several virtues, but extensive range is not one of them. As I mentioned above, the G1 X flash's effective range is no more than about 23 feet at the wide-angle zoom setting. The range is reduced to about 10 feet at the 112mm telephoto position, because the light emitted by the flash is "cropped" by the tighter view, and less of the illumination is used to expose the photo. In other words, every time the flash fires, it sends out the same size or width beam of light; it does not vary the shape of the beam to match the zoom factor of your shot. So, if you are taking a wide-angle shot, the flash may not fully cover the area in the scene, or, if you have zoomed your lens in for a telephoto shot, a good portion of the flash's coverage may be "wasted" by falling outside of the field of view of the lens.

This range is less powerful than the larger external flash units available for the PowerShot. Therefore, you need to be mindful of the fact that the built-in flash can be a useful tool for filling in shadows and grabbing snapshots indoors, but it's not a substitute for a stronger, dedicated unit such as those used by photojournalists and wedding photographers.

When you're deciding whether the built-in flash is likely to be of use in a particular situation, here are a couple of important factors to keep in mind: distance and ISO setting. The farther away your subject is from the camera, the greater the light fall-off, thanks to the inverse square law discussed earlier. Keep in mind that a subject that's twice as far away receives only one-quarter as much light, which is two f/stops worth. Also, the higher the ISO sensitivity, the more photons captured by the sensor. So, doubling the sensitivity from ISO 100 to 200 produces the same effect as, say, opening up your lens from f/8 to f/5.6.

Available Settings for the Built-in Flash

Now it's just about time to get into the details of how to work with the settings for the PowerShot G1 X's built-in flash. As I've indicated, though, the flash system with this camera is remarkably sophisticated for a compact camera, and I need to go over a few general points about how the flash settings are structured before I discuss the details of the various settings.

The main point to bear in mind when working with the built-in flash is that your choices of flash settings will change, depending on other choices you have made in setting up the camera for your shot. There are three levels of decisions you can make when you're deciding how the built-in flash should operate, and all three decisions, one after the other, have an impact on how the flash will operate when you press the shutter button to take the picture.

First, you choose a shooting mode; second, you can press the Flash button to choose a general status for the flash; and third, if you're using flash, you can use the Flash Control submenu to make further choices about how the flash will operate when and if it fires. Of course, you don't have to consciously make all three of those choices; if you don't think about them yourself, the camera will use its default settings and make the choices for you. But I'm assuming you are the sort of photographer who wants to take control over such decisions. So let's look at those choices in more detail now.

Mode Dial: Shooting Mode

The shooting mode you select with the mode dial can have considerable influence over the behavior of the flash. In some modes (for example, the Fireworks and Sports versions of SCN mode), the flash is forced off and there's nothing you can do to turn it on—except switch out of Fireworks or Sports mode. In many of the SCN modes and Auto mode, the camera will initially set the flash to Auto, but will let you override that choice. However, in those more automatic shooting modes, although you can choose whether the flash is on or off, your other choices of flash behavior, such as controlling flash output and shutter sync, are limited. In the most advanced shooting modes, M, Av, Tv, and P, most of the decisions about the use of flash are completely within your control.

When the internal flash is elevated, press the right cursor/Flash button and a selection menu pops up on the screen showing the available flash modes. Table 10.1 shows your choices. I'll explain what each mode does next.

Flash Control Submenu: Other Settings

While using the right cursor/Flash button to select a flash mode, you can press the MENU button at any time to produce the Built-in Flash Settings screen, shown in Figure 10.8. It has six options, five of which are shown in Figure 10.8. In the Flash Control submenu you can pick from an array of further options for how the flash will operate if it does fire. This array of options will vary according to the other choices you have made. Right now, I'm going to discuss all of the possible choices that can be made from this submenu, even though you're never going to see all of the choices at any one time.

As a reminder, there are three ways to get to the Flash Control submenu: select Flash Control from the Shooting menu; press the right cursor/Flash button once lightly, then the MENU button; or hold down the right cursor/Flash button until a different Flash Control submenu appears. In all cases, the flash must be elevated to access this menu. If you just need the Flash Output/Flash Exposure Compensation setting, you can select that item by pressing the FUNC./SET key and selecting the Flash item (seventh entry down on the FUNC. menu).

Table 10.1 Flash Modes

Exposure Mode	Flash Options
Manual - M	Flash On/Flash Off
Aperture Priority - Av	Flash On, Slow Syncro, Flash Off
Shutter Priority - Tv	Flash On, Flash Off
Program mode - P	Auto, Flash On, Slow Synchro, Flash Off
Auto	Auto, Flash Off
SCN	
Movie Digest (For still photos only)	Auto, Flash On, Slow Synchro, Flash Off
Portrait/Landscape/Kids & Pets/Smart Shutter/Beach /Underwater/Foliage/Snow/ Stitch Assist	Auto, Flash On, Flash Off
Sports/High speed Burst HQ/Night Scene/ Fireworks	Disabled
Creative Filters	
Nostalgic/Fisheye/Miniature/Toy Camera/ Monochrome/Super Vivid/Poster Effect/ Color Accent/ Color Swap/	Auto, Flash On, Flash Off
HDR	Disabled
Movie Mode	Disabled

Here are all the choices that may be available on the Flash Control submenu, depending on the context:

■ **Flash Mode.** This option can be set to either Manual or Auto. Now, here's a slightly tricky point to be aware of: This is one of two uses of the term "Auto" in connection with the operation of the flash, with two different meanings. Here is what "Auto" means in this case: Unlike the setting of Auto as opposed to On or Off, which controls *whether* the flash will fire, this setting of Auto controls *how* the flash will be fired—that is, through automatic exposure control, or manual setting of the flash output (which we'll discuss next). In many cases, such as with the Auto shooting mode and almost all of the SCN modes, this option is not available on the Flash Control submenu, because the camera sets Flash mode to Auto without

Figure 10.8
The Built-in
Flash Settings
screen.

asking you. Also, when the shooting mode is set to Manual, the camera sets Flash mode to Manual, again without consulting you. The only times this setting is available for you to set are when the Shooting mode is set to Av or Tv.

■ **Flash Exposure Compensation.** This setting is available only when Flash mode (see above) is set to Auto, meaning the camera will use its metering to determine the intensity of the flash exposure. The Flash Exposure Compensation setting is analogous to the standard exposure compensation setting. Although the camera will initially determine the correct flash exposure, you have the option of dialing in positive or negative amounts of flash output, relative to that automatic setting. The adjustment is displayed numerically in 1/3 EV steps, up to 2 full steps positive or negative. When the Flash mode is set to Manual, this option stays available, except that its name changes to Flash Output, discussed next. See Figure 10.9.

■ **Flash Output.** As noted above, this setting is the counterpart to Flash Exposure Compensation, when Flash mode is set to Manual (see Figure 10.10). In that case, you can dial in the amount of flash intensity, except that, because the flash exposure will be manual, you are actually determining the *absolute* amount of flash to be emitted, rather than the relative amount, as with Flash Exposure Compensation. When using the built-in flash, your choices for Flash Output are Minimum, Medium, or Maximum. If you use that setting, you are responsible for setting the

Figure 10.9
The Flash Exposure Composition mode setting on the Flash Control sub-menu can be set to either Auto or Manual, which determines whether or not the camera uses metering to determine the flash output.

Figure 10.10
When Flash mode is set to Manual, the Flash Output setting is available for you to set at Minimum, Medium, or Maximum.

camera so that the image is properly exposed; the camera will not be using any automatic exposure settings to determine the proper flash output. Up to 22 different output levels are possible with the Speedlite 580EX II, and up to 19 output levels with other Speedlites.

■ **Shutter Sync.** You can choose 1st-curtain sync, which fires the flash as soon as the shutter is completely open (this is the default mode). Alternatively, you can select 2nd-curtain sync, which fires a pre-flash used to measure exposure as soon as the shutter release is pressed down all the way, but before the shutter opens, and then triggers a second flash at the end of the exposure, just before the shutter starts to close. This action allows photographing a blurred trail of light of moving objects with sharp flash exposures at the beginning and the end of the exposure, as I described earlier in this chapter. This setting is available in the M, Av, Tv, and P shooting modes, as well as in the Quick Shot shooting mode on the PowerShot G1 X. I discussed 2nd-curtain sync earlier in regards to using it to reverse the direction of "ghost" images caused by a secondary ambient light exposure.

■ **Red-Eye Correction.** This setting is available in most SCN shooting modes, but not for the advanced modes, P, Av, Tv, and M. With this option, the camera attempts to apply digital corrective measures to remove red areas near the eyes. You should note that, although all images you take will be processed somewhat by the camera for sharpness, noise, contrast, and the like, this option applies a form of processing that goes beyond those normal adjustments in that it can actually alter the content of the image, so you should be sure you want to take that risk before activating it. Remember that this option also can be applied to images after the fact, through the Playback menu.

■ **Red-Eye Lamp.** This option, also, is available in the great majority of shooting modes. This feature is distinct from Red-Eye Correction; this one causes the camera to shine its bright lamp into the subject's eyes for an instant before the flash in an effort to cause his or her pupils to contract (assuming the subject is looking at the camera), thereby reducing the red-eye effect, as I explained in Chapter 4.

■ **Safety FE.** This setting is available in the Av, Tv, and P shooting modes on the G1 X. It is available only when Flash mode is set to Auto, meaning the flash intensity is determined through the camera's autoexposure system. This setting, which can be set either On or Off, acts as a safety net. If the camera senses that the image will be overexposed, if this option is activated, the camera adjusts the aperture or shutter speed to reduce the exposure so as to avoid blowing out the highlights. There is one other aspect of this setting that you should bear in mind. On the G1 X, it is possible to set the shutter speed as high as 1/2,000th second, even when using flash. However, if Safety FE is set to Off, then the highest shutter speed that can be used with flash is 1/500th second.

- **Slow Synchro.** This setting is available for you to set in a few shooting modes, including Av and P. In several other modes, it is set to On and cannot be changed. When this option is turned on, the camera will set the shutter speed slower than it otherwise would, in order to allow time for the ambient light to expose the background, so the final image is not overwhelmed by the portion that is illuminated by the flash. This option is accessed through the Flash button on the G1 X. When Slow Synchro is available on the G1 X, it appears as one more option along with Auto, On, and Off on the Flash button's menu of options.

Using Built-In Flash with the Various Shooting Modes

We have now explored all of the options that are available for using the PowerShot G1 X's built-in flash. As we have seen, although the little unit is not very powerful in terms of its flash intensity, it comes armed with an impressive set of control options that make it a very versatile and useful tool. Now, to make it clearer how these settings work in practice, I'm going to go through the various shooting modes briefly to point out just how the built-in flash acts in those modes, and what flash settings are available in each of them.

Auto Mode

When the PowerShot G1 X is set to the Auto shooting mode, the built-in flash will initially be set to Auto, and it will fire when needed to provide extra illumination in low-light situations, or when your subject matter is backlit and could benefit from some fill flash—with a few exceptions. You have the option of turning the flash off, which is good if you're in a location with a "no-flash zone." However, you cannot force the flash to be on; if you want flash, you have to rely on the camera's native intelligence to figure out if the flash will actually be fired. You can activate Red-Eye Correction and the Red-Eye Lamp. Other settings, such as Flash Exposure Compensation, are not available.

Program Mode

In P mode, just about all of the flash control options are available for you to set. However, you cannot set Flash Mode to Manual, and, therefore, you cannot control the absolute amount of flash (Flash Output). You can, however, adjust the relative amount of flash (Flash Exposure Compensation) and you can control the flash's other settings.

Manual, Aperture Priority, and Shutter Priority Modes

In M, Av, and Tv modes, virtually all of the flash control settings are available, except that you can't set the flash to Auto (the "Auto" meaning that the camera decides whether to fire the flash); if you want the flash to fire in either of these shooting modes, the flash has to be set to On. The other flash control settings are almost all available, although, on the G1 X, Slow Synchro is not available in M or Tv mode. Flash mode cannot be set to Auto (the "Auto" meaning the camera determines the amount of flash) in M mode.

SCN Modes and Special G1 X Modes (Low Light and Quick Shot)

In the various SCN modes there are various flash control options, depending on the nature of the shooting scenario. On the G1 X, in Sports and Fireworks modes the flash is always turned off. In most of the SCN modes the flash is set to Auto, and the only options available from the Flash Control menu are Red-Eye Correction and Red-Eye Lamp.

If you happen to be shooting a sports or fireworks photo and do want to use flash for some reason, you will have to switch to another shooting mode. However, if you're using any one of the automatic modes (including Auto) and decide that you definitely *don't* want the flash to fire—in a museum with a "no flash" rule for example—you're in luck. With the PowerShot G1 X Canon has expressed its confidence in the ability of its users to make their own decisions about turning off the flash. So, unlike the situation with some other compact cameras, with the PowerShot G1 X, you always have the option of turning the flash to its "Off" setting, ensuring that it will not fire, even if you enter the museum's simulation of the inside of King Tut's tomb and the door clanks shut behind you.

Using FE Lock

If you want to lock flash exposure for a subject that is not centered in the frame, you can use the FE Lock button (*) to lock in a specific flash exposure. First, you have to make sure the flash is set to On, not Auto. Then, depress and hold the shutter button halfway to lock in focus, center the viewfinder on the subject you want to correctly expose, and press the * button. The pre-flash fires and calculates exposure, displaying the * on the LCD screen to show that the exposure is locked. Then, recompose your photo and press the shutter down the rest of the way to take the photo. Of course, this procedure works only when the camera is using its automatic metering to determine the flash exposure. It will work at all times in P mode; when you're using Tv or Av mode, you need to make sure that Flash mode is set to Auto. (It won't work in M mode, because the Flash mode is always set to Manual in that shooting mode.)

Using External Electronic Flash

Canon offers a broad range of accessory electronic flash units that will work with the PowerShot G1 X. For such a small camera, many of them are a bit of overkill, and they are larger than the G1 X itself. (See Figure 10.11.) They can be mounted to the flash accessory shoe, or used off-camera with a dedicated cord that plugs into the flash shoe to maintain full communications with the camera for all special features. They range from the Speedlite 580EX II, which can correctly expose subjects up to 24 feet away at f/11 and ISO 200, to the 270EX, which is good out to 9 feet at f/11 and ISO 200. (You'll get greater ranges at even higher ISO settings, of course.)

A special case is the Canon Speedlite 600EX-RT, which was announced as I was writing this chapter. It's too soon to know whether the PowerShot G1 X will support this high-end flash unit, which costs almost as much as the camera itself. Odds are it will work just fine, but not using the new radio-controlled modes. While it's unlikely that anyone will purchase the 600EX-RT specifically for use with the G1 X, I expect many Canon G1 X owners who also have more advanced EOS digital SLRs (such as the 5D Mark III) will want to get extra use of their flash with the PowerShot, too.

Another special case, for those who do a lot of macro photography, are the Canon Macro Twin Lite MT-24EX, and Macro Ring Lite MR-14EX, which clip onto the front of the camera, attaching to the Macro Light Adapter MLA-DC1. To use the adapter, you'll need to remove the protective ring covering the bayonet around the lens. Just press the button located to the lower right of the lens (as seen when you're holding the camera with its lens facing you). It will twist right off.

When you attach one of the compatible Canon Speedlites, you will notice some changes in the displays on the LCD screen and menus of the PowerShot G1 X. First, once the external flash is attached, the built-in flash is disabled and cannot be elevated, let alone

Figure 10.11
Some of Canon's larger Speedlites are bigger than the PowerShot G1 X itself.

fire or be controlled, even if the external flash is turned off. Second, once the non-slave external unit is attached and turned on, you will see an orange-red lightning bolt on the right side of the screen, indicating that an external flash is attached. You will never see any other flash icon, such as the icon for Auto or Off, because those settings would have no meaning once you have decided to use an external flash. Also, the Flash Control submenu will have different settings, depending on what flash unit you have attached. For example, you likely will have a greater range of Flash Exposure Compensation and Flash Output settings available than with the built-in flash, and there may be a setting for Hi-speed sync, along with 1st-curtain and 2nd-curtain sync.

Here are some details about the various external flash units that are compatible with the PowerShot G1 X.

Speedlite 270EX

This Canon Speedlite (shown in Figure 10.12) is small enough at five ounces to fit in a pocket, and, instead of zooming, uses two fixed coverage levels for 28mm and 50mm focal lengths. It offers bounce-lighting capabilities, and uses two AA batteries, which provide enough power to recycle the unit in four seconds between flashes.

Figure 10.12
The Canon 270EX is small and makes a good add-on flash for the PowerShot G1 X.

Speedlite 270EX II

This $170 ultra-compact unit is Canon's most fully featured entry-level Speedlite, and suitable for G1 X owners who want a simple strobe for occasional use, without sacrificing the ability to operate it as a wireless slave unit. With a GN of 89, it provides a little extra pop for fill flash applications. It has vertical bounce capabilities of up to 90 degrees, and can be switched between Tele modes to Normal (28mm full-frame coverage) at a reduced guide number of 72.

The 270EX II functions as a wireless slave unit triggered by any Canon EOS unit or flash (such as the 580EX II) with a Master function. It also has the new flash release function, with a two-second delay that lets you reposition the flash. There's a built-in AF-assist beam, and this 5.5-ounce, 2.6 × 2.6 × 3–inch unit is powered by just two AA-size batteries.

Speedlite 320EX

This $249 flash has a GN of 105. Lightweight and more pocket-sized than the 430EX II or 580EX II, this bounceable (both horizontally and vertically) flash has some interesting features, including a built-in LED video light that can be used for shooting movies, or as a modeling light or even AF-assist beam when shooting with Live View. Canon says that this efficient LED light can provide up to four hours of illumination with a set of AA batteries. It can be used as a wireless slave unit, and has a new flash release function that allows the shutter to be triggered remotely with a two-second delay.

Speedlite 430EX II

This affordable electronic flash is nearly four times as powerful as the 270EX, and has zoom coverage from 24mm to 105mm. If you want to use this with your dSLR, too, it has a wide-angle pullout panel that covers the area of a 14mm lens on a full-frame camera, and automatic conversion to the cropped frame area of some Canon digital cameras. The 430EX also communicates white balance information with your dSLR camera, and has its own AF assist beam. It, too, uses AA batteries, and offers recycle times of 0.1 to 3.7 seconds for 200 to 1,400 flashes, depending on subject distance.

Speedlite 580EX II

This flash is the second-most powerful unit the company offers, and probably is a bit of overkill for the PowerShot G1 X. It's slightly more than twice as powerful as the 430 EX II, and has a zoom flash head that covers the full frame of lenses from 24mm wide angle to 105mm telephoto. (There's a flip-down wide-angle diffuser that spreads the flash to cover a 14mm lens's field of view, too.) The unit offers full-swivel, 180 degrees in either direction, and has its own built-in AF assist beam. Powered by economical AA-size batteries, the unit recycles in 0.1 to 6 seconds, and can squeeze 100 to 700 flashes from a set of alkaline batteries. (See Figure 10.13.) Its guide number is 190 at ISO 100 and the 105mm flash zoom setting.

Figure 10.13
The Canon Speedlite 580EX II is a powerful shoe-mount flash.

Speedlite 600EX-RT

This unit was introduced to replace the 580EX II, and has the same basic features as its predecessor, with some new touches. For example, where previous Canon flash units used pre-flashes to communicate with Canon cameras, the 600EX-RT adds radio communication to the mix (although it can still use the older system to link with cameras introduced prior to 2012).

It can control five groups of flashes, includes a filter holder (light orange and dark orange are included to balance the flash with incandescent illumination), and includes beefier construction (including a re-designed hot shoe), an improved back-panel LCD, and an upgrade to the built-in AF assist beam to increase compatibility with cameras like the Canon EOS-1D X and EOS-5D Mark III.

Its guide number is a bit higher, although Canon's specs don't make that obvious. It's rated at GN 197 at ISO 100, but with the flash head at 200mm. That means it reaches farther out into the inky blackness than the 580EX II (which is spec'ed using a 105mm zoom setting). Indeed, the 600EX-RT is the first Canon flash unit to *have* a rating for a 200mm (full frame) focal length. The unit actually zooms to embrace the fields of view of all lenses from 20mm to 200mm, which helps justify its $629 (street) price tag. This is likely to be a luxury item for most Canon photographers, whether they are using the G1 X or not.

More Advanced Lighting Techniques

As you advance in your Canon PowerShot G1 X photography, you'll want to learn more sophisticated lighting techniques, using more than just straight-on flash, or using just a single flash unit. Entire books have been written on lighting techniques. I'm going to provide a quick introduction to some of the techniques you should be considering.

Using External Flash Units

Your PowerShot G1 X can easily trigger external flash units, including those of the non-Canon variety, such as studio flashes. The secret is to use a radio control or optical device to trigger the external units. The accessory flashes must have receivers, of course. Optical slave units are being replaced by radio units, like the one shown in Figure 10.14.

Although traditional optical triggers are inexpensive (the transmitters can cost $30, and many studio flash units have optical receivers built-in), they have some drawbacks when used with modern digital cameras. For example, those who try to use their camera's built-in flashes to trigger optical slaves are often surprised to discover that their camera's pre-flash sets off the slave flash *before* the picture is taken. Not all slaves have a so-called "digital" mode that ignores the pre-flash and waits for the main flash.

Figure 10.14
Radio controls allow your PowerShot to trigger external flash units.

Radio transmitters are virtually foolproof. They cost more, and require a transmitter on at least one of the slave flash units (the others can often be triggered by the flash of the one with the receiver) but may include perks like the ability to adjust the output level of the remote flash units at the camera transmitter. (I like Radio Poppers for that reason.) (www.radiopopper.com.)

Diffusing and Softening the Light

Direct light can be harsh and glaring, especially if you're using the flash built into your camera, or an auxiliary flash mounted in the hot shoe and pointed directly at your subject. The first thing you should do is stop using direct light (unless you're looking for a stark, contrasty appearance as a creative effect). There are a number of simple things you can do with both continuous and flash illumination.

- **Use window light.** Light coming in a window can be soft and flattering, and a good choice for human subjects. Move your subject close enough to the window that its light provides the primary source of illumination. You might want to turn off other lights in the room, particularly to avoid mixing daylight and incandescent light.

- **Use fill light.** Your PowerShot G1 X's built-in flash makes a perfect fill-in light for the shadows, brightening inky depths with a kicker of illumination when it's switched on.

- **Bounce the light.** As I noted, some external electronic flash units mounted on the PowerShot G1 X usually have a swivel that allows them to be pointed up at a ceiling for a bounce light effect. You can also bounce the light off a wall. You'll want the ceiling or wall to be white or have a neutral gray color to avoid a color cast.

- **Use reflectors.** Another way to bounce the light is to use reflectors or umbrellas that you can position yourself to provide a greater degree of control over the quantity and direction of the bounced light. Good reflectors can be pieces of foamboard, Mylar, or a reflective disk held in place by a clamp and stand. Although some expensive umbrellas and reflectors are available, spending a lot isn't necessary. A simple piece of white foamboard does the job beautifully. Umbrellas have the advantage of being compact and foldable, while providing a soft, even kind of light. They're relatively cheap, too, with a good 40-inch umbrella available for as little as $20. (See Figure 10.15 for an example.)

- **Use diffusers.** Some other vendors offer clip-on diffusers like the one shown in Figure 10.16, that fit over your electronic flash head and provide a soft, flattering light. These add-ons are more portable than umbrellas and other reflectors, yet provide a nice diffuse lighting effect.

Figure 10.15
A reflector like an umbrella makes the perfect diffuse illumination for informal soft-focus portraits like this one.

Figure 10.16
Some soft boxes use Velcro strips to attach to third-party flash units (like the one shown) or any Canon medium-sized or larger external flash.

Downloading and Editing Your Images

Taking the picture is only half the work, and, in some cases, only half the fun. After you've captured some great images and have them safely stored on your Canon PowerShot G1 X's memory card, you'll need to transfer them from your camera and memory card to your computer, where they can be organized, fine-tuned in an image editor, and prepared for web display, printing, or some other final destination.

Fortunately, there are lots of software utilities and applications to help you do all these things. This chapter will introduce you to a few of them.

What's in the Box?

Your Canon PowerShot G1 X came with software programs on CD for both Windows PCs and Macs. Pop the CD into your computer and it will self-install a selection of these useful applications and utilities. Manuals for the key programs are included on CD, too, but here's a summary of what you get on the Canon Digital Solutions disk: ZoomBrowser EX/Image Browser, Camera Window, PhotoStitch, Digital Photo Professional, Movie Uploader for YouTube, and the PowerShot G1 X Camera User Guide.

ZoomBrowser EX/ImageBrowser

This is an image viewing and editing application for Windows PCs (the equivalent program for Macs is called ImageBrowser and performs the same functions). You can organize, sort, classify, and rename files, and convert JPEG files in batches. This utility is especially useful for printing index sheets of groups of images. It can also prepare images for e-mailing. It works with RAW Image Task for converting CR2 files to some other format, and it can be used to select images for merging using PhotoStitch.

When you connect your G1 X to your computer using a USB cable, ZoomBrowser first loads the CameraWindow DC utility, shown in Figure 11.1. There are three functions with this window. You can import images from the camera, choosing to preview the images to be transferred by date shot (as in Figure 11.2), by folder on the memory card, only the images that have not yet been transferred, or all the images on the memory card. Click on the images you'd like to transfer, then click the Import button in the lower-left corner of the window. The CameraWindow utility can also be used to make certain limited camera settings from your computer. You can select a start-up image, choose sounds, or select a theme, as shown in Figure 11.3.

Once you've transferred photos, you can do simple editing using the ZoomBrowser window that appears when you close CameraWindow. (See Figure 11.4.) The simple image-editing facilities of ZoomBrowser allow red-eye correction, brightness/contrast and color correction, manipulating sharpness, trimming photos, and a few other functions. For more complex editing, you can transfer images directly from this application to Digital Photo Professional, Photoshop, or another image editor.

Figure 11.1

ZoomBrowser EX's CameraWindow DC utility pops up when you connect the camera to your computer with a USB cable.

Figure 11.2
Select which
files on the
memory card to
download from
the camera to
the computer.

Figure 11.3
You can change
camera settings
from your
computer.

Figure 11.4
ZoomBrowser allows organizing your images and performing simple fixes.

PhotoStitch

This Windows/Mac utility allows you to take several JPEG images and combine them to create a panorama in a single new file. You can choose the images to be merged in ZoomBrowser and then transfer them to PhotoStitch, or operate the utility as a stand-alone module and select the images using the standard File > Open commands (see Figure 11.5).

Digital Photo Professional

While far from a Photoshop replacement, Digital Photo Professional is a useful image-editing program that helps you organize, trim, correct, and print images. You can make RAW adjustments, correct tonal curves, color tone, color saturation, sharpness, as well as brightness and contrast. Especially handy are the "recipes" that can be developed and saved so that a given set of corrections can be kept separate from the file itself, and, if desired, applied to other images (see Figure 11.6).

Movie Uploader for YouTube

This is a simple utility that does nothing but allow you to create a list of movies that you've shot with your PowerShot G1 X, and then queue them for uploading to YouTube. You can assign a title to your video, append a description, mark each with a Publish checkmark when they're ready to go, and then click Upload. You'll be asked for your YouTube username (which you can register permanently with the utility) and password; then click Log In to begin. (See Figure 11.7.)

Figure 11.5
Panoramas are easy to create with PhotoStitch.

Figure 11.6
Digital Photo Professional will never replace Photoshop, but it has some basic image-editing features.

Figure 11.7
Movie Uploader
for YouTube
makes it easy to
upload all your
PowerShot G1
X videos.

Transferring Your Photos

While it's rewarding to capture some great images and have them ensconced in your camera, eventually you'll be transferring them to your laptop or PC, whether you're using a Windows or Macintosh machine. You have three options for image transfer: direct transfer over a USB cable; automated transfer using a card reader and transfer software such as ZoomBrowser EX/ImageBrowser or, if you've installed it, Adobe Photoshop Elements Photo Downloader; or manual transfer using drag and drop from a memory card inserted in a card reader.

Direct Transfer

There are some advantages to transferring photos directly from your G1 X to a computer. The destination computer doesn't need to have a card reader; all it requires is a USB port. So, if you have the USB cable that came with your camera, you can transfer photos to any computer that has the Canon utility software installed. However, direct transfer uses your G1 X's internal battery power, while removing the card and transferring the photos with a card reader installed on the destination computer does not.

You can select which images are transferred to the computer, or transfer all the images, both RAW and JPEG, that are on the memory card. Just connect your camera to the computer using a USB cable, and either the Canon software will pop up or another file transfer program you may have installed, such as the Photoshop Elements Photo Downloader Utility will appear. Or, the file transfer program built into your computer's operating system may offer to do the job.

Elements' downloader includes a simple dialog box, like the one shown in Figure 11.8, and a more advanced set of choices. In the simple dialog box, you can choose the destination folder, whether to rename files (and a filename template if you do decide to rename them), and the choice of deleting the original photos from your memory card after they've been transferred, or leaving them on the card. I prefer the latter; it's best not to erase images until you're *positive* they've been transferred correctly and, in any case, reformatting the memory card in your camera rather than just deleting its old files is a better choice for starting over with a "clean" card.

Figure 11.8
You can rename images as they are downloaded using Photoshop Elements' downloader.

The advanced dialog box lets you choose individual files to download, selecting from a thumbnail preview of the image on your camera. You can apply advanced options, such as automatic red-eye repair, or import the images into a suggested Elements "photo stack" (a group of like images organized for easier browsing). You can even add a copyright notice to the data embedded within your images.

Using a Card Reader and Software

You can also use a memory card reader and software to transfer photos and automate the process using the Canon utility, Photoshop Elements' Photo Downloader, or the downloading program supplied with some other third-party applications. This method is more frugal in its use of your G1 X's battery and can be faster if you have a speedy USB 3.0 or FireWire card reader attached to an appropriate port.

The installed software automatically remains in memory as you work, and it recognizes when a memory card is inserted in your card reader; you don't have to launch it yourself. With Photoshop Elements Photo Downloader, you can click Get Photos to begin the transfer of all images immediately or choose Advanced Dialog to produce a dialog box like the one shown in Figure 11.9, and then select which images to download from the memory card by marking them with a check. You can select the photos you want to transfer, plus options such as Automatically Fix Red Eyes. Start the download, and a confirmation dialog box like the one in Figure 11.10 shows the progress.

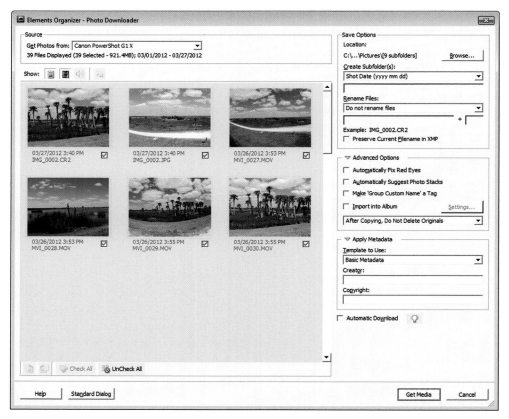

Figure 11.9
With Advanced view activated, Photoshop Elements' Photo Downloader allows you to select the photos you want to copy to your computer and apply some options such as new filenames or red-eye fixes automatically.

Figure 11.10
The Photo Downloader's confirmation dialog box shows the progress as images are transferred.

Dragging and Dropping

The final way to move photos from your memory card to your computer is the old-fashioned way: manually dragging and dropping the files from one window on your computer to another. The procedure works pretty much the same whether you're using a Mac or a PC.

1. Remove the memory card from the PowerShot G1 X and insert it in your memory card reader.

2. Using Windows Explorer, My Computer, or your Mac desktop, open the icon representing the memory card, which appears on your desktop as just another disk drive.

3. Open a second window representing the folder on your computer that you want to use as the destination for the files you are copying or moving.

4. Drag and drop the files from the memory card window to the folder on your computer. You can select individual files, press Ctrl/Command+A to select all the files, or Ctrl/Command+click to select multiple files.

Editing Your Photos

Image manipulation tasks fall into several categories. You might want to fine-tune your images, retouch them, change color balance, composite several images together, and perform other tasks we know as image editing, with a program like Adobe Photoshop, Photoshop Elements, or Corel Photo Paint.

You might want to play with the settings in RAW files, too, as you import them from their CR2 state into an image editor. There are specialized tools expressly for tweaking RAW files, ranging from Canon's own Digital Photo Professional to Adobe Camera Raw, and PhaseOne's Capture One Pro (C1 Pro). A third type of manipulation is the specialized task of noise reduction, which can be performed within Photoshop, Adobe Camera Raw, or tools like Bibble Professional. There are also specialized tools just for noise reduction, such as Noise Ninja (also included with Bibble) and Neat Image.

Each of these utilities and applications deserves a chapter of its own, so I'm simply going to enumerate some of the most popular image-editing and RAW conversion programs here and tell you a little about what they do.

Image Editors

Image editors are general-purpose photo-editing applications that can do color correction, tonal modifications, retouching, combining of several images into one, and usually include tools for working with RAW files and reducing noise. So, you'll find programs like those listed here good for all-around image manipulation.

The leading programs are as follows:

Adobe Photoshop/Photoshop Elements. Photoshop is the serious photographer's number one choice for image editing, and Elements is an excellent option for those who need most of Photoshop's power, but not all of its professional-level features. Both editors use the latest version of Adobe's Camera Raw plug-in, which makes it easy to adjust things like color space profiles, color depth (either 8 bits or 16 bits per color channel), image resolution, white balance, exposure, shadows, brightness, sharpness, luminance, and noise reduction. One plus with the Adobe products is that they are available in identical versions for both Windows and Macs

Corel Photo Paint. This is the image-editing program that is included in the popular CorelDRAW Graphics suite. Although a Mac version was available in the past, this is primarily a Windows application today. It's a full-featured photo retouching and image-editing program with selection, retouching, and painting tools for manual image manipulations, and it also includes convenient automated commands for a few common tasks, such as red-eye removal. Photo Paint accepts Photoshop plug-ins to expand its assortment of filters and special effects.

Corel Paint Shop Pro. This is a general-purpose Windows-only image editor that has gained a reputation as the "poor person's Photoshop" for providing a substantial portion of Photoshop's capabilities at a fraction of the cost. It includes a nifty set of wizard-like commands that automate common tasks, such as removing red-eye and scratches, as well as filters and effects, which can be expanded with other Photoshop plug-ins.

Corel Painter. Here's another image-editing program from Corel for both Mac and Windows. This one's strength is in mimicking natural media, such as charcoal, pastels, and various kinds of paint. Painter includes a basic assortment of tools that you can use to edit existing images, but the program is really designed for artists to use in creating original illustrations. As a photographer, you might prefer another image editor, but if you like to paint on top of your photographic images, nothing else really does the job of Painter.

Corel PhotoImpact. Corel finally brought one of the last remaining non-Adobe image editors into its fold when it acquired PhotoImpact. This is a general-purpose photo-editing program for Windows with a huge assortment of brushes for painting, retouching, and cloning, in addition to the usual selection, cropping, and fill tools. If you frequently find yourself performing the same image manipulations on a number of files, you'll appreciate PhotoImpact's batch operations. Using this feature, you can select multiple image files and then apply any one of a long list of filters, enhancements, or auto-process commands to all the selected files.

RAW Utilities

Your software choices for manipulating RAW files are broader than you might think. Camera vendors always supply a utility to read their cameras' own RAW files, but sometimes, particularly with those point-and-shoot cameras that can produce RAW files, the options are fairly limited.

The third-party solutions are usually available as standalone applications (often for both Windows and Macintosh platforms), as Photoshop-compatible plug-ins, or both. Because the RAW plug-ins displace Photoshop's own RAW converter, I tend to prefer to use most RAW utilities in standalone mode. That way, if I choose to open a file directly in Photoshop, it automatically opens using Photoshop's fast and easy-to-use Adobe Camera Raw (ACR) plug-in. If I have more time or need the capabilities of another converter, I can load that, open the file, and make my corrections there. Most are able to transfer the processed file directly to Photoshop even if you aren't using plug-in mode.

This section provides a quick overview of the range of RAW file handlers, so you can get a better idea of the kinds of information available with particular applications. I'm going to include both high-end and low-end RAW browsers so you can see just what is available.

Digital Photo Professional

Digital Photo Professional, introduced earlier in this chapter, is preferred by many for Canon digital cameras like the PowerShot G1 X.

DPP offers much higher-speed processing of RAW images, rivaling third-party standalone and plug-in RAW converters in speed and features. It supports both Canon's original CRW format and the newer CR2 RAW format used by the G1 X, along with JPEG and other file formats.

You can save settings that include multiple adjustments and apply them to other images, and use the clever comparison mode to compare your original and edited versions of an image either side by side or within a single split image. The utility allows easy adjustment of color channels, tone curves, exposure compensation, white balance, dynamic range, brightness, contrast, color saturation, ICC Profile embedding, and assignment of monitor profiles. A new feature is the ability to continue editing images while batches of previously adjusted RAW files are rendered and saved in the background.

IrfanView

At the low (free) end of the price scale is IrfanView, a Windows-only freeware program you can download at www.irfanview.com. It can read many common RAW photo formats. It's a quick way to view RAW files (just drag and drop to the IrfanView window) and make fast changes to the unprocessed file. You can crop, rotate, or correct your image, and do some cool things like swap the colors around (red for blue, blue for green, and so forth) to create false color pictures.

Phase One Capture One Pro (C1 Pro)

If there is a Cadillac of RAW converters for Nikon and Canon digital camera cameras, C1 Pro has to be it. This premium-priced program does everything, does it well, and does it quickly. If you can't justify the price tag of this professional-level software, there are "lite" versions for serious amateurs and cash-challenged professionals called Capture One digital camera and Capture One digital camera SE.

Aimed at photographers with high-volume needs (that would include school and portrait photographers, as well as busy commercial photographers), C1 Pro is available for both Windows and Mac OS X, and supports a broad range of Canon digital cameras. Phase One is a leading supplier of megabucks digital camera backs for medium and larger format cameras, so they really understand the needs of photographers.

The latest features include individual noise reduction controls for each image, automatic levels adjustment, a "quick develop" option that allows speedy conversion from RAW to TIFF or JPEG formats, dual-image side-by-side views for comparison purposes, and helpful grids and guides that can be superimposed over an image. Photographers concerned about copyright protection will appreciate the ability to add watermarks to the output images. See www.phaseone.com.

AfterShot Pro

One of my personal favorites among third-party RAW converters is AfterShot Pro (formerly Bibble Pro). It supports one of the broadest ranges of RAW file formats available (which can be handy if you find yourself with the need to convert a file from a friend or colleague's non-Canon camera), including NEF (Nikon), CRW/CR2 (Canon), ORF (Olympus), DCR (Kodak), RAF (Fuji), PEF (Pentax), and ARW (Sony).

The utility supports lots of different platforms, too. It's available for Windows, Mac OS X, and, believe it or not, Linux. AfterShot Pro works fast because it offers instantaneous previews and real-time feedback as changes are made. That's important when you have to convert many images in a short time. AfterShot Pro's batch-processing capabilities also let you convert large numbers of files using settings you specify without further intervention.

Its customizable interface lets you organize and edit images quickly and then output them in a variety of formats, including 16-bit TIFF and PNG. You can even create a web gallery from within AfterShot Pro. I often find myself disliking the generic filenames applied to digital images by cameras, so I really like AfterShot Pro's ability to rename batches of files using new names that you specify. AfterShot Pro is fully color managed, which means it can support all the popular color spaces (Adobe sRGB and so forth) and use custom profiles generated by third-party color-management software.

BreezeBrowser

BreezeBrowser was long the RAW converter of choice for Canon digital camera owners who run Windows and who were dissatisfied with Canon's lame antique File Viewer Utility (which has been gone from the scene for many years now). It works quickly and has lots of options for converting CRW and CR2 files to other formats. You can choose to show highlights that will be blown out in your finished photo as flashing areas (so they can be more easily identified and corrected), use histograms to correct tones, add color profiles, auto rotate images, and adjust all those raw image parameters, such as white balance, color space, saturation, contrast, sharpening, color tone, EV compensation, and other settings.

You can also control noise reduction (choosing from low, normal, or high reduction), evaluate your changes in the live preview, and then save the file as a compressed JPEG or as either an 8-bit or 16-bit TIFF file. BreezeBrowser can also create HTML web galleries directly from your selection of images. See www.breezesys.com.

Adobe Photoshop

The latest version of Photoshop includes a built-in RAW plug-in that is compatible with the proprietary formats of a growing number of digital cameras, both new and old. This plug-in also works with Photoshop Elements.

To open a RAW image in Photoshop, just follow these steps (Elements users can use much the same workflow, although fewer settings are available):

1. Transfer the RAW images from your camera to your computer's hard drive.

2. In Photoshop, choose Open from the File menu, or use Bridge or the Elements Organizer.

3. Select a RAW image file. The Adobe Camera Raw plug-in will pop up, showing a preview of the image, like the one shown in Figure 11.11.

4. If you like, use one of the tools found in the toolbar at the top left of the dialog box. From left to right, they are as follows:

   ■ **Zoom.** Operates just like the Zoom tool in Photoshop.

   ■ **Hand.** Use like the Hand tool in Photoshop.

   ■ **White Balance.** Click an area in the image that should be neutral gray or white to set the white balance quickly.

   ■ **Color Sampler.** Use to determine the RGB values of areas you click with this eyedropper.

   ■ **Crop.** Pre-crops the image so that only the portion you specify is imported into Photoshop. This option saves time when you want to work on a section of a large image, and you don't need the entire file.

- **Straighten.** Drag in the preview image to define what should be a horizontal or vertical line, and ACR will realign the image to straighten it.

- **Retouch.** Used to heal or clone areas you define.

- **Red-Eye Removal.** Quickly zap red pupils in your human subjects.

- **ACR Preferences.** Produces a dialog box of Adobe Camera Raw preferences.

- **Rotate Counterclockwise.** Rotates counterclockwise in 90-degree increments with a click.

- **Rotate Clockwise.** Rotates clockwise in 90-degree increments with a click.

5. Using the Basic tab, you can have ACR show you red and blue highlights in the preview that indicate shadow areas that are clipped (too dark to show detail) and light areas that are blown out (too bright). Click the triangles in the upper-left corner of the histogram display (shadow clipping) and upper-right corner (highlight clipping) to toggle these indicators on or off.

6. Also in the Basic tab you can choose white balance, either from the drop-down list or by setting a color temperature and green/magenta color bias (tint) using the sliders.

7. Other sliders are available to control exposure, recovery, fill light, blacks, brightness, contrast, vibrance, and saturation. A check box can be marked to convert the image to grayscale.

8. Make other adjustments (described in more detail below).

Figure 11.11
The basic ACR dialog box looks like this when processing a single image.

9. ACR makes automatic adjustments for you. You can click Default and make the changes for yourself, or click the Auto link (located just above the Exposure slider) to reapply the automatic adjustments after you've made your own modifications.

10. If you've marked more than one image to be opened, the additional images appear in a "filmstrip" at the left side of the screen. You can click on each thumbnail in the filmstrip in turn and apply different settings to each.

11. Click Open Image/Open Image(s) into Photoshop using the settings you've made, or click Save Image at the bottom left to save the settings you've made without opening the file.

The Basic tab is displayed by default when the ACR dialog box opens, and it includes most of the sliders and controls you'll need to fine-tune your image as you import it into Photoshop. These include:

- **White Balance.** Leave it As Shot or change to a value such as Daylight, Cloudy, Shade, Tungsten, Fluorescent, or Flash. If you like, you can set a custom white balance using the Temperature and Tint sliders.

- **Exposure.** This slider adjusts the overall brightness and darkness of the image.

- **Recovery.** Restores detail in the red, green, and blue color channels.

- **Fill Light.** Reconstructs detail in shadows.

- **Blacks.** Increases the number of tones represented as black in the final image, emphasizing tones in the shadow areas of the image.

- **Brightness.** This slider adjusts the brightness and darkness of an image.

- **Contrast.** Manipulates the contrast of the midtones of your image.

- **Clarity.** Use this slider to apply a hybrid type of contrast enhancement to boost midtone contrast.

- **Vibrance.** Prevents over-saturation when enriching the colors of an image.

- **Saturation.** Manipulates the richness of all colors equally, from zero saturation (gray/black, no color) at the −100 setting to double the usual saturation at the +100 setting.

Additional controls are available on the Tone Curve, Detail, HSL/Grayscale, Split Toning, Lens Corrections, Camera Calibration, and Presets tabs, shown in Figure 11.12. The Tone Curve tab can change the tonal values of your image. The Detail tab lets you adjust sharpness, luminance smoothing, and apply color noise reduction. The HSL/Grayscale tab offers controls for adjusting hue, saturation, and lightness and converting an image to black-and-white. Split Toning helps you colorize an image with sepia or cyanotype (blue) shades. The Lens Corrections tab has sliders to adjust for chromatic aberrations and vignetting. The Camera Calibration tab provides a way for calibrating the color corrections made in the Camera Raw plug-in. The Presets tab (not shown) is used to load settings you've stored for reuse.

Figure 11.12 More controls are available within the additional tabbed dialog boxes in Adobe Camera Raw.

Glossary

Here are some terms you might encounter while reading this book or working with your Canon PowerShot G1 X.

additive primary colors   The red, green, and blue hues that are used alone or in combinations to create all other colors that you capture with a digital camera, view on a computer monitor, or work with in an image-editing program, such as Photoshop.

ambient lighting   Diffuse, non-directional lighting that doesn't appear to come from a specific source but, rather, bounces off walls, ceilings, and other objects in the scene when a picture is taken.

analog/digital converter   The Canon DIGIC 5 electronics built into the G1 X that convert the analog information captured by the camera's sensor into digital bits that can be stored as an image bitmap.

angle of view   The area of a scene that a lens can capture, determined by the focal length of the lens. Lenses with a shorter focal length have a wider angle of view than lenses with a longer focal length.

anti-alias   A process that smoothes the look of rough edges in images (called *jaggies* or *staircasing*) by adding partially transparent pixels along the boundaries of diagonal lines that are merged into a smoother line by our eyes. *See also* jaggies.

Aperture priority   A camera setting, called Av (for Aperture value), that allows you to specify the lens opening or f/stop that you want to use, with the camera selecting the required shutter speed automatically based on its light-meter reading. This setting is represented by the abbreviation Av on the G1 X's mode dial. *See also* Shutter priority.

artifact   A type of noise in an image, or an unintentional image component produced in error by a digital camera during processing, usually caused by the JPEG compression process in digital cameras.

aspect ratio   The proportions of an image as printed, displayed on a monitor, or captured by a digital camera.

autofocus   A camera setting that allows the Canon PowerShot G1 X to choose the correct focus distance for you, based on the contrast of an image (the image will be at maximum contrast when in sharp focus).

Automatic exposure bracketing   Automatic exposure bracketing takes a series of pictures at different exposure increments to improve the chances of producing one picture that is perfectly exposed.

back lighting   A lighting effect produced when the main light source is located behind the subject. Back lighting can be used to create a silhouette effect, or to illuminate translucent objects. *See also* front lighting and side lighting.

barrel distortion   A lens defect that causes straight lines at the top or side edges of an image to bow outward into a barrel shape. *See also* pincushion distortion.

blooming   An image distortion caused when a photosite in an image sensor has absorbed all the photons it can handle so that additional photons reaching that pixel overflow to affect surrounding pixels, producing unwanted brightness and overexposure around the edges of objects.

blur   To soften an image or part of an image by throwing it out of focus, or by allowing it to become soft due to subject or camera motion. Blur can also be applied in an image-editing program.

bokeh   A term derived from the Japanese word for blur, which describes the aesthetic qualities of the out-of-focus parts of an image. Some lenses produce "good" bokeh and others offer "bad" bokeh. Some lenses produce uniformly illuminated out-of-focus discs. Others produce a disc that has a bright edge and a dark center, producing a "doughnut" effect, which is the worst from a bokeh standpoint. Lenses that generate a bright center that fades to a darker edge are favored, because their bokeh allows the circle of confusion to blend more smoothly with the surroundings. The bokeh characteristics of a lens are most important when you're using selective focus (say, when shooting a portrait) to deemphasize the background, or when shallow depth-of-field is a given because you're working with a macro lens, a long telephoto, or a wide-open aperture. *See also* circle of confusion.

bounce lighting   Light bounced off a reflector, including ceiling and walls, to provide a soft, natural-looking light.

bracketing   Taking a series of photographs of the same subject at different settings, including exposure and white balance, to help ensure that one setting will be the correct one.

buffer   The digital camera's internal memory where an image is stored immediately after it is taken until it can be written to the camera's non-volatile (semi-permanent) memory or a memory card.

burst mode   Known as continuous shooting modes in the PowerShot, burst shooting is the digital camera's equivalent of the film camera's motor drive, used to take multiple shots within a short period of time, with each shot stored in a memory buffer temporarily before writing it to the media.

calibration   A process used to correct for the differences in the output of a printer or monitor when compared to the original image. Once you've calibrated your scanner, monitor, and/or your image editor, the images you see on the screen more closely represent what you'll get from your printer, even though calibration is never perfect.

Camera Raw   A plug-in included with Photoshop and Photoshop Elements that can manipulate the unprocessed images captured by digital cameras, such as the Canon PowerShot G1 X's .CR2 files. The latest versions of this module can also work with JPEG and TIFF images.

camera shake   Movement of the camera, aggravated by slower shutter speeds, which produces a blurred image. You can minimize camera shake by using the PowerShot's image stabilization feature.

Center weighted metering   A light-measuring device that emphasizes the area in the middle of the frame when calculating the correct exposure for an image. *See also* Spot metering and Evaluative metering.

chromatic aberration   An image defect, often seen as green or purple fringing around the edges of an object, caused by a lens failing to focus all colors of a light source at the same point. *See also* fringing.

circle of confusion   A term applied to the fuzzy discs produced when a point of light is out of focus. The circle of confusion is not a fixed size. The viewing distance and amount of enlargement of the image determine whether we see a particular spot on the image as a point or as a disc. *See also* bokeh.

close-up lens   A lens add-on accessory that allows you to take pictures at a distance that is less than the closest-focusing distance of the lens alone.

color correction   Changing the relative amounts of color in an image to produce a desired effect, typically a more accurate representation of those colors. Color correction can fix faulty color balance in the original image, or compensate for the deficiencies of the inks used to reproduce the image.

compression   Reducing the size of a file by encoding using fewer bits of information to represent the original. Some compression schemes, such as JPEG, operate by discarding some image information, while others, such as RAW, preserve all the detail in the original, discarding only redundant data.

contrast   The range between the lightest and darkest tones in an image. A high-contrast image is one in which the shades fall at the extremes of the range between white and black. In a low-contrast image, the tones are closer together.

dedicated flash   An electronic flash unit, such as the Canon 270EX Speedlite, designed to work with the automatic exposure features of a specific camera.

depth-of-field   A distance range in a photograph in which all included portions of an image are at least acceptably sharp. With the Canon PowerShot G1 X, you can see the available depth-of-field at the taking aperture by pressing the depth-of-field preview button, or estimate the range by viewing the depth-of-field scale found on many lenses.

diaphragm   An adjustable component, similar to the iris in the human eye, that can open and close to provide specific-sized lens openings, or f/stops, and thus control the amount of light reaching the sensor or film.

diffuse lighting   Soft, low-contrast lighting.

digital processing chip   A solid-state device found in digital cameras, such as the DIGIC 5 chip in the PowerShot G1 X, that's in charge of applying the image algorithms to the raw picture data prior to storage on the memory card.

diopter   A value used to represent the magnification power of a lens, calculated as the reciprocal of a lens's focal length (in meters). Diopters are most often used to represent the optical correction used in a viewfinder to adjust for limitations of the photographer's eyesight, and to describe the magnification of a close-up lens attachment.

Evaluative metering   One system of exposure calculation used by the PowerShot G1 X that looks at many different segments of an image to determine the brightest and darkest portions. *See also* Center weighted metering and Spot metering.

exchangeable image file format (Exif)   Developed to standardize the exchange of image data between hardware devices and software. A variation on JPEG, Exif is used by most digital cameras, and includes information such as the date and time a photo was taken, the camera settings, resolution, amount of compression, and other data.

Exif   *See* exchangeable image file format (Exif).

exposure   The amount of light allowed to reach the film or sensor, determined by the intensity of the light, the amount admitted by the iris of the lens, the length of time determined by the shutter speed, and the ISO sensitivity setting for the sensor.

exposure values (EV)   EV settings are a way of adding or decreasing exposure without the need to reference f/stops or shutter speeds. For example, if you tell your camera to add +1EV, it will provide twice as much exposure by using a larger f/stop, slower shutter speed, or both.

fill lighting   In photography, lighting is used to illuminate shadows. Reflectors or additional incandescent lighting or electronic flash can be used to brighten shadows. One common technique for outdoors is to use the camera's flash as a fill.

filter   In photography, a device that fits over the lens, changing the light in some way. In image editing, a feature that changes the pixels in an image to produce blurring, sharpening, and other special effects. Photoshop includes several interesting filter effects, including Lens Blur and Photo Filters.

focal length   The distance between the film and the optical center of the lens when the lens is focused on infinity, usually measured in millimeters.

format   To erase a memory card and prepare it to accept files.

fringing   A chromatic aberration that produces fringes of color around the edges of subjects, caused by a lens's inability to focus the various wavelengths of light onto the same spot. Purple fringing is especially troublesome with backlit images.

front lighting   Illumination that comes from the direction of the camera. *See also* back lighting and side lighting.

f/stop   The relative size of the lens aperture, which helps determine both exposure and depth-of-field. The larger the f/stop number, the smaller the f/stop itself.

graduated filter   A lens attachment with variable density or color from one edge to another. A graduated neutral-density filter, for example, can be oriented so the neutral-density portion is concentrated at the top of the lens's view with the less dense or clear portion at the bottom, thus reducing the amount of light from a very bright sky while not interfering with the exposure of the landscape in the foreground. Graduated filters can also be split into several color sections to provide a color gradient between portions of the image.

gray card   A piece of cardboard or other material with a standardized 18 percent reflectance. Gray cards can be used as a reference for determining correct exposure or for setting white balance.

HDMI (High Definition Multimedia Interface)   An interface for transmitting audio and video information between a source, such as a digital camera or television tuner, to an output device, such as a high-definition television (HDTV) monitor.

high contrast   A wide range of density in a print, negative, or other image.

highlights   The brightest parts of an image containing detail.

histogram   A kind of chart showing the relationship of tones in an image using a series of 256 vertical bars, one for each brightness level. A histogram chart, such as the one the Canon PowerShot G1 X can display, typically looks like a curve with one or more slopes and peaks, depending on how many highlight, midtone, and shadow tones are present in the image.

hot shoe   A mount on top of a camera used to hold an electronic flash, while providing an electrical connection between the flash and the camera.

hyperfocal distance   A point of focus where everything from half that distance to infinity appears to be acceptably sharp. For example, if your lens has a hyperfocal distance of four feet, everything from two feet to infinity would be sharp. The hyperfocal distance varies by the lens and the aperture in use. If you know you'll be making a grab shot without warning, sometimes it is useful to turn off your camera's automatic focus, and set the lens to infinity, or, better yet, the hyperfocal distance. Then, you can snap off a quick picture without having to wait for the lag that occurs with most digital cameras as their autofocus locks in.

image rotation   A feature that senses whether a picture was taken in horizontal or vertical orientation. That information is embedded in the picture file so that the camera and compatible software applications can automatically display the image in the correct orientation.

image stabilization   A technology that compensates for camera shake, usually by adjusting the position of the camera sensor (with some vendors) or, in the case of Canon's PowerShot G1 X cameras, lens elements that shift in response to movements of the camera.

incident light   Light measured as it falls on a surface, as opposed to light reflected from that surface.

International Organization for Standardization (ISO)   A governing body that provides standards used to represent film speed, or the equivalent sensitivity of a digital camera's sensor. Digital camera sensitivity is expressed in ISO settings.

interpolation   A technique digital cameras, scanners, and image editors use to create new pixels required whenever you resize or change the resolution of an image based on the values of surrounding pixels. Devices such as scanners and digital cameras can use interpolation to create pixels in addition to those actually captured, thereby increasing the apparent resolution or color information in an image.

ISO   *See* International Organization for Standardization (ISO).

jaggies   Staircasing effect of lines, most easily seen at large magnifications, that are not perfectly horizontal or vertical, caused by pixels that are too large to represent the line accurately. *See also* anti-alias.

JPEG   Short for Joint Photographic Experts Group. A file "lossy" format that supports 24-bit color and reduces file sizes by selectively discarding image data. Digital cameras generally use JPEG compression to pack more images onto memory cards. You can select how much compression is used (and, therefore, how much information is thrown away) by selecting from among the Standard, Fine, Super Fine, or other quality settings offered by your camera. *See also* RAW.

Kelvin (K)   A unit of measure based on the absolute temperature scale in which absolute zero is zero; it's used to describe the color of continuous-spectrum light sources and applied when setting white balance. For example, daylight has a color temperature of about 5,500K, and a tungsten lamp has a temperature of about 3,400K.

lag time   The interval between when the shutter is pressed and when the picture is actually taken. During that span, the camera may be automatically focusing and calculating exposure. With digital cameras like the Canon PowerShot G1 X, lag time is generally very short.

latitude   The range of camera exposure that produces acceptable images with a particular digital sensor or film.

lens flare   A feature of conventional photography that is both a bane and a creative outlet. It is an effect produced by the reflection of light internally among elements of an optical lens. Bright light sources within or just outside the field of view cause lens flare. Flare can be reduced by the use of coatings on the lens elements or with the use of lens hoods. Photographers sometimes use the effect as a creative technique, and Photoshop includes a filter that lets you add lens flare at your whim.

lighting ratio   The proportional relationship between the amount of light falling on the subject from the main light and other lights, expressed in a ratio, such as 3:1.

lossy compression   An image-compression scheme, such as JPEG, that creates smaller files by discarding image information, which can affect image quality.

maximum burst   The number of frames that can be exposed at the current settings until the buffer fills.

midtones   Parts of an image with tones of an intermediate value, usually in the 25 to 75 percent brightness range. Many image-editing features allow you to manipulate midtones independently from the highlights and shadows.

neutral color   A color in which red, green, and blue are present in equal amounts, producing a gray.

neutral-density filter   A gray camera filter that reduces the amount of light entering the camera without affecting the colors. The PowerShot G1 X has a feature that acts as a neutral-density filter built into the camera.

noise   In an image, pixels with randomly distributed color values. Noise in digital photographs tends to be the product of low-light conditions and long exposures, particularly when you've set your camera to an ISO rating higher than about ISO 800.

noise reduction   A technology used to cut down on the amount of random information in a digital picture, usually caused by long exposures at increased sensitivity ratings. In the Canon PowerShot G1 X, noise reduction is automatically applied for long exposures.

overexposure   A condition in which too much light reaches the film or sensor, producing a dense negative or a very bright/light print, slide, or digital image.

pincushion distortion   A type of lens distortion in which lines at the top and side edges of an image are bent inward, producing an effect that looks like a pincushion. *See also* barrel distortion.

polarizing filter   A filter that forces light, which normally vibrates in all directions, to vibrate only in a single plane, reducing or removing the specular reflections from the surface of objects. Such filters tend to increase the contrast between colors and make blue skies more dramatic, most strongly when the sun is located at a 90-degree angle from the direction the camera is pointed.

RAW   An image file format, such as the CR2 format in the Canon PowerShot G1 X, which includes all the unprocessed information captured by the camera after conversion to digital form. RAW files are very large compared to JPEG files and must be processed by a special program such as Canon Digital Photo Pro or Adobe's Camera Raw filter after being downloaded from the camera.

saturation   The purity of color; the amount by which a pure color is diluted with white or gray.

selective focus   Choosing a lens opening that produces a shallow depth-of-field. Usually this is used to isolate a subject in portraits, close-ups, and other types of images, by causing most other elements in the scene to be blurred.

self-timer   A mechanism that delays the opening of the shutter for some seconds after the release has been operated.

sensitivity   A measure of the degree of response of a film or sensor to light, measured using the ISO setting.

shadow   The darkest part of an image, represented on a digital image by pixels with low numeric values.

sharpening   Increasing the apparent sharpness of an image by boosting the contrast between adjacent pixels that form an edge, whether done in the camera or in image-editing software.

shutter   In a conventional film camera, the shutter is a mechanism consisting of blades, a curtain, a plate, or some other movable cover that controls the time during which light reaches the film. Digital cameras may use actual mechanical shutters for the slower shutter speeds (less than 1/200th second) and an electronic shutter for higher speeds.

Shutter priority   An exposure mode, represented by the letters Tv (Time value) on the G1 X's mode dial, in which you set the shutter speed and the camera determines the appropriate f/stop. *See also* Aperture priority.

side lighting   Applying illumination from the left or right sides of the camera. *See also* back lighting and front lighting.

slave unit   An accessory flash unit that supplements the main flash, usually triggered electronically when the slave senses the light output by the main unit, through radio waves, or through a pre-burst emitted by the camera's main flash unit.

slow synchro   An electronic flash synchronizing method that uses a slow shutter speed so that ambient light is recorded by the camera in addition to the electronic flash illumination. This allows the background to receive more exposure for a more realistic effect.

specular highlight   Bright spots in an image caused by reflection of light sources, often from shiny surfaces.

Spot metering   An exposure system that concentrates on a small area in the image. *See also* Center weighted metering and Evaluative metering.

time exposure   A picture taken by leaving the shutter open for a long period, usually more than one second. The camera is generally locked down with a tripod to prevent blur during the long exposure.

tungsten light   Light from ordinary room lamps and ceiling fixtures, as opposed to fluorescent illumination.

underexposure   A condition in which too little light reaches the film or sensor, producing a thin negative, a dark slide, a muddy looking print, or a dark digital image.

vignetting   Dark corners of an image, often produced by using a lens hood that is too small for the field of view, a lens that does not completely fill the image frame, or generated artificially using image-editing techniques.

white balance   The adjustment of a digital camera to the color temperature of the light source. Interior illumination is relatively red; outdoor light is relatively blue. Digital cameras like the PowerShot G1 X set correct white balance automatically or let you do it through menus. Image editors can often do some color correction of images that were exposed using the wrong white balance setting, especially when working with RAW files that contain the information originally captured by the camera before white balance was applied.

Index

Like the Book?

Let us know on Facebook or Twitter!

facebook.com/courseptr

twitter.com/courseptr

Like us on Facebook or Follow us on Twitter to learn about upcoming books, promotions, contests, events and more!